THE
23rd
PSALM

THE
23rd
PSALM

A Holocaust Memoir

THE TWENTIETH ANNIVERSARY EDITION

GEORGE LUCIUS SALTON
with ANNA SALTON EISEN

Foreword by MICHAEL BERENBAUM

[M]

MANDEL VILAR PRESS

This book is typeset in Minion Pro 11/14. The paper used in this book meets the minimum requirements of ANSI/NISO Z39.48-1992 (R1997). ∞

Designed by Sophie Appel
Cover drawing by George Lucius Salton
Unless otherwise noted, all images in this book are from the author's collection.

Publisher's Cataloging-in-Publication Data

Names: Salton, George Lucius, author, with Salton Eisen, Anna, co-author
Title: The 23rd Psalm: A Holocaust Memoir / The Twentieth Anniversary Edition
Description: Simsbury, Connecticut. Mandel Vilar Press, 2022
Identifiers: ISBN: 9781942134848 (pbk.)
E-ISBN 9781942134855 (ebook)
Subjects: Salton, George Lucius Memoir / Jews / Poland / Tyczyn (Rzeszów) /
    Biography / Holocaust, Jewish (1939–1945) / Personal narratives / Slave labor /
    Concentration camps including Rzeszów, Płaszów, Flossenbürg / Colmar /
    Sachsenhausen / Braunschweig / Ravensbrück / Wöbbelin
The Twentieth Anniversary Edition / Foreword by Michael Berenbaum / Postscript,
    George Salton speeches about his book and life / Color insert includes
    concentration camp original art by George Salton, historical photographs, and
    map of concentration camps
Classification LCC DS135.P63 S2457 2022

Printed in the United States of America
22 23 24 25 26 27 28 29 30 / 9 8 7 6 5 4 3 2 1

Mandel Vilar Press
19 Oxford Court, Simsbury, Connecticut 06070
www.americasforconservation.org | www.mvpublishers.org

To my wife, Ruth,
to my children, Henry, Alan, and Anna,
and to my grandchildren,
Daniel, Sarah, Benjamin, Joshua, Erica, and Aaron,
whose love and goodness
I cherish.

A Psalm of David

The Lord is my shepherd; I shall not want.
    He maketh me to lie down in green pastures;
    He leadeth me beside the still waters.
He restoreth my soul;
He leadeth me in the paths of righteousness for His name's sake.
    Yea, though I walk through the valley of the shadow of death,
    I will fear no evil, for Thou art with me;
    Thy rod and Thy staff, they comfort me.
Thou preparest a table before me in the presence of mine enemies;
Thou anointed my head with oil; my cup runneth over.
    Surely goodness and mercy shall follow me all the days of my
        life;
    And I shall dwell in the house of the Lord forever.
                   —Psalm 23, *Jewish Family Bible*

◆ FOREWORD ◆

We must be grateful to George Lucius Salton for writing his Holocaust memoir, which reflects the observational powers and the unflinching honesty of a fourteen-year-old boy who would later become an engineer and an outspoken advocate for oppressed humanity.

Like many memoirs, this one is divided into three parts—*before*, *during*, and *after*—yet the bulk of Salton's work details his multilayered and complex experiences during the Holocaust. His life *before* is a prelude, setting the scene. His life *after* is a coda—he could not leave the story unfinished because every reader will be interested in what happened to Lucek Salzman (George Lucius Salton's pre-Americanized name). However, this is a *Holocaust* memoir.

The standard Holocaust narrative for Polish Jews is ghettoization, deportation, death camp—and for those who did not die, the near impossible struggle for survival. But Lucek Salzman's experience was different. When his parents were deported to Belzec from the Rzeszów ghetto, fourteen-year-old Lucek remained in the ghetto, then was sent from one labor camp to another and, at the end of the war, from one concentration camp to another when these camps were overwhelmed and had ceased to function, making daily life even more difficult. Salton writes in intricate detail of each step on his journey, each assignment, each of the many moments of crisis, and of the men with whom he shared his struggle. He also depicts his perpetrators, often by name, and the industries that exploited his enslavement.

Salton's memoir was difficult to write and also difficult to read, not because he is unclear but because he describes so precisely the conditions he faced, the crises he encountered, the degradation he endured, and the misery he withstood, so that we too, his readers, must feel some of what he felt. To read this memoir properly we must avoid the psychological numbness that he must have experienced. We can't shut down but must remain open to truly grasp the importance of his work.

As I read Salton's memoir, I kept thinking of another scientist who was engulfed by the Holocaust, Primo Levi, who found himself deported to a concentration camp. He applied his talent for observation much as Lucek did. However, Lucek, though mechanically gifted and scientifically inclined, was a child, while Levi was a trained chemist who could more easily move from the particular experience to the principle that it illustrated. Yet we must be grateful to have young Lucek's detailed observations.

Salton's memoir is honest—painfully, brutally honest. The true mark of such honesty is his abandonment of a narrative depicting his own heroism and strength, and his willingness to discuss experiences that make him and his readers uncomfortable. We learn of desperation from Salton's memoir. Toward the end of the work he describes cannibalism.

"Do you know what you are eating?" "Potatoes with meat," I said, hoping that he would go away. "No. Not meat. Human flesh cut from the dead. They are cannibals."

I remember the first time I heard of such cannibalism. I conducted a long interview with a survivor, after which he asked that we turn off the camera and shut down the recording. In soft, hesitant tones, he whispered, "We were so hungry that we even ate the dead."

Salton does not spare himself. Hoping his Polish fellow inmate who told him what he was eating would go away and keep his mouth shut, Lucek wanted what one might call plausible deniability, not admitting to his own desperation, to how low he had sunk.

Another instance of painful honesty is his depiction of friendship. But first let me offer some context. Throughout Lucek's multiple, seemingly unending, ordeals, he is buoyed by friendships. First, there was the love that he experienced from his older brother, Manek, who had been admonished by his mother just before their final deportation to take care of Lucek, which Manek did with admirable dedication and courage until the brothers were forcibly separated, and Manek went off on his own. Later, Lucek received support from friends, including young men from his hometown of Tyczyn or his ghetto of Rzeszów. One survivor I knew well as a friend, Mike Jacobs, observed: "No one survived alone." Everyone needed someone to keep them from the abyss, to help them in an inevitable moment of weakness, to keep them from becoming a muselman, one who had given in to despair, who had nothing left, a walking dead man.

Yet, lest the reader feel sentimental about friendships forged under oppression, Salton observes: "I had learned to always cling to friends I could trust and not to rely on strangers. I could count on Emil Ringel, and he could rely on me. In all except the most desperate circumstances, we would not steal each other's shoes."

No romantic depiction here, but an honest understanding that in extreme moments slave laborers will do anything—anything and everything—to survive.

Salton reminds me of what Elie Wiesel wrote in his novel *Day:*

Suffering brings out the lowest, the most cowardly in man. There is a phase of suffering you reach beyond which you become a brute: beyond it you sell your soul—and worse yet the soul of your friends—for a piece of bread, for some warmth, for a moment of oblivion, of sleep. Saints are those who die before the end of the story.

Salton is less poetic, more personal, more engaged, and so much less abstract that you feel his anguish. You know he is telling the truth, the painful truth.

There are important pieces of historical information in Salton's recounting of Lucek's experience. Lucek was enslaved by German corporations, including the prestigious Mercedes Benz. Historians recount that German corporations invested 700 million in 1942 Reichsmarks in the slave labor complex Auschwitz III (Buna Monowitz). Those decisions were made in corporate boardrooms far from Auschwitz, not necessarily by Nazis but by prominent executives who ran great corporations before the war and often after it. They presumed that slavery would be an ongoing part of the German economy, not only in wartime but for the indefinite future. They simply wanted to cash in, to earn more profits for themselves and for their companies. Salton recounts that the Mercedes employees who supervised his work were just as cruel, just as driven, just as antisemitic as those men who were chosen, trained, and indoctrinated for the SS. He was also enslaved by the Hermann Göring Werke, the German conglomerate that provided one-eighth of Germany's steel output during the war. It was created to provide a Nazi-controlled military industrial complex for the regime that would be uncompromised by private interests. By the end of 1941, the Göring Werke was the largest company in Europe, and probably in the whole world, with a capital of 2.4 billion in 1941 Reichsmarks and about half a million workers. Lucek Salzman was one of those workers.

Joseph Borkin, who wrote an important study of slave labor, *The Crime and Punishment of I. G. Farben,* writes: "They oiled the machines, they did not feed the prisoners." He could have used Lucek's experience and George Salton's memoir as his proof text. There was a sameness to the treatment Lucek experienced: virtually identical inhumane living conditions and virtually identical cruelties perpetrated by the slave masters of the different industries and corporations. Factory foremen don't ordinarily behave this way; the conditions alone did not cause such behavior; it was the ideology that supported treatment of these laborers, especially the Jews, as subhuman, surely deserving of their enslavement.

In one camp, Lucek was assigned to work on aircraft, which was essential to the war effort. His supervisors were Luftwaffe, German Air Force officials. Though they did not go through SS training and indoctrination, they too were capable of great cruelty. Lucek's experience with them refutes the all too comfortable position of those who want to differentiate honorable German soldiers from SS personnel—as Helmut Kohl and Ronald Reagan tried to do at Bitburg.

Almost all survivors claim that they survived because of a four-letter word, *luck*, which implies that someone wiser, stronger, and more deserving was in the wrong place at the wrong time and did not make it. The prisoner was shot with greater accuracy or beaten with extra intensity; a bomb was dropped, even an Allied bomb, in the wrong place and the prisoner was murdered or killed and the survivor was spared. There is no answer to why. We can barely count the number of times that Lucek was on the verge of death, or the moments where he ran out of strength and was just not going to make it when a friend offered him solace, a small piece of bread, a place to lie down, a drink of water.

Yet Lucek did not survive merely by luck. Read this book and see the pattern that developed. Unable to go to school, he was trained as a locksmith's apprentice. His mechanical skills made him useful. His work was apparently good.

Prisoners had two conflicting survival strategies: volunteer for nothing or volunteer for everything. Lucek chose the latter. When a master asked for people with specific skills, Lucek stepped forward whether he had those skills or not. He tried repeatedly to prove himself useful to his masters. In a rational world, if a slave is useful to his masters, he will not be killed. In the Nazi universe, usefulness did not necessarily assure survival because the slave was not a capital investment but a consumable raw material to be discarded in the process of manufacture. The product was all important, the workers dispensable, virtually interchangeable. Recall: "They oiled the machines, they did not feed the workers." In the Nazi mindset, some slaves were considered "life unworthy of living," or "useless eaters," which is how the Nazis spoke of people whom we humanely describe as having "special needs." The Jews were considered a cancer, whose elimination was essential to the well-being of German society.

Volunteering and making himself useful was one way that Lucek fought for survival. He demonstrated his skills. Even though he was but a child, Lucek could distinguish between those who were relentlessly cruel for sport or for the joy of punishing their prey, and those who had moments of compassion or at least moments when the zeal to punish or kill gave way to laziness or indifference. He had a knack for making friends who could help him and whom, in turn, he could help. These friendships were not only essential to his continued existence, but they were indispensable to his survival as a person. They preserved his humanity, at least some of it.

Knowing that his food was inadequate and that he would always be hungry, Lucek tried not to eat at once all the food that he was given; he disciplined himself, often unsuccessfully, to preserve some for later. Jewish readers will recall that in the very first moments of the Passover seder, one breaks the middle matzo and hides the larger piece for later. This ritual is a reminder of slavery, for when food is scarce and inadequate, one sets aside some food for another occasion, when one is even more hungry.

Lucek described another survival strategy. Some French prisoners would cut their bread unevenly, giving one person almost a third of a loaf and others ever smaller portions of bread, day-by-day for ten days; but on the tenth day the rotating prisoner would have a feast, a third of a loaf of bread, and be satisfied, albeit just for a day. These French prisoners understood that indefinite starvation is almost unendurable; but one could endure nine days of deprivation if, at the end, there was one moment of satiation. Lucek's misfortune was that he did not stay with that group for the requisite ten days.

Like many survivors, Lucek believed that he was at the end. Had liberation by the Allied armies tarried, had the Germans held out a bit longer, he would not have made it. His words are poignant, powerful:

> One afternoon I was wandering around outside the barracks, waiting for the bread line to form. I passed a barracks window and saw the reflection of a face in the dirty glass, a familiar prisoner who looked like a muselman with sunken eyes, hollow cheeks, broken teeth, a skinny neck, and shaved head. I turned to see who was standing beside me, but no one was there. I was looking at myself.
>
> I despaired. I had sworn to myself and tried so hard not to become a muselman and now I could see that it was too late.

I must confess that when I first read Salton's memoir, twenty years ago, I was perplexed by the title *The 23rd Psalm*. Unlike the psalmist, Lucek walked through the valley in the presence of death—not its shadow—and he feared evil. Rightfully so! For God was absent and there was no comfort.

Yet he lived to tell the tale and for this we must forever be grateful.

Michael Berenbaum
American Jewish University
Los Angeles, CA

THE 23rd PSALM

◆ PROLOGUE ◆

After more than fifty years I have returned to Poland. I sit in the back of a taxi, riding the six miles from Rzeszów to Tyczyn and look out the window at the bleak familiar roads. As we approach the town I recognize the places that marked my childhood. The forests give way to streets bordered by shabby houses stooped with age. I see the homes and shops that once belonged to friends and neighbors. The taxi drops me at the center of town, the market square. It is lined with the same narrow houses and small stores. Today I will just be a stranger in the square, a foreign tourist taking pictures of rundown houses and overgrown gardens.

In my rusty Polish I try to converse with an old man walking down the sidewalk. I greet him and say that I used to live here before the war and that I have come back after so many years. He walks away before I can tell him my name. I approach other elderly people, hoping someone might remember my family. No one wants to bother with a tourist. Nothing is said about the war or the Jews who once lived here.

I cross the market square, determined to find a narrow cobblestone alley that led to the old stone synagogue. I stop to ask a shopkeeper how to find the old Tyczyn synagogue, and he shrugs his shoulders as he tells me that the town has never had a synagogue.

I walk to the street where I lived with my parents and my brother. I stand at the top of the sloping, crooked hill and feel my heart beating and tears welling up in my eyes. I turn a last corner and see my house. It is an old abandoned wreck. The gardens are trampled and barren, and the giant tree that stood in front of the house has been cut down to a stump. It is my house, with its sienna tile roof and cream stucco walls. I see the original door, handsomely carved from dark wood. Without touching it, I can feel the doorknob in my hand. I remember the house as it used to be. I see my father, tall and handsome in his lawyer's robe, rushing off to the courthouse in the morning. I remember the afternoons that I played in the streets with my friends, and I hear my mother's voice calling me to come for dinner. I remember how my brother, Manek, always left his bicycle leaning up against the front of the house.

An older, heavyset Polish woman steps out onto the second floor balcony and looks down at me. She does not know that I played up there, outside my parents' bedroom, when I was just a child. I call out to her in Polish that I lived in this house when I was a small boy and ask if I might come inside for a minute to look around. "No," she tells me, "the house is being remodeled and I cannot let anyone in." She slips quickly inside and shuts the door. In an instant my chance is over. I had not dared to hope that the house would still be standing, and here I am, crying and fumbling with my camera.

I walk back to the market square, turning to look at my house, to capture it in my mind. I get into the taxi and direct the driver to take me back to Rzeszów. He drives down the hill, past the park where I played and the pond where I skated when the leaves had fallen from the trees and the water had turned to ice. We pass the shops and homes of people I once knew and who once knew me. Everyone is gone. I remember how I was chased from this town and realize that I will always be a stranger here. I can never escape the memories, never leave them in some house or town, and they shall never let me go. The wall that I have carefully built between the past and present has crumbled and fallen down, and suddenly everything has changed, and nothing has changed at all.

◆ *1* ◆

Igrew up in a small Polish town named Tyczyn. It was close to Rzeszów, a larger city and our county seat. In Tyczyn were the grade school that I attended and the local court where my father practiced law. The high school, county court, railway station, fancy restaurants, and movie theaters were all in Rzeszów, about six miles away. Three thousand people lived in Tyczyn, and a third of them were Jewish. Most were either quite poor or of modest means. They lived simple and quietly religious lives. Some families owned small shops, or the men worked as tailors, shoemakers, or other tradesmen. A few made a living peddling their wares in nearby villages. Few Jews in our town were professionals. Our lives were comfortable, and we felt we were a welcome part of the community. Tyczyn was an ideal place to grow up. Its smallness allowed me to know every corner, house, and alley, every bend in the river, each grassy place to play, and the best hills to sled in winter. As I grew, I grew to know and love my town.

My father, Dr. Henry Salzman, practiced law in the local court in Tyczyn and the county court in Rzeszów. He was born in the neighboring town of Łańcut, on a farm estate owned by my grandfather, after whom I was named. My father had three brothers and five sisters.

My mother's name was Anna. Her parents, the Hutterers, owned a sawmill in a wooded village fifty miles east of Tyczyn, on the bank of the river San. My mother had one older sister, Pauline, and two brothers, Henry and Benek. Pauline married a doctor and moved to Vienna with their two children. Henry became a businessman, and Benek studied dentistry in France. We were a large, close-knit family and gathered on many festive occasions.

When my father met my mother, she was a young widow with an infant son, Manek. Her first husband had died before the baby was born. My mother cared for the baby alone until she married my father. She lovingly nicknamed my father Henryk, and he called her Andzia. I was born on January 7, 1928, when my brother was six. I was named Lucjan Salzman and nicknamed Lucek. Ours was a close and loving family. I brought my endless questions and youthful problems to my strong and wise father, and my bruises and bad dreams to my tender and loving mother. As a teenager, Manek was tall, blond, and handsome. He was a talented artist and musician and very popular. He helped me with my homework and taught me how to ride a bicycle and how to swim in the river.

My early years passed, and I flourished in the warm circle of family. I worked hard to be a good student and earned high marks in school. I had many friends, both Catholic and Jewish. I loved books and especially those about the brave Polish army that defeated the Russians in the great battle of Warsaw, and the Polish knights who rescued Vienna during the Turkish siege. My father was a reserve officer in the Polish army and captivated me with his tales of war.

But some painful and sobering incidents reminded me that, to my Catholic friends, I was a Jew first and not a Pole. On the playground they called other children fools and ugly. I was called a dirty Jew. Our teacher led our class in morning and afternoon Catholic prayers. The Catholic students stood with their hands clasped, looking toward heaven, while we Jewish students were required to stand with our arms folded and eyes downcast. These were reminders that we were not only different but also less in the eyes of the Gentiles.

One day my teacher told our class that all people, except Jews and Gypsies (the Roma), had ethnic origins. "What about the Jews?" a Catholic student asked. "Where do they come from?" "No one knows," my teacher answered. "They come from nowhere and they have no roots. They are mongrels." During recess some boys called me a dirty mongrel Jew. That night I asked my father why Jews had no roots. He explained that it was not true and that we were from an ancient biblical people, the Semites. I told him what my teacher had said. He was furious and determined to speak to the principal, who was his old high school classmate. A few days later my teacher stared at me while he told the class in a sarcastic voice that he was mistaken when he said that Jews were mongrels and that they were actually of Semitic stock.

My closest friends and playmates lived in my part of town. Most boys were Catholic, except Mayer Rab, who was also Jewish. We formed a soccer team and played against other teams in town. In the winter we had snowball fights and skated on the frozen pond. In the summer we swam and fished in the river. In the fall we wandered in the local forests to play and eat wild berries. We roamed the fields and stole apples from the orchard. On rainy days we visited each other's homes and played cards and chess. We traded books about Tarzan and Tom Sawyer, about cowboys and Indians and Polish heroes. The local parish priest, who was also a high school classmate of my father's, asked me to drill my Catholic friends in the Latin verses of the catechism that they recited as altar boys. The priest often teased that I would serve as an altar boy if my friends didn't learn their lines.

But even among my friends, antisemitism kept surfacing. I remember a lazy, warm spring afternoon when I was sitting on the porch of the Roskiewiczes' house. I must have been about nine. A few schoolmates were there, including one of my best friends, Jurek Roskiewicz. Jurek's mother, a teacher, was telling us about her childhood. I was half listening until I heard the word *Jews*.

"Always beware of Jews," she said. "Especially in the spring. I was coming home from my grandma one night when I was about six years old. I passed a big old house where some Jews lived. Two old men with long beards and black coats and hats jumped out from the bushes and started dragging me to their house. I screamed and kicked until I got free and ran away as fast as I could. My mother told me that I was lucky because the Jews kill Christian children every spring to get blood to make matzos." The boys listened in horror.

I ran home and confronted my parents. "Why do we kill Christian children for our matzos?" I told my father the story that I had heard, and he shook his head in disgust and disbelief. He said this lie had been started centuries earlier by evil haters of Jews. The accusation was untrue and denied by popes and cardinals, kings and presidents, by righteous people of every nation. Still, many Christians repeated and accepted the ugly story. I was upset that my own friends would believe such an ugly lie about the Jews.

The summer of 1939 was a peaceful stretch of sunshine and blue skies. Oceans of wheat turned gold and covered the countryside. In the gardens apples and pears grew heavy and ripe. I was eleven. It was the start of my summer vacation. Going back to school in September seemed very far away. The fifth grade was behind me, and the next year would be my last before I began high school. I ventured out early every morning to find my friends. A few times I traveled to Rzeszów by myself, where I visited my uncle Kalman, who introduced me to the excitement and attractions of the city.

Rzeszów had a Jewish tennis club. Children went there to socialize and play tennis. I would walk to the tennis club and look through the fence at the teenagers playing and laughing. I was eager to grow up and join their world on the other side of the fence.

In July I was introduced to a Hebrew tutor my parents had hired to prepare me for my bar mitzvah when I turned thirteen. I had a few lessons and memorized some Hebrew letters and words. My family was not very religious. We celebrated the holidays in our home and sometimes attended synagogue. My bar mitzvah would be a milestone in my Jewish education, and I would have new responsibilities as a Jewish adult in our community.

Manek applied for admission to the well-known Aeronautical Engineering College in Katowice. His grades were excellent, and he had strong recommendations from his teachers. To our dismay, his application was rejected. Inquiries revealed that the school did not accept Jews. Father asked some friends who had served with him in the Polish army and now held important government positions to help get Manek admitted. They wrote letters and made phone calls and visits on his behalf. One afternoon a special messenger delivered an acceptance letter to our house. Manek was thrilled to be accepted and to move to

Katowice, where a favorite uncle, my mother's brother Benek, lived and worked as a dentist. My parents had reservations about Manek's attending a school that did not accept Jews. Still, this was what Manek wanted, and we were glad for him.

This was the summer that I discovered girls. I tried to keep my first crush a secret. I saw one special and favorite girl many times but never dared to speak to her. Her name was Esther, and she was about fourteen. She was beautiful. Her family lived in a small house near the synagogue. Her father was a religious man who worked as a scribe and traded in religious items. I was determined to meet Esther and to speak to her. I often combed my hair, polished my shoes, put on my best clothes, and walked through the market square in the hope of catching a glimpse of her and getting her to notice me. One day I saw Esther standing alone on the sidewalk outside a shop. I nervously approached her and wanted to say something to impress her. I managed only to mumble and blush with embarrassment. Esther looked up at me and gave me the most beautiful smile. Before I could regain my composure, her mother came out of the store and motioned Esther to follow her. As she walked away, Esther turned to me and said in a sweet voice, "Goodbye, Lucek." Her mother gave me a sharp and a questioning look. All I could think of was that Esther knew my name. I was in love.

The joys of summer and my infatuation with Esther did not stop me from sensing the uneasiness in our lives. I overheard my parents talking about Jews being expelled from Germany and stories of restrictions and persecutions. Mother's sister, Pauline, wrote that her family was experiencing discrimination in "German" Vienna and that they were trying to emigrate to the United States. My parents talked about leaving Poland. Father felt that as a lawyer, tied to the language and laws of Poland, it would be impossible for him to find work in other countries. He did think that we should have the option to leave if times became really bad. He registered our family with the American consulate in Kraków and filed for papers to emigrate to the United States. Manek was anxious about college. Father told him that the annual Polish quota for emigration to the United States was small and that Manek would probably be able to start and finish school before our turn came.

"They need aeronautical engineers in America," Father told Manek, "more than they need Polish lawyers."

My parents and their friends gathered around our radio to listen to angry German speeches. The news each day threatened our future. Toward the end of the summer a Polish organization known as the Endecja started organizing anti-Jewish activities. They put up posters with antisemitic slogans and ugly cartoons of Jews. We were angry and insulted. Many of our Catholic neighbors found it all quite amusing. We could only hope that this would pass as quickly as it had come.

In August my parents and their friends fretted about the news on the radio and headlines in the newspapers. I learned that the Germans were demanding a piece of Poland as a route from Germany to East Prussia and Danzig. I heard Polish proclamations on the radio that not an inch of Polish land would be given up and that, if war came, the Polish army would smash the Germans on the way to Berlin. The threat of war was in the air. My friends and I sensed our parents' concern, but we also felt excited about a victory over the German army.

Manek warned me that my father might be called back to military duty as a reserve officer. My father discussed the situation with us at dinner. "I'm worried there might be war," he said as we sat around the table. He stopped cutting the loaf of bread that Mother had placed before him. "I am afraid that a war will be hard for Poland and especially hard for us Jews." My visions of brave Polish soldiers riding into Berlin faded. "Chances are that I will be called early," my father continued. "Manek may also have military duty." Manek had participated in the high school's junior officer-candidate program. My father turned to me and smiled. "You may have to take care of your mother for a while." I was scared that my father and Manek would be sent away. My mother put her arms around my shoulders and said with assurance, "Lucek and I will manage just fine."

Father told us that during World War I, the Germans were better behaved than the other armies that moved across Poland. "The Jews could even communicate with them in Yiddish." He shook his head. "Now, I don't know. From what we hear about Hitler and what he is doing to the Jews in Germany and Austria, it could be much different and more dangerous." My mother looked troubled. "I remember during the last war, when the Russians were coming. So many people put their families and belongings into wagons and drove into the night. They lived in the fields and forests or had to find shelter in some deserted barn. Back in town, their homes were looted. Staying home is safest." Father echoed her feelings. "We have a roof over our head and beds to sleep in. We are not strangers. We have friends here in Tyczyn."

The newspapers and radio carried stories about the likelihood of war. The Polish government refuted the constant German threats. We heard about alliances between Poland, France, and England. My parents met with friends and discussed the dangers late into the night. I would stand in the hallway to listen and try to understand what was happening. They spoke of Kristallnacht, a terrible night of violence staged against the Jews in Germany. No one knew what to expect or how to prepare. My parents decided to stockpile food.

At the end of August mobilization notices were posted on the store windows and distributed on the streets. My father received his notice at work. He was a staff officer and would have to report in one month in Tarnów, a town forty miles west. Other, younger men had to report right away. Many were schoolteachers, and the government announced that schools, scheduled to open in September, would be closed until further notice. I was not upset, but we all felt bad for Manek, whose plans to start college seemed unlikely. He tried to hide his disappointment from our parents. The next day other notices went up. High school students aged sixteen and older who had participated in junior officer-candidate programs had to stand by for military duty. My mother now worried about my father and my brother.

Grandmother telephoned from Katowice, where she was staying with Uncle Benek. She said that if the war started, she would come to stay with us. Benek, Uncle Henry, and his wife, Nadzia, would come too. That night my mother made plans to accommodate the four visitors. Manek, Uncle Benek, and I would share one bedroom. We would move two beds into the dining room for Grandmother, Henry, and Nadzia. Normally, Grandmother's visit would have been a happy occasion. This visit confirmed our premonition about the troubles ahead.

On September 1, 1939, Germany invaded Poland. Urgent voices in the kitchen woke me early in the morning. I could hear the radio and my parents talking with some visitors. I came into the kitchen and my father said, "Germany has attacked Poland. We are at war." He and the others looked solemn. A neighbor said, "There are rumors that they may use poison gas against us, and there are not enough gas masks for all the people in Tyczyn. We should get gas masks as soon as the stores open." My father turned to Manek, "The Germans could drop bombs. Get a pick and a shovel. Take Lucek and start digging a bomb shelter out back." We had received a civil defense flyer with designs for a small family shelter. My father, the only Jewish member of the city council, would have to spend most of the day in emergency council meetings.

Manek and I got the pick and shovels and started digging. The ground was hard and full of roots. We made little progress. Before long my mother called us into the house. She had heard from Grandma. They were leaving Katowice immediately and should be here by morning. My mother worried that the trains could be bombed. We had furniture to move, beds to set up, and drawers to empty. We had no time for idle worry. War had not brought marching troops, military bands, or fluttering flags, only fears, rumors, and uncertainty.

Grandmother, Uncle Benek, Uncle Henry, and Nadzia arrived after a long and difficult journey. Our house was cramped, and before long everyone became tense and disagreeable. At the market square and on the street corners I could feel the tension building from day to day. People gathered in anxious groups to exchange news from relatives serving in the army or living close to where the fighting was taking place. A few small units of Polish soldiers passed through town. They marched in the streets and rode on horse-drawn wagons. On cloudless days we could see airplanes flying overhead.

A small Polish army unit was stationed in Tyczyn in the city hall building. The soldiers organized a registration of all male high school students for military assignment. Manek registered and was told to stand by for orders. Father was busy with city council meetings. He was still trying to get gas masks for us. His military reporting date was only three weeks away. News reports on the radio and in the papers declared that the Germans had attacked Poland from Slovakia in the south, from Germany in the west, and from East Prussia in the north. The Germans were advancing on all fronts, and the Polish army was retreating. Everyone was shaken, and the Jews were especially fearful. The Polish government issued instructions that all military-age men should prepare to join the Polish army.

Groups of weary Polish soldiers began moving east through Tyczyn. They were followed by groups of civilians. This became the time to decide whether we would leave our homes to follow the retreating Polish army. In our house the discussions and debates lasted into the night. Benek and Manek decided to head east, ahead of the Germans. They would try to find safe accommodations and then send for us to follow them. Father insisted that the rest of the family stay in Tyczyn and not become refugees. That evening my mother helped Manek pack some food and clothing in a backpack. Father wrote letters to relatives in the town of Lwów and gave them to Manek, along with some Polish złotys and US dollars.

Early the next morning Manek, Benek, and friends of my father's, the lawyer Wiener and his wife, bid us a tearful farewell and hitched a ride on one of the horse-drawn wagons. We stood in front of our house and watched them disappear around the bend of the road leading toward Błażowa. Grandmother and Mother cried. I stood with my father and held back my tears.

All that day and into the night Polish soldiers retreated through town. We stood on the streets and gave them food and water and wished them God's blessings for a victory over the Germans. By the next morning only a few stragglers appeared on the street. By noon the soldiers of the local army garrison and the Polish police had packed their belongings and weapons and driven off in wagons. We civilians were alone.

Late that afternoon looters broke into the liquor store and got wildly drunk. They broke into apartments and carried out furniture, dishes, and clothing. We stayed in our house with our doors locked and curtains drawn. My father and Uncle Henry were ready to defend us if the looters tried to break in. They brought some heavy walking canes down from the attic to use in a fight. They pushed the dining room credenza in front of our entry door. My father loaded his army pistol. We stayed awake all night. The looters did not come to our house. We could hear them in the streets, drunk and yelling. The next morning the streets were empty. We stayed in all day, away from the doors and windows.

✦ 2 ✦

Just before noon on the tenth day of war, the German army drove through Tyczyn. The soldiers rode on motorcycles, half-tracks, tanks, artillery pieces, and trucks, all marked with black crosses. They drove through Tyczyn in relentless pursuit of the retreating Polish army. I watched them through a window at the front of the house. My parents and grandmother stood with me. Grandmother was upset and left to join Uncle Henry and Nadzia, who had been ill for several weeks, in another room.

Some neighbors stood outside watching the German troops pass by. Mr. Luszczak and his two daughters were there; so were the local judge and his wife, my parents' bridge partners and friends. I saw Mr. Krieger, a Jewish neighbor. Down the street I saw my friends the Szpala boys. The people of Tyczyn watched the Germans chase after our soldiers. I went outside and stood shoulder to shoulder with my friends and neighbors. In our sad faces, clenched jaws, and teary eyes was the heartbreak of defeat. For a moment we were one people, Polish Christians and Jews. Together we mourned the loss of our freedom.

The German troops moved through Tyczyn for two days. Our lives returned to a state of quiet uncertainty and worry. Many men had left with the Polish army or were refugees in the east. At least no Germans were stationed in Tyczyn. During the next few weeks German administrators and police became established in neighboring Rzeszów. The Germans from Rzeszów came to Tyczyn occasionally but stayed only a few hours. They appointed a German resident of Tyczyn as the new mayor and transferred two Polish police officers from Rzeszów to maintain civil order. The courthouse and the school remained closed. The Germans issued a decree that all Poles had to turn in their radios and weapons. We carried our radio, Manek's air rifle, and one of Father's pistols to city hall. Manek and I had buried his other pistol in the garden where we had dug the start of our bomb shelter.

The fighting in Poland ended. The Germans occupied western and central Poland, and the Russians occupied eastern Poland. Many people who had fled east with the retreating Polish army were in the Russian zone. Manek and Benek were there, and we waited anxiously for news. Some of those who had moved east with the Polish army started returning. We got word that Manek and Benek were safe on the Russian side. They were in a small town where Benek had friends. We were told that the new German-Russian border was open, that people could cross in either direction. We heard stories that the Germans were forcing Jews living near the border to cross to the Russian zone.

We also heard rumors that German troops were physically abusing Jews in small Polish towns. Again we faced the question of whether we should cross to the Russian side. This was the difficult matter among our Jewish friends and neighbors. Many families were afraid to remain under German control. Others insisted that the stories of Jews being abused had not been confirmed and that, even if they were true, were probably only isolated incidents. They recalled their experiences during World War I when the German troops were well commanded and disciplined. Families at home during that war were better off than those that became refugees. My father pointed out that the Russians might not treat us any better than the Germans. Many believed that these troubles would not last long. The French and the English would eventually come to our rescue. Before long we heard that crossing the new border was difficult. My father decided that we would stay home.

One morning German troops arrived in Tyczyn. We heard that German soldiers and trucks were on the market square and would be quartered in the Tyczyn courthouse. Our house was within sight of the courthouse, and I watched the Germans arrive. I saw soldiers in uniforms with a skull on their caps. Father said that they were the SS and dangerously violent and antisemitic. The German soldiers stopped a few men on the street and forced them to unload heavy boxes from their trucks and carry them into the courthouse. I saw some boys, including some of my Christian friends, watching from the sidewalk.

My parents and their friends decided that it was safest for Jewish adults to stay inside. The Germans had not bothered any of the younger boys, so I was allowed to go out. I watched the Germans from the distance, peering from around a corner or from behind a tree. A few soldiers walked up the street to the market square. My Christian friends followed them closely, and I followed carefully behind. At the square the Germans stormed into a Jewish shop. They came out cursing, kicking, and dragging two elderly, bearded Jews. The German soldiers beat them with truncheons and forced them to crawl on the street like animals. They threw off their black hats and tore their clothing as they pushed the Jews about. Some Jewish women pleaded with the Germans to stop. The Germans hit the women with the truncheons and drove them away. They forced the old men to stand at attention with bruised and bloody faces, while the Germans tore and cut off their beards and side curls with scissors and wire cutters. I could not bear to hear the shouts of the Germans and the cries of the Jewish women. Then I heard laughter coming from a group of Poles watching the spectacle. I knew the Jewish men and women being beaten and abused. I knew them from their stores, from passing them on the streets, from our synagogue. A Polish man walked by and saw me at the edge of the market square. "Don't go there," he warned me. "They are beating up the Jews."

The Germans turned to the circle of Poles and spoke with them. Some soldiers and SS started walking toward the alley with the Poles behind them. I ran down the alley past the synagogue and hid behind a small house. They came to the synagogue door. When they saw that it was locked, they shot at the door and kicked it open. Some German soldiers and the SS stormed in through the broken door. I watched in frozen silence. The SS and the soldiers came out of the synagogue carrying the sacred Torah scrolls and armfuls of prayer books. They threw the books and Torahs to the ground and used them to make a bonfire.

The fire grew, and black smoke drifted toward the sky. The Germans shouted with joy, and the Poles, the people of my town, my neighbors and friends, two of them my classmates, did a little dance and cheered. I turned and ran home. I ran between small old houses, through back-yards and gardens and down the alleys. I ran into my house, up the stairs, and threw myself onto my bed. I closed my eyes, but I could still see our prayer books and our Torahs burning. I could still hear the cries as the men were beaten.

Grandmother saw me run up the stairs and called Mother to come after me. I told her that I had seen Jews beaten on the market square and the Germans break into the synagogue and burn our prayer books and Torahs. "The Poles were laughing, even boys from my school." My father came, and my mother told him what had happened. He turned to me and said, "Do not despair. These were not the only Torahs. There are Torahs in England, France, America, Palestine, and, yes, even in Tyczyn. The Torah, our precious teaching, cannot be destroyed by fire."

That evening a few of Father's friends and clients came to our house. They were shaken by what had happened and feared for their families' safety. The question of leaving to cross to the Russian side was again the topic of conversation. There were no easy answers. They decided to try to find out whether there was any way to get out of Tyczyn safely and cross the border. Late that night, well past midnight, our friends left our home in the darkness, uncertain of what the next day would bring.

In the morning we sat in the kitchen. My mother was dressed but still wore her slippers. She stood at the stove boiling water for tea. My father sat at the table with me. Grandmother, Uncle Henry, and Nadzia were still in their rooms. There was a loud banging on our front door. My father rushed to open it and found two German officers in black uniforms. Behind them stood two Polish police officers. "Dr. Salzman?" one of the Germans asked. "Yes," my father answered. "Gestapo. Come with us! At once!" they shouted in German. Both my parents tried to find out why and where he was being taken. The Germans ignored their pleas and questions. They allowed my father to take his coat and hat and escorted him to a car waiting outside. They ordered the rest of us to stay inside. I heard car doors slam and the cars drive away. In less than a minute my father was gone. Grandmother and my uncle came into the kitchen. My mother was crying as she told them what had happened. Grandmother put her arms around my mother.

My mother stepped back from my grandmother. "Take care of Lucek and the house. I am going to Rzeszów to help Henryk." My mother, an elegant and delicate lady who played the piano and the zither, who took pride in the fame of her Viennese pastry, changed into a wife of great strength and courage. She would go anywhere, plead with anyone, and do anything to help my father.

My mother quickly packed a small bag with my father's toiletries and clothing. She said, "I have to get to Rzeszów. I am sure they took him there. I might have to stay for a few days. I will stay with Kalman and try to let you know what is happening." She held my face in her hands and kissed me. "Be good. I love you. I have to go. Please do not be afraid. I promise I will come back and bring Father." She turned and walked out the door. I was brokenhearted yet proud to see her bravery and determination to bring my father home.

The hours after she left were long and empty. A few neighbors and friends, Jews and Gentiles, came over after they found out what had happened. I spent the afternoon and almost all the next day standing by the front door, waiting for news and hoping for the return of my parents. I felt utterly alone and helpless, but I could do nothing but wait. Two days later someone slipped an envelope under our door. It was a short note from my mother. She wrote that my father was being held by the Gestapo in a prison in Rzeszów. She had tried to visit him and bring him some food and his belongings, but she was not allowed to see him. She was able to learn why Father was arrested and hoped that with luck and help she might be able to get him released. We continued to wait for news or their return.

My mother came back two days later, weary from the hard journey. She had gotten a short ride in a peasant's cart and walked the rest of the way. She told us about Father's arrest and what she would do to help him. Through friends in Rzeszów she was able to contact a Polish police officer who worked in the prison. He told the story behind

Father's arrest, which had its beginnings back in September, after the Polish authorities had left and before the Germans had arrived. Some thieves had looted a number of empty apartments, among them the apartment of the lawyer Wiener and his neighbors, a Polish couple who were staying with relatives in a nearby village. When the couple returned, they discovered that their apartment had been looted. They reported the theft and the names of people whom they suspected, who were then arrested and locked up in the Rzeszów prison. During an interrogation one of the thieves, a man named Rozmus, offered to share vital information with the Germans to lessen the harshness of his treatment. Rozmus told them that during the Polish retreat from Tyczyn, he and others who had served in the Polish army were approached by a Polish reserve officer who asked them to join an underground resistance unit. Rozmus told them that the Tyczyn lawyer Dr. Salzman was the ringleader.

My mother made many trips to Rzeszów to bring my father food and try to visit him. The German troops and SS stationed in Tyczyn had left, and my mother could move freely in town to look for people who might help her. She spoke to veterans of the Polish army who wrote statements denying that my father had tried to recruit them. She presented the statements to the Gestapo and pleaded with them to reconsider. They did not respond. The long nights in our home became unbearable as we pictured my father held in a dark dungeon, abused and alone and beyond our reach.

Other difficult problems demanded my mother's time and attention. We were warned that the Germans would search homes and that it would be dangerous if any Jewish men were living with us. We made arrangements for Uncle Henry and Nadzia to move in with another family. Money became a problem. Since his arrest Father's income had stopped, the banks were closed, and our small reserve of cash had lost its value because of inflation. My mother started selling our warm clothes, silver, and jewelry for a few złotys to buy food. I sensed her growing despair as she sold or traded our valuable possessions.

My mother was gone most of the time. I spent the days visiting my friends in the neighborhood. I was not the only one whose father was missing. The Germans had arrested Mr. Roskiewicz. Other men were still in the east with the Polish army. School was closed, and we spent empty hours talking about the war. Some neighbors asked us to harvest fall apples and pears in exchange for a share of the crop. My friends told me that they had heard that school would open in a few days. That evening my mother returned from Rzeszów. I told her about school, and she welcomed the news as a sign of better times. She valued education and wanted me to have something of a normal life.

Everyone at home helped me to prepare for school. They washed and ironed my clothes. I polished my shoes and collected pencils and pens. My mother spent precious money to buy some paper and a notebook. On the first day of school I put my supplies in my backpack and walked the familiar streets and shortcuts, greeting friends and classmates along the way. In school there was the normal confusion of a first day. I found my sixth-grade class and saw my old teacher, the one who had questioned the ethnic origins of Jews. He looked at me strangely and asked me to step out into the hallway. He faced me with embarrassment and sadness. He put his hands gently on my shoulders and told me that he was sorry but Jews were not allowed to attend school. He stood silently as I walked out of the school. The streets were still filled with students, and I was the only one walking the other way. I avoided the others, but I could hear them whispering as I rushed home. My mother was upset, but there was nothing to be done.

My mother came up with a plan to free Father from prison. She would get written testimony from Germans living in Tyczyn who knew my father and Rozmus. The challenge would be getting recognized *Volksdeutscher*, individuals of German nationality, to testify to the Gestapo in defense of a Jew. The huge risk was that one of the Germans would back Rozmus's testimony. Nothing else had worked, and the passing of time lessened Father's chances for surviving the Gestapo prison. Mother approached three German families in Tyczyn. One was the Heggenbergers. They owned a chimney-sweeping business and lived near our house. Mother pleaded with them and offered them money. They and two other families agreed to sign a statement supporting Father. My mother typed the defending letters in German on our old typewriter. After they signed them, she traveled to Rzeszów to deliver them to the prison. The Gestapo officer would not accept the testimony unless the three Volksdeutscher would come in person. My mother rushed back and again pleaded with the three Tyczyn Germans to help her. A few days later the three Germans traveled to Rzeszów with my mother to appear before the Gestapo. She was exhausted when she returned that evening but hopeful that Father would soon be free to come back to us. The Germans had spoken firmly in Father's defense. The Gestapo questioned them intensely and said they would make a decision in a few days. After so many months of painful longing and worry, we finally felt hope that Father's horrible imprisonment would end and we would be reunited.

We stood by the windows anxiously every day, waiting and watching for Father's return. There was no sign of him, and our hope turned to despair. My mother made the difficult trip to Rzeszów again, but she was still not allowed to visit my father. The Gestapo ordered her to return to Tyczyn and await their decision. The days grew shorter and turned cold as autumn turned to winter. The gray days added to our gloom. There were new problems and shortages. The Poles entered the synagogue and chopped up the wooden benches, tables, and window frames for firewood. Wind blew through the gaping doors and missing windows, and for a few days the charred pages of the prayer books flew into the cold air.

A few Jewish high school students organized a study group. They planned to return to school when the occupation ended and did not want to fall behind in their studies. They met in each other's homes, assigned each other homework, and graded it. They began to teach classes for the younger Jewish children. My mother convinced me to attend the classes. She felt that my father would want me to continue to learn and would be pleased when he returned. I found comfort and support from the families and tutors who shared in and understood the misery of our days.

At home we gathered in the kitchen to try to keep warm. We talked endlessly of my father and tried to convince each other that the delay in his release must be due to some problems of paperwork and not a sign that we had failed. We tried not to speak about our poverty or the escalating restrictions imposed upon us by the German District Administration. One evening I sat at the kitchen table working on my studies as my mother and grandmother tried to turn some leftover potatoes into a meal. We heard a soft knock at the front door and hurried to open it, silently wishing that it might be my father, but found Manek standing there looking tired, thin, and shabby. We shouted with joy and disbelief and cried as we fell into each other's arms. My mother and Grandmother were overcome with relief that he had returned to us safely. Our excitement and celebration quickly turned to a quiet sorrow. Manek did not know about my father's arrest and imprisonment. He held his head in his hands and wept as my mother told him all that had taken place. She tried to offer him hope that Father would soon return, but her tears betrayed her.

Grandmother was anxious to hear news of Benek and the others who had moved east in search of safety and shelter. Manek told us that Benek had found work as a dentist in a hospital in Turka. He wanted Grandmother, Henry, and Nadzia to join him. My mother supported the plan and hoped that when my father returned, we might all be together.

We led Manek to his bed in the next room. He was exhausted and slept through the night and most of the next day. We tiptoed around the house and spoke in whispers so as not to wake him. My mother had a new look on her face, and she had a new energy as she worked to prepare a meal fit for a son's homecoming. Secretly, I prayed that his return was a good omen that my father would soon be free and we would be together again as a family.

When Manek finally awoke, we gathered around the kitchen table. My mother had prepared some soup and bought some bread to celebrate his return. As he ate, we told him about the changes that had taken place in Tyczyn: the German occupation, the destruction of the synagogue, the closing of the school to Jewish children, and the severe restrictions and shortages of food and fuel. Manek was upset at the news. With my father gone, Manek felt responsible for somehow easing the difficulties of our life. He told us how he had traveled east with

Benek on foot, by horse-driven wagons, and finally on a crowded train. They got to Lwów just before the Russians occupied it. The city was crowded with refugees. It was extremely difficult to find a place to stay or to purchase food. Entire families were sleeping on the streets, in stairways, and in the park. Manek and Benek had found our relatives, who wanted to offer to help, but their homes were already crowded with other friends and relatives. After a few days Manek and Benek decided to travel to Turka, a town west of Lwów where Benek had friends from high school. Benek found work in the dental department of the hospital. Manek tried to find work, but there were many desperate refugees, and after days of trying he found that nothing was available. He stayed in a room that Benek had rented from a Polish family. Soon Manek's money was gone.

Many refugees started returning to their own towns and villages. Manek had heard that Germans were abusing Jews in some towns and forcing those living close to the new border to cross to the Russian side. He worried about our family and decided to return to Tyczyn. Benek asked Manek to bring a message saying that Grandmother and Henry should join him in Turka. He had gotten a small raise and would look for an apartment where they could all live. He felt confident that he would be able to arrange for a job for Henry in the hospital.

Late one night Manek left to return to Tyczyn. He walked through the dark woods, spent his last money to cross the river in a small boat, and was lucky to hitch a ride in a peasant's cart. After traveling without rest or sleep for two days, he had come home.

Grandmother and Henry discussed moving across the border to live with Benek in Turka. Henry wanted to go, but Grandmother did not want to leave us while my father was still being held in the Gestapo prison. Henry and Nadzia left a few days later for Turka. They traveled late at night with only a few belongings and some food for the journey. A few weeks later Grandmother relented and agreed to join them. We had received messages from Benek that conditions were better, and my mother promised Grandmother that we would join them as soon as my father was released. Grandmother left late one night, guided by a paid peasant who would escort her across the border, where Benek and

Henry would meet her. For days afterward my mother was sad and upset, and the house was quiet and lonely without Grandmother.

As news got out about Manek's return, neighbors began to come to our house to ask about others who had traveled east and had not returned or sent word to their families still in Tyczyn. Manek tried to reassure them, telling them that many refugees were on the Russian side and that while it was relatively safe there, crossing the border and sending messages home was difficult. He had heard that regular mail service would start between the Russian and German areas and that our neighbors should hear from loved ones soon. They clung to his words with great hope.

Manek met with some of his old friends. He hoped to find out more about Father's situation and try to find a way to help secure his release. Manek's friends told him about the Germans' treatment of Jews and the restrictions and punishments imposed in Tyczyn and Rzeszów. He felt desperate to find a way to earn some money to buy food for us. With another friend he decided to open a bicycle repair shop. Bicycles had become an important mode of transportation, and both he and his friend had fixed their own bicycles for years. With Manek home, my mother decided to travel to Rzeszów and stay with some friends while she continued to try to help my father. She was torn about leaving us, but we convinced her that we would care for ourselves and that doing whatever she could to bring Father home was the best thing for all of us. Early the next morning she packed her suitcase and left for Rzeszów.

Manek and I were on our own. He became my protector during our mother's absence. He went to work at the bicycle repair shop every day, and occasionally he took me with him and gave me odd jobs to distract me from the constant worry about my parents. We bought bread and some food from neighbors who knew we were alone. In the evenings we prepared simple and meager meals in the kitchen and sat by the stove to keep warm.

German officials and police from Rzeszów came to Tyczyn every few days to meet with our Volksdeutscher mayor. During these visits the Germans always found some Jews, usually older men and women, and publicly humiliated them. They forced Jews to kneel down to polish their shoes, to crawl on all fours like animals, or to behave like fools. All while the Germans cursed and hit the elderly Jews with riding whips and rubber truncheons. Manek and I cautiously made our way through the back streets and alleys.

Winter came, and the streets were covered with snow. The wind swept drifts against the houses and leafless trees. Manek and I moved our beds to the kitchen so that we could conserve the wood and coal to heat our house. One morning I awoke in the cold kitchen and sat up in my bed. The light was on, and Manek was sitting at the table fully dressed. He saw me and whispered, "Mother and Father are home."

I wanted to shout as I jumped out of my bed and looked into my parents' darkened bedroom. I could see them sleeping in each other's arms. Quietly, I closed the door and turned to my brother. We clung to each other.

◆ 3 ◆

My father spent several days in bed resting and accepted few visitors. Friends brought potatoes, vegetables, and even some meat so that my mother could make him a few hearty meals to restore his strength. She brought him trays with soup and tea and spent hours at his side, holding his hands and watching him sleep. He had changed drastically during his imprisonment. He had lost a lot of weight and seemed frail and weary. We tried to cheer him with stories of Manek's bicycle shop and hopeful news of the war, while we avoided speaking of the difficult and terrible events that had taken place during his absence. My father listened quietly and sometimes turned his face from us to hide the pain and anguish in his eyes.

Every few days the Germans posted and distributed throughout the town new orders and restrictions with severe penalties for disobedience. Some directives limited Jews' use of telephones, buses, and trains. Others declared shops and streets off limits and set out specific rules prescribing the way Jews had to greet Germans on the street, including avoiding direct eye contact. We had to look down and step off the sidewalk while the Germans passed. The decrees closed the legal and medical practices of Jews and dismissed Jews from all government jobs. The daily struggles to feed the family, keep the house warm, and remain safe continued. My father was sick, ravaged by pains from severe stomach ulcers, which he had developed in the Gestapo prison. My mother tried to prepare bland healing meals for him from potatoes and ground wheat. He was bedridden and miserable, both physically and emotionally. He wanted to support and protect our family, but he could do little until he recovered. He never spoke of his experience in the Gestapo prison. I never found out about the terrible things that destroyed his health and broke his spirit. My mother left the house each morning to sell and trade our few remaining valuables. She had made essential contacts with the Poles who wanted to take advantage of our desperate situation. One day I noticed that she was no longer wearing her watch, and soon after her wedding ring disappeared. We never asked her about them and pretended not to notice. Day by day our lives were changing, and all we had accumulated and accomplished was slipping away.

A large group of Jewish refugees from Kalish, a town in western Poland, arrived in Tyczyn. They had been driven out by the Germans and sent on foot to find new places to live. Entire families appeared, ragged and hungry, looking for shelter. Jewish families took them in whenever we could and shared our meager meals and abundant misery. They brought stories of German persecution and brutality in Kalish and other cities. Fear and doom spread over the town like a dark sky before a storm.

The Germans decreed that a Judenrat, a Jewish council, be established in Tyczyn. The mayor selected and questioned five men, who were then approved by the German police. Goldman, from a wheat-merchant family, was appointed the chairman. All the men of the Judenrat were established residents and Jewish leaders. They worked out of an office in the Tuchmans' house on the market square. The Judenrat would serve as the contact between the Jewish community and the mayor and Germans from Rzeszów. The Germans ordered the Judenrat to organize a group of orderlies to ensure Jewish compliance with all orders and regulations from the German authorities. Manek was asked to volunteer. He agreed in hope of helping our Jewish community organize and deal more effectively with the Germans.

One of the first tasks for the Judenrat was to register all Jews older than twelve who were living in Tyczyn and the surrounding villages. On a designated day we were ordered to appear at the Judenrat office. This was the first time that my father had left the house since his return from prison. I walked with him to the market square. He was weak, and his steps were slow and painful. Standing in line for such a long time was difficult for him. After several hours our turn came, and we gave our names and dates and places of birth to a German official sitting behind a desk. The German checked our names against lists from city hall and the Judenrat. He barked and shouted questions at us and got angry when we did not understand the questions and answer quickly enough. My turn came, and I stood facing the German police officer. I gave him my last and first name. He shouted at me in German, and I had no idea what he was saying. My father, standing in line behind me, quickly translated that they wanted to know my *Beruf*, my occupation. The German shouted at my father to stand away and not to speak. I quickly said that I was a student, and the German shouted at me again and motioned for me to move to another line to have my picture taken. I waited for my father, and we slowly walked home. The registration had taken his strength. For the next few days he was even sicker and weaker.

A week later a new identification document, called a *Kennkarte*, was issued to all residents of Tyczyn. Each had a photograph, name, date and place of birth, and religion. The Kennkarten issued to Christians were printed on light blue paper, and those issued to Jews were yellow. The issuance of the Kennkarte was followed by a decree that all Jews older than fourteen had to wear an armband on their right arm. The specific instructions said that it had to be a white band nine to ten centimeters wide, with a large blue Star of David on it, and that it was to be worn above the elbow. The penalty for violating the order would be arrest and severe punishment. My mother cut a white sheet into armbands and stitched on a Star of David cut from blue cloth. We had to wear these at all times, even in our homes. We were now always marked as Jews.

Before the winter snows had melted, the Germans issued a new directive. Within a week all Jewish men and boys older than twelve had to appear at the Judenrat office to identify their craft, profession, and current place of work. The rumor was that Jewish men and boys without jobs would be subject to work assignments or sent to forced-labor camps in a distant forest, construction project, or mine. It became vital for everyone to have a job or valid excuse for not working. My father got a medical certificate from a physician stating that he was disabled. Manek showed that he was working as a Judenrat orderly and in the bicycle repair shop. Those who could not prove that they were working were assigned to hard labor jobs—paving and repairing roads or draining the swamps outside town. I was too young to claim that I was a craftsman and decided to find work as an apprentice in a shop in town.

My parents found me a job as an apprentice to Mr. Gorzelec, a master locksmith and blacksmith. I started work and registered at the Judenrat as an apprentice locksmith. He had three other apprentices, Catholic teenage boys who had worked for him for nearly a year. My first job was to sweep and clean the shop and to carry Mr. Gorzelec's toolbox on house calls to repair locks and hinges. He taught me to make keys and hinges out of the red-hot metal. The work was hard, hot, and dirty and a constant reminder of how our lives and fortunes had fallen.

Jewish parents struggled to feed, clothe, and shelter their children. We were still able to sell and trade our dwindling possessions to the Poles. In the evenings the Jewish teenagers tutored the children. Those few who had anything left to share gave to charity to help the very old and most needy Jews.

We received a letter from Turka. Grandmother, Uncle Henry, and Nadzia had arrived safely. Benek and Henry were working at the hospital. Nadzia's health was slowly improving, and Grandmother was keeping house for them. There were shortages, and they were doing the best they could. My mother wrote back, telling them that Father was home. We knew that the German authorities were censoring our letters, so we could not divulge many details of our difficult lives and our feeble attempts to manage.

A letter arrived from Mother's sister, Pauline, in America. This was the first news from her since before the war. She and her husband, Julius, and their children, Henry and Erika, were living in New York City. Julius was studying for an examination that would allow him to practice medicine. My cousins were in school. Pauline wrote that it was possible to send food packages to occupied Poland through Portugal and that she had sent one to us. My mother wrote back asking for medicine for Father, and tea and coffee, which we could trade for food.

A few weeks later a package arrived for us at the post office. It was full of tea, cocoa, and coffee, cans of meat, jars of jam, and small boxes of dried fruit. After our dinner of potatoes and vegetables, we enjoyed a taste of the chocolate cookies that came from the United States. We would trade the other foods for flour, bread, potatoes, and other essentials. My mother sold and traded the food from America carefully. Once or twice she got an egg for each of us. She was able to get some milk and oatmeal to help ease my father's chronic stomach pains. The arrival of the package from the United States reminded us that even though we felt isolated and alone, we had not been forgotten.

In town people spoke about an expected spring offensive by the French and English armies in the West that would defeat the Germans. Mr. Gorzelec told us that the French and English were waiting for the fields and roads to dry up. They would attack, and Germany would ask for peace, just as in the last war. I had heard the same predictions from others. My father felt sure that the French and English would defeat the Germans but that it would take a year or longer. "We must do everything we can to survive," he said. "When the war is over, we will all go to Palestine or America. We should have gone before."

Spring and the Passover holiday were approaching, the first Passover since the start of the war. The Passover holiday was always a special time of festive seder meals and visits to Grandmother's house in Lesko Łukawica. At our home or Grandmother's we always had special dishes, including my favorites: gefilte fish and chicken soup with matzo balls. Every year my mother would order the Passover matzos from a special bakery in Rzeszów. They would be delivered to our house a few days before the holiday, wrapped in white linen and kept in a large basket in the pantry. Our home was always filled with joyous anticipation as my mother worked with labor and love to orchestrate our seders. With our poverty, the shortage of food, and the constant menace of the Germans, I did not give much thought to the coming holiday. I could not help but be saddened that we would not celebrate Passover this year. My mother announced that we would do whatever was possible and that we would observe Passover. We would not neglect our Judaism. We were living out the Passover theme of bondage and needed to hear how liberation was always a possibility. "We will have a seder," my mother said. "Lucek will ask the four questions, and Dad will answer them. No feast, no fish, no beef, and no desserts, but maybe I can get a chicken and make a little soup. And we will have matzos. We may not have enough for all the days, but we will have matzos for our seders. We will bake them ourselves."

My mother ordered three kilograms of Passover flour from the baker Leibowitz and arranged for us to take a turn at his special oven. Manek and I would go along to help. The following Sunday my mother, Manek, and I walked up the alley that led to the Leibowitz house. We carried the small sack of flour, and the basket and white sheet in which we had kept the matzos in the past. In a back room of the house Jewish men, women, and children were baking matzos under Mr. Leibowitz's direction. We kneaded matzo dough in wooden bowls and rolled it out on flour-covered tables. In the corner the matzos were baking in a large, wood-fired stone oven. The room was crowded, the air filled with the aroma of baking matzo and with lively conversations. Mother was kneading dough with other women. Manek stood at the stove and used a long wooden shovel to place the flat pieces of dough into the oven and remove the golden baked matzos. I rolled a small toothed wheel over the flat dough before it was baked. When our matzos were ready, we wrapped them in the white linen and put them in our basket. We continued working to help bake matzos for the other families. Walking home that afternoon, I felt cheered from the communal baking. Despite all the troubles that had come our way because we were Jews, I was glad to be a part of the Jewish people and proud that we had not abandoned our traditions.

We had a seder that year. The food was modest, but we lit candles and drank a little wine. We had soup and chicken and the matzos that we baked ourselves. I asked the four questions, and my father answered them. We read the Passover Haggadah and told the story of the Israelites' bondage and liberation from Egypt.

German soldiers from an infantry division were stationed in Tyczyn again. They imposed new hardships and indignities on the Jews. Every day a group of Jewish men had to assemble to work for the German soldiers. They loaded and unloaded supplies, cleaned the soldiers' quarters, and washed their trucks. Whenever we passed a German soldier in town, we had to step off the sidewalk and bare our heads. Jews were prohibited from being out after dark in the section of town where the soldiers had pitched their tents.

One evening I came home from the locksmith shop and found my parents in an unusually cheerful mood. My mother had received another letter from America with news that food packages were on the way. My father was fluent in German and had been hired by two Gentile lawyers to translate legal briefs and appeals. As a Jew, my father was not allowed to practice law. Now he had found a way to earn some money. Manek left after dinner to visit his friends. My parents and I sat in our dining room. The window was open to the warm, quiet evening. My father turned to my mother and said, "Andzia, I feel like tonight is special somehow. Please for me, would you play the piano? It has been so long since we have had any music in this house. Please, play Beethoven's *Pathétique*." My mother held my father's cheek in her hand and looked at him with sadness and love. She moved to the piano and began to play. My father and I sat together watching, listening, and remembering the lovely musical evenings of the past.

Someone knocked at the door. My mother stopped playing, and my father went to open it. Two German officers stood in the doorway. "We heard you playing," one of them said. "It is all right. We just wanted to come and see who was playing so well. Please, continue playing. We will just stay a while." My father offered the soldiers chairs. My mother nervously returned to the piano and began to play. The captain made polite conversation with my father. He said that he was from Vienna and that the other soldier was a lieutenant from the Austrian Tyrol. My father and the lieutenant spoke about the Tyrolian villages set high up in the Alps; my father knew them from his days as an officer during the last war. The captain asked my mother to play a popular song and began to sing along.

Ja, ja, das Chianti Wein,
Es lads Uns alle ein,
So lass Uns lustig sein,
By golden Chianti Wein.
[Yes, yes, the Chianti wine,
It invites us all in,
So, let us be joyous
By the golden Chianti wine.]

I sat and listened to the music and conversation, captured by the peaceful moment. The German harshness was not in evidence this evening. After a while the soldiers stood up to leave and thanked my mother for performing such a beautiful concert for them. "Thank you," my father responded. "We enjoyed this too. Even though we are from here and you come from Austria, we are all human beings." "No! No!" The captain shook his head. "We are not the same. We are superior Germans and you are only Jews!" We were stung by his words.

❖ 4 ❖

Several weeks went by, filled with the daily struggle to find food and avoid the German soldiers on the street. One day the Polish newspaper that the Germans published in Kraków flashed a bold headline in red ink: FRANCE SURRENDERS TO GERMAN FORCES! ENGLISH TROOPS TRAPPED IN DUNKIRK!

This was terrible news. Germany had occupied Denmark, Norway, Holland, and Belgium. France had surrendered. The English had been cut off at Dunkirk and had retreated. Italy had made a pact with Germany and entered the war against France and England. The German military seemed to be invincible. No English troops were moving north from Hungary to rescue us. With the German victory no one could think of a country in Europe that had the might or the desire to come to our aid. The future of Poland and our future were bleak.

In the locksmith shop Mr. Gorzelec was distraught. We bent over our work and tried to avoid his temper. "I don't want to hear any mention of Paris or Dunkirk today!" he insisted. "We have work to do! I will not allow any lazy boys to work in my shop!" We worked swiftly and silently, though our hearts were heavy with worry. That night I found an atlas among Manek's books and searched for a map of Europe. I found Germany, France, and Italy, the Low Countries, Scandinavia, and Russia. They were all under German control or allied with Germany. And we were here in Tyczyn, a tiny speck too small to even be on the map, in the middle of immense enemy territory. I felt like we were drifting in a little boat, in the middle of a stormy ocean, with no oars and no sight of land.

German troops moved into Tyczyn and were quartered in houses and apartments throughout town. They moved into our home and took over two bedrooms, my father's office, and the waiting room. Twelve or fifteen soldiers were living under our roof. We tried to stay out of sight while they were around. They insulted and cursed us and ordered us to do their chores. We cleaned their rooms, polished their boots, and washed their laundry. Sometimes in the evenings they would get drunk, and then we would stay away from the house for hours. My parents, my brother, and I moved into the kitchen and the dining room. We carried most of our furniture and belongings up into the attic and pushed two small beds and a dresser into the dining room. We traded our better furniture to neighbors and local farmers in exchange for firewood, potatoes, and flour. During the next few days the farmers arrived in filthy wagons and carried off our piano and polished mahogany furniture.

More German combat troops were stationed in Tyczyn. Every morning they demanded that the Judenrat provide a group of Jewish workers for menial jobs. On the streets they stopped Jewish men and women marked by the Jewish armbands and made them do all kinds of demeaning work and humiliated them by ordering them to scrub the sidewalks with their handkerchiefs. One German, the *Unteroffizier* Pitchkie, was a hateful and cruel soldier who supervised the Jewish workers. The German soldiers jokingly called him the "king of the Jews." He took pleasure in hitting and kicking the Jewish workers. He forced them, along with any other Jews he grabbed on the street, to march in step until they were exhausted. Sometimes he made them strip to their underwear and do calisthenics. The German soldiers and some of the Tyczyn Poles followed him around and laughed at his violent antics.

No Jew was safe from Pitchkie. I traveled the back alleys and went through people's yards just to avoid him. I was too young to have to wear a Jewish armband and hoped that this would save me from harm. A few times he singled me out, but I pretended that his shouts and commands were not directed at me and walked on. I was lucky that he let me go. Someone must have told him that I was a Jew. One time he spotted me walking near the market square. He shouted and pointed his gun at me and yelled for me to join a group of Jews whom he had rounded up for one of his tirades. He ordered us to march and run and march again until I was ready to drop. I was filled with dread and panic, and my feet were swollen and burned with blisters. When he finally let us go, he pointed his pistol at me and warned me that he would remember me.

Pitchkie was riding his motorcycle though town when he spotted me walking home from the apprentice shop. He stopped and roughly pulled me onto the back of his motorcycle and took me for a terrifying, reckless ride. He drove off the road and over rocks and ruts. I held on to the sides of the bike, afraid to touch him. Pitchkie laughed and hollered and drove his motorcycle over the worst Tyczyn streets until I finally fell off. I ran home covered with cuts and bruises, bleeding and humiliated. I vowed that I would be more careful to avoid him and that I would outrun him if he tried to get me again.

One morning I left home for the shop, hopeful that he would not be out on the streets so early. I walked down a deserted road and saw him with a group of German soldiers. He saw me and started yelling, "You boy! Dirty Jew! Come here!" I started running as fast as I could. Two German soldiers ran after me and grabbed me. They kicked me and dragged me along the ground back to Pitchkie. They pulled me up and bent me over a wooden bench, and Pitchkie began whipping me with his rubber truncheon. I had never felt such horrible pain, and I could hear myself screaming like a wounded animal. The German soldiers whipped me and laughed at my shrieks. A group of Poles watched me being beaten but stood silent as I cried out in pain. They finally let me go, and I staggered toward the locksmith shop.

That night I did not tell my parents what Pitchkie had done to me. My father was in bed sick again, and my mother was worried about our growing troubles. I was upset and shaken, but I could not bring myself to tell them. I knew that they would be crushed and heartbroken that not even children were safe in our town. Later that evening when we got into bed, I told Manek what had happened to me. He looked at the marks left by the truncheon and put some cream on my cuts and scrapes. He wrapped his arms around me and promised to look after me and to make sure that this did not happen again. I turned to the wall in the darkness and cried. Even though I was only twelve, I knew that I would have to take care of myself.

Through the summer of 1940 and into the early days of fall, life for the Jews became increasingly difficult as the Germans added restrictions and directives. Jews were no longer allowed to travel from Tyczyn to Rzeszów without specific written documents from the police. We were forbidden to visit neighboring villages, where we had been able to buy or barter our belongings for food. Families who lived in separate towns were cut off from each other. It was nearly impossible and dangerous to request a travel permit from the police. A few desperate Jews removed their armbands and traveled to other towns. Some Poles recognized their Jewish neighbors and denounced them to the police. The Jews caught were arrested, beaten, and sent to forced-labor camps. Jewish businesses and stores were turned over to Gentile Polish managers, while the Jewish owners were forced out or reduced to menial jobs. The Germans organized a system to ration food and allowed the Jews pitifully less than the Poles. Poverty and hunger invaded our Jewish homes. My father's health worsened, and he suffered chronic stomach pains. Without medicine or a bland diet his condition deteriorated. He kept working, translating legal documents, but his earnings amounted to only a few złotys.

The travel restrictions curtailed my mother's attempt to sell and trade our belongings to the Poles. She was desperate to earn some money for our family. Mrs. Gruber, the Jewish widow of the pharmacist, had been my mother's friend for years. They joined with a local Polish man who had gotten sugar and sugar beets from the black market and started making hard candies to sell in town. They made the candy in Mrs. Gruber's apartment above the drugstore. My mother spent two or three long days there each week. We looked after my father and waited anxiously for her to return at night.

The weather turned cold, and the first snow fell. People stopped riding their bicycles, and Manek's shop had no work. He used his spare time to help my mother sell and deliver the candy. I kept working in the locksmith shop. I was not paid, but the job kept me from being sent to a forced-labor camp. Mrs. Gorzelec was kind enough to offer me some of the soup she cooked for her husband each day. By eating at work, I was able to eat less of the meager meals that my mother prepared at home. I felt that I was helping my parents and brother to survive on what little we had. On many days we had no food in our house, and we went to bed hungry.

Snow fell upon snow, and frigid winds sculpted impassable drifts. The freezing air invaded our home. We would gather in the kitchen at night wearing layers of clothing and huddle near the wood stove until we fell asleep and the fire burned out. In the mornings the windows were icy. Farmers stopped coming to town to sell and barter their crops. The food rations were available only sporadically. We could have bought food on the black market if we had any money. Jewish parents stood on the streets and begged for food for their starving children.

We received another package from Aunt Pauline and sold the delicacies for some money. She wrote a letter saying that they were doing well in the United States. Our spirits were lifted. We were desperate and glad to know that Jews who had fared better than we were trying to help us. We also received a letter from our cousin Julek Birman, who had been deported by the Russians to a remote labor camp in Siberia. We were relieved that my grandmother and uncles had avoided deportation and were still managing to survive in Turka.

In the beginning of January 1941 my family planned a surprise for me after our evening meal. My mother brought out a tray of cupcakes, and everyone wished me a happy birthday. I could not believe my eyes at the incredible feast. How had she managed to give me such a treat during this terrible time of rationing? I was thirteen years old. My father promised me that one day our troubles would end, the synagogue would reopen, and I would have a bar mitzvah. He told me that under Jewish law, I was a man now and a responsible adult of the Jewish community. I did not want to spoil the moment by telling him that I had not considered myself to be a child since the day the Germans came to town more than a year before.

Gestapo and SS soldiers started coming to Tyczyn every few days. They met with the Tyczyn mayor and the Judenrat. Stories reached us from Rzeszów that the Germans were viciously mistreating the Jews. We heard that the Gestapo had arrested and executed members of the Rzeszów Judenrat for not cooperating with the German administration. The Germans had forced the Rzeszów Jews to pay a large fine as a punishment and compensation for the behavior of the executed members of the Judenrat. The German police searched the homes of the Judenrat, looking for valuables and illegal possessions. They confiscated their little food and clothing for no reason at all.

One afternoon, while Manek and I were away, the German police searched our home. I came home in the evening from the locksmith shop and found my parents distraught. My mother had been crying. They would not tell me what the Germans had said or done during the search, except that they had taken Father's typewriter, Manek's camera, some books, and a few pieces of china. When the Gestapo and SS came to town, the Jews would alert each other, and entire families would run to hide in attics, sheds, and even in the surrounding fields and forests. When the Germans caught any Jews hiding, they beat and arrested them. Sometimes we hid for hours in the black night along the banks of the Stryj River. We crouched in the dark and cold until we heard the German trucks leaving for Rzeszów. Parents kept their children close to home and were ready to flee at the slightest hint of danger.

Spring arrived in Tyczyn. The fruit trees blossomed, and the meadows carried the songs of birds. Light rains washed the cobblestone streets, which glistened in the noontime sun. In the locksmith shop we finished some soup that Mrs. Gorzelec had served the apprentices. Mr. Gorzelec took his lunch in his apartment over the shop. We kept the fire in the forge burning and rested quietly until Mr. Gorzelec returned. I had been in the shop for almost a year and had learned all about locks. Mr. Gorzelec was a strict boss but treated me fairly. I had become friendly with the other boys and felt comfortable and relatively safe. The other boys were older and more experienced. They were helpful and never made an issue of my being Jewish. The German police had come to the shop only a few times for minor requests or repairs. The shop became a haven from the reality of the terrible situation in town.

Among the Jews who came to Tyczyn after being expelled from Kalish by the Germans was a pretty blonde woman named Hanka. She was married and had two little daughters. The family was quite poor and lived in a single room in a shack on the outskirts of town. Hanka's husband tried to earn money by doing odd jobs. Hanka stood on the street corner behind the Tyczyn church and sold small packages of sunflower seeds. She was there with her young daughters every day, in any weather, from early in the morning until late at night.

A Polish neighbor who worked as a carpenter and specialized in wooden coffins came into the shop quite upset. "The Germans just shot and killed the Jewess Hanka from Kalish! The one that sold sunflower seeds! They shot her and left her next to Golomb's barn," he shouted. The carpenter opened the door and motioned for us to follow him. The other boys and I walked after him to Golomb's barn. A few people stood around Hanka's body. She was lying face down in the mud with her dress pulled up above her brown stockings. Her face was turned to the side, and her eyes were open. Her nose and mouth lay in a pool of blood, which was spreading from under her head. Her hair kerchief had been pulled down around her neck. Her golden blonde hair was streaked with blood. From a brown paper bag sunflower seeds spilled all around her and into the blood. An old Polish woman pulled Hanka's dress down and covered her legs. She took the bloody kerchief off Hanka's neck and laid it over her face.

No one seemed to know what to do. I was frightened. I had never seen a dead person before. Soon others came over and asked what had happened. Someone explained that the German police had spotted Hanka selling her sunflower seeds and ordered her to come to them. Hanka had grabbed her daughters and tried to run. Two Germans chased her and shot her in the back. She fell and tried to crawl to Golomb's barn, but the Germans kicked her in the head, and then one of them stepped on her back with his heavy boots and shot her in the back of her head. Her little girls had run off crying after they saw their mother murdered in the street.

A member of the Judenrat arrived with men from the Jewish burial society. They carried a wooden pallet and some white sheets. One Jew recognized me and gently but firmly told me to leave. I returned to the locksmith shop, while the other apprentices stayed to watch the body be taken away. In the shop Mr. Gorzelec was upset. He had heard about Hanka's death and told me that the Germans had killed another Jew in Tyczyn, the old man Wachs. They had entered his iron shop near city hall and found him working for the new Polish manager. The Germans dragged Wachs out into the middle of the market square and beat him to his knees and then shot him in the back of his head. Then the German police got into their cars and drove away, leaving his body in the street. Mr. Gorzelec dismissed me for the rest of the day. I left before the other apprentices returned from Golomb's barn.

My parents and Manek were sitting in the kitchen when I got home. The story of Hanka and Mr. Wachs's killings had spread through town. My father said, "These are new dangers. If the German police are going to kill Jews at will and without reason, then we are all in terrible trouble. We will have to be even more careful. We need to find a place to hide and be ready every time the Germans come to town."

A few days later Mr. Gorzelec announced that he was closing his shop. He thanked us for our work and gave us each a letter acknowledging the length and quality of our apprenticeship and a recommendation for future employment. Many people were surprised by his decision. Some thought that it was because of his poor health, while others, including me, thought that his outspoken criticism of the Germans might have gotten him into trouble and that he had decided that it was best to leave town. My job was over, but I had learned a vocation that might help me find other work.

✦ 5 ✦

In early May 1941 a large detachment of German soldiers arrived in Tyczyn. They were stationed in people's homes and barns and lived in tents in the woods and orchards. They parked their trucks, tanks, and artillery pieces in grassy yards, along the banks of the river, and in the park. They were busy training and working on their vehicles and weapons and did not have much contact with us. Some German soldiers still sought out Jews to publicly mistreat them. No Jew was safe on the street or at home. The Germans would accost the religious Jews with beards and tear and cut the hair from their faces. Some Germans who knew about Jewish customs and laws would force Jews to eat pork or go about with their heads uncovered.

One day as I was on my way home, I came upon a huge German soldier standing over my father and pointing a gun at his head. My father was on his knees polishing the soldier's boots. The soldier saw me staring and waved me away with his gun. My father looked up at me and hissed in an urgent voice to walk away. I walked a short distance and then looked back at my father polishing the German's boots. I waited behind a corner of a building until my father was released. He came to where I stood, and as we hurried home, he told me not to be upset by what I had seen. We had to overlook these events and focus on staying alive. He told me that one day justice would prevail and punishment would come to the Germans for what we had endured.

The Judenrat was required to provide a specific number of workers each day to the German military. Almost everyone ended up working for the Germans at some point. Father's health was failing again, and he was again excused from work for medical reasons. My mother was also excused because she was almost forty, and the Germans wanted only young women for work. Manek's work at the bicycle shop was not enough to keep him from being assigned to the Germans at least every second week. I no longer worked in the locksmith shop and got assigned to work for the German soldiers. I chopped wood, washed trucks, carried crates, scrubbed floors, and unloaded supplies. One day I was in a group of Jews who were ordered to attach large wooden road signs to telephone poles and trees. The signs were in different colors and had large black numbers painted on them. I had no idea what the numbers meant. The signs were heavy and difficult to carry up the ladders. The soldiers kicked and punched us as we worked for an entire day without a break.

That evening I told my parents that I had to find full-time work to keep me from being assigned to the Germans. Two days later my father heard of work with a gardener at a large estate at the edge of town. The job would probably last only until after the fall harvest. I would be paid a small wage and kept from the forced-labor assignments. We hoped that I might be allowed to take home a few vegetables as part of my wages. The estate was large and employed dozens of full-time workers. The Polish owner had gone away at the beginning of the war and had not returned. The German administration had taken over the estate, which was now run by a German manager. On my first day I recognized Zbigniew Ziarnecki, a young man with a university degree in agronomy who knew my family and had helped me get the job at the estate. He had taken a great risk because he was also concealing from the Germans that he was half Jewish. His father had converted to Catholicism before the war, but this did not affect the German designation that only one Jewish grandparent meant that a person was Jewish.

I was the only Jew working at the estate. The other workers took little interest in my presence. I turned the soil with a hoe, shoveled, and pushed it in a wheelbarrow, and I weeded and seeded the garden beds. I worked six days each week and got paid a small wage every Saturday. I was occasionally allowed to take a few carrots, peas, and potatoes.

In late June 1941 Germany launched a major surprise attack on the Soviet Union. Overnight all the German soldiers left Tyczyn with their vehicles and equipment and headed east. During the months that followed, the German-controlled newspapers detailed many German military successes and predicted the imminent collapse of the Soviet army. The Germans took many towns and overran the part of Poland that the Russians had occupied since 1939. The news of German victories was terribly disheartening.

We heard many stories of German violence against the Jews in the territories captured from the Russians. We heard terrible reports of massacres of large groups of Jews by the Germans and Ukrainians. We learned of bloody pogroms and mass attacks in Lwów, Białystok, and other large towns. The Jews were being forced to move into ghettos. In the smaller towns and villages German killing squads marched the Jews into the woods and shot them. Many Jews in my town refused to believe that this could be happening. They could believe that Jews were forced into ghettos. They could believe that pogroms existed. They had seen Jews killed for no reason. The Germans had killed Hanka from Kalish and Old Man Wachs. But they could not believe that the Germans would shoot the entire Jewish population of a town and leave them in mass graves.

In Rzeszów, Dr. Ehaus, who was from Vienna and known to be a fanatical Nazi and a vicious hater of Jews, was the new German district officer and administrator. Jewish families were evicted from their homes and ordered to move into shabby buildings in the oldest part of Rzeszów. That area became a closed Jewish ghetto that was guarded like a prison. We feared that we might also be forced to move to the Rzeszów ghetto.

Polish refugees started returning from the towns in eastern Poland that had been under Russian control but were now occupied by the Germans. The Tyczyn city hall organized lodging for the newcomers in the homes and apartments that German soldiers had recently vacated as they departed for the Russian border. My parents received notice to pay their overdue municipal taxes and warnings that we might be evicted from our home to accommodate Polish refugees. My parents

entered into an agreement with a Polish man that gave him full owner-
ship of our house but allowed us to remain there. The new owner, Mr.
Wodzinski, decided to rent out rooms in our house. We were soon living with a woman who was a teacher and her young daughter, an older
woman who worked as a midwife, and a family with two children.

Fall came and the Gestapo and SS from Rzeszów began to appear
in Tyczyn almost every week. They searched Jewish homes, confiscated
valuables, and made demands on the Judenrat for forced labor. They
posted further restrictions for the Jews. They organized another registration of Jews aged thirteen to sixty. Many Jews were arrested, and the
Jewish community was fined for all violations of the restrictions. More
Jews were shot and killed.

Manek turned nineteen and had a girlfriend named Ruth. She had
moved to Tyczyn from Kalish with her parents and two sisters. Manek
went to see her almost every evening. On Sundays, when the weather
was good, they took long walks along the river, outside town and away
from the Germans. My parents were happy that in these terrible times
Manek had still found love.

Our spirits sank with the gloomy cold and rainy skies. We had
lived under German occupation for more than two years. My job with
the estate gardener ended after the fall harvest. Manek's bicycle shop
would soon close for the winter months. I decided to approach some
Polish friends and ask if they could help me find a job. I had seen these
boys on only a few occasions. I went to Jurek Roskiewicz's house one
morning and found him, the Szpala brothers, and two other boys sitting on the back porch. They were talking about soccer and fishing and
were planning an outing. They were surprised to see me. They asked
about my family's situation and how we had avoided being arrested or
shot by the Germans. I could sense a distance between us. Even though
we lived in the same town, we were now worlds apart. Their parents
still worked in the factories, stores, and shops as they had before the
war. They went to church and to the cinema. They swam in the river in
the summer and skated in the winter.

Tadek Gliwa, a friend a few years older than I, came around from the
front of the house. He was happy to see me, but his expression changed

to dismay as he noticed my tattered clothes and impoverished appearance. I told them that I had been working for a gardener and that my job had ended. I explained that my family was in need of food and money. I could sense their discomfort as I spoke of our circumstances. Tadek told me that his uncle Jan farmed a small plot and needed workers to harvest potatoes. Tadek and his sister would be working for him. He promised to ask his uncle that evening if I could work in exchange for some potatoes. After arranging to meet him early the next morning, I went home. That evening I told my parents that I would spend the next day with the Gliwas but did not tell them that I might have found work. I was not sure whether the day would bring a chance to earn potatoes for our family.

I got up before dawn the next morning, quietly left the house, and went to the Gliwas'. Tadek was happy to tell me that his uncle had given permission for me to work in his field and that I would be given potatoes at the end of the day. This was great news. I walked with Tadek and his sister to the potato field at the outskirts of town. His uncle gave us and the other workers instructions, and we began our work. I broke off the brown, dried potato stalks and collected them into a pile. I dug the hard ground with a hoe and used my hands to pull out the potatoes. Tadek's uncle used a wheelbarrow to move the potatoes to a wagon. We worked all day, stopping only for lunch. Tadek's aunt baked a few potatoes in a burning pile of potato stalks. We worked until dark. Jan praised my work and gave me a large sack of potatoes. It was too heavy to carry, and he kindly lent me his wheelbarrow until the next morning. I rushed home, anticipating my parents' reaction when they saw what I had done.

I wheeled the sack of potatoes to the back of our house, then went in and quietly asked Manek to come outside. He helped me carry the heavy sack into the kitchen. My parents looked up with surprise. I told them about my work and good fortune. My mother hugged me with tears in her eyes. She had decided to sell a special ring that my father had given her in order to buy food for our family. Now she would be able to keep it for a while longer.

"Lucek," my father said. "What you have done today shows me that you are no longer a child. You have acted on your own to help our family. You cannot believe how proud I am of you." I was happy to bring them some relief and already thinking about ways that I could help again. I did find other work, harvesting potatoes, cabbage, turnips, and beets for local Poles who grew vegetables in small gardens close to town. They had no farm equipment and used workers they could pay with a share of the harvest. That fall my family had extra food, and we were even able to store some potatoes and vegetables in our cellar to help us prepare for the shortages of the coming winter.

The winter of 1941–42 was our third winter since the start of the war. Cold winds, ice, and snow kept people inside their homes. My father's health worsened. He was thin and drawn, his complexion gray, his hair falling out in clumps and turning white. He pretended that he was feeling well, but we knew that he was suffering. We hid our worries by acting as if he was improving. We tried to encourage him with exaggerations of good news. He was too ill to be burdened with the truth of our desperate situation. My mother had lost much weight but still looked beautiful. Her eyes revealed a fierce determination to get our family through each crisis. She asked us to carry her old foot-pedal sewing machine down from the attic. She tried to earn a little money sewing blouses and dresses for the Polish women in town. She could not compete with the established seamstresses in town, and after spending money on material and thread, she had little profit. Before long she sold the sewing machine for a few sacks of flour.

In November we learned that the Germans, stuck in Russian snow, had failed to take Moscow. The Germans were not invincible. But the few positive stories about the war did not affect our daily struggle. We heard rumors that Jews would be sent to a labor camp in the Jasło forests to cut down trees for firewood. In December we heard the unbelievable news that Japan had attacked the United States and that America was now at war with Germany. We celebrated that the Americans had joined in the fight against Germany. We realized that we would no longer receive any packages or letters from my aunt Pauline in New York. Veterans of the last war recalled how the Americans had helped defeat the Germans within a year. We had hope for the future, but our situation here in Tyczyn grew worse every day, and a year was too long to wait for rescue.

My birthday came, and I turned fourteen on January 7, 1942. There was no way to have any sort of celebration, but we shared dreams of a lavish party for my next birthday. Manek played the "Sto Lat" on his harmonica, the traditional Polish birthday song for a hundred years of life. My mother handed me a white armband with a blue Star of David and gently told me that I was now required to wear it. I took it and put it in my pocket. I would not start to wear it today, on my birthday. My father warned me to be careful and that the punishment if I was caught without my armband could risk our lives.

The snow did not keep the Gestapo and SS from coming to Tyczyn. They demanded that the Judenrat provide Jewish workers for compulsory labor in work camps in the Rzeszów region. They searched Jewish homes and arrested and beat Jews at random. They shot and killed four elderly Jews on the street, then dumped their bodies in the woods. One day the Germans marched fourteen Jewish men to the Jewish cemetery and executed them. Their bodies were found strewn among the tombstones. I decided not to wear my Jewish armband so that I could move about the streets to run errands. I was malnourished, had not grown much, and did not look fourteen. I walked when it seemed safe and ran when I had to. The police never stopped me for being without my armband, and when local hoodlums spotted me, I was able to outrun them. Because I was walking and running through the snow, and my feet were still growing, my only pair of shoes fell completely apart. We had no money to buy me shoes. My mother searched the attic and found her old ice skates. I tried them on, and the shoes fit me. A Jewish neighbor, who had worked as a shoemaker, removed the blades from the bottom of the boots and nailed on makeshift heels. We gave him my old leather shoes to use to repair or make shoes for other desperate Jewish children.

By the middle of winter we were hungry and cold all the time. We had sold and traded most of our warm clothes and wore layers of the tattered pieces that remained. My mother fed us potatoes and a gluey gruel that she cooked from wheat kernels and flour. Bread became our dessert. I longed for moist, black, crusty peasant bread. My mother began to ration our food to make it last as long as possible. Manek and

I ate our small portions without complaining or asking for more. Some nights, when the pains in our stomach kept us awake, we would distract each other by dreaming up elaborate menus. We looked through an old pastry cookbook that we found in the attic and tortured ourselves by imagining that we could taste the sumptuous desserts.

We had little wood or fuel for cooking and keeping our rooms warm. We had chopped our fence down for firewood the previous winter. We had traded most of our wooden furniture, or the Germans had confiscated it. My father was able to get a small homemade stove made of bricks. It could hold two small pots on top, and it did not take much wood to heat. We placed it on a small metal table by the kitchen window and fed its exhaust pipe out through a hole cut in the windowpane. We were all living in the kitchen, which we shared with the other families living in our house. We washed ourselves in icy water and only laundered alternating pieces of our clothing, which took days to dry draped next to the small stove. We lit a small fire a few times a day and kept it burning just long enough to cook our potatoes and gruel.

Manek went to see Ruth every day. Sometimes he would take me along. The conditions in Ruth's house were no better than ours. Her parents had lost all hope and were convinced that the Jews would not survive this war. I stopped going with Manek. I did not want to hear their dire predictions. I stayed home to help my mother with her chores and keep my father company to try to take his mind off his sickness. Many Jews were ill and dying without the medicines that they needed. I stood guard over my father, helpless and desperate that he should get well. Friends came, and their visits cheered him, even though the bits of news that they shared were not good. They told us that, in Rzeszów, the Germans made the Jews build walls, fences, and gates around the section of town that was now called the ghetto. In January soldiers locked and guarded the large iron gates. Only Jews with approved outside jobs and passes were allowed to leave the ghetto to work. All the other Jews were locked inside the crowded ghetto, separated from the Polish population. Many Jews were arrested and executed when they were caught outside the ghetto walls illegally.

We heard reports that Jews living in large towns in eastern Poland, such as Lwów and Białystok, were forced into Jewish ghettos. My cousins, the Talers, were in the Lwów ghetto. We had no news from my grandmother or my uncles. We assumed that they had been moved to a ghetto and could not use the mail or send out any messages.

We heard stories that Jews in many of the small towns and villages had simply disappeared. Entire Jewish communities had vanished and left relatives frantic with worry and dread.

The Germans stepped up their directives and demands. Fur coats and small fur pieces had to be immediately surrendered to city hall. They would view refusal as interference with German war efforts and severely punish those who disobeyed. My mother had sold her fur coat and short fur jacket long ago. She had sewn a few remnant fur pieces onto the collars of our winter coats. She removed them, and Manek delivered them to city hall.

About a week later the daughter of a Jewish neighbor came to warn us that German police were searching Jewish homes for furs. They had beaten and arrested the Jewish furrier. We had no furs but still feared a German search. She had just left when the front door burst open, and two armed SS men and two Polish police officers armed with rifles cornered us in the kitchen. My parents and I jumped up and stood at attention. One of the Germans shouted, "Dirty shit Jews! We are sure you have furs! We'll shoot you, you swine dogs!" Father started to speak, but a German hit him in the face with his truncheon and shouted, "Keep your mouth shut, you shitty Jew! I did not tell you to say anything!" Father staggered back, and blood ran out of his mouth and nose and dripped down the front of his shirt. My mother moved toward my father. The other SS man took out his gun and shouted at her, "Do not move, you Jewish whore, you swine!" I stood frozen against the wall. My mother mouthed to me in Polish not to speak. The Germans ordered the Polish police to search our home. The Poles moved quickly through the rooms. We could hear them opening closet doors and pulling out drawers. An SS man opened a kitchen cabinet. Inside were some dishes and a few books. He used his truncheon to push the books out onto the floor. He stepped on the books and tore

them with the heel of his boot. We watched, terrified to do or say anything. My father held a handkerchief to his bloody face.

After a few minutes the police came back into the kitchen and
reported that they had found no furs. They turned to leave, and one of
them spotted a photograph hanging on the wall. It was of my father's
family, taken before World War I. The fourteen people in it were sitting
and standing against a background of trees. My grandfather sat on a
chair in the middle, his face pleasant and earnest, his long white beard
flowing to his chest. My grandmother and their daughters, in high-
necked dresses and upswept hair, sat to the side of the men. Behind
them stood their sons and their daughters' husbands in suits and
stiff-collared shirts. My father, the youngest son, stood smiling and
handsome with his thick black hair. My grandparents had died before
I was born, and I knew them from this photograph. The German
knocked the photograph off the wall with his stick. The glass shattered,
and the black frame broke open. The Germans and the Polish police
turned and left. My mother rushed to my father. The torn photograph
lay on the floor.

The spring of 1942 arrived with warm weather that brought us
relief from the winter winds and temperatures. Our food shelves were
barren, and we were always hungry. The farmers returned to town to
shop and to take advantage of the desperate Jews. My mother had sold
and traded all our valuables except a few small pieces of silver, two
silver candlesticks, and some jewelry that she had hidden by sewing it
into our clothing.

The Germans declared victory in Russia and North Africa. We
were unshaken in our conviction that Germany would eventually lose
this war, but our salvation seemed far away. Poles told stories about the
Germans who had massacred Jews in the small towns and villages. We
heard that in the Rzeszów ghetto they had searched for Jewish commu-
nists and arrested and executed dozens of Jews.

One of my father's older sisters came to Tyczyn. She brought her
daughter, Stefa, and her young husband. They had lived in Kraków
before the war and had moved to Tarnów to escape the Germans.
When the Jews in Tarnów were forced into a ghetto, they had fled to

Tyczyn. I had not met them before. My aunt and cousins were eager to establish legal residence in Tyczyn without attracting the attention of the police. My father helped them get on the official list of Tyczyn's Jewish residents. They stayed in our house for a few days. They were lucky to find a small room to rent in the Grubers' house.

6

German SS and Polish police moved into Tyczyn and began to patrol the streets in pairs. The Jews were concerned, for any change brought fresh worries about the future. We could not get any information from the Judenrat and the Polish policemen we knew. My father insisted that we stay close to the house. My mother put together a small package with food, extra clothing, and blankets in case we had to run to the woods to hide from the Nazis.

After much discussion my parents agreed to let me go to our neighbors for news. The streets were deserted. The Jews and the Poles were avoiding the soldiers and police. I ran through our neighbor's backyard, climbed over a low wire fence, and softly knocked on the back door of Jewish neighbors, the Krugers. They had no information to share. I went to another Jewish family, the Rabs, who also had no news. I went to the door of a Catholic neighbor. He had been out that morning and had seen many German soldiers gathered in front of the Tyczyn police station. I knew that my parents would be upset with me, but I made my way through the back alleys toward the police station. I hid behind a fence at the house of a Polish teacher. I could see the police station. Parked out front were German military trucks and cars adorned with Nazi flags. A group of uniformed Germans stood about. One spotted me and shouted for me to come forward. I had my armband on. I turned and ran without looking back. That day they were not going to catch me. I ran with all my might and speed. I ran until I was breathless and could run no more. I threw myself on the ground behind some bushes and lay listening for the sounds of the soldiers. I lifted my head and peered through the bushes. I could feel my heart pounding in my chest. Luckily, no one was after me.

I cautiously made my way home. My mother was relieved to see me. I told my parents about my visits to the neighbors but not my encounter with the soldiers. I had learned that I could save myself from the Germans. I sat on a bench in the kitchen with my mother. She leaned against me and held me in her arms. It had been so long since I had been the young boy who knew safety in his mother's embrace. That evening someone stopped by our house to tell us that the commander of the SS unit had sent orders to the Judenrat to assemble for a meeting the next morning. I watched my father pace and my mother wring her hands in worry and feared that they knew more than they were sharing with me. Manek had left after dark to see his beloved Ruth.

I could not fall asleep and waited for Manek to come home. He arrived a few hours later and lay down on the bed next to me. I listened to my parents toss in their bed and whisper to each other. As the dawn was breaking, I heard a strange knocking outside our house. I looked out the window and saw a policeman nailing a white paper to the telephone pole in front of our house. Manek came and stood next to me. We dressed and quietly slipped out the front door. Two other men were standing by the telephone pole, reading the white paper. It was an official document, embellished with a swastika and written in German and Polish. It was typed and carried the seal and signature of the German district administrator. It read: "Within one week, all Jews residing in Tyczyn and vicinity must relocate to the Rzeszów Ghetto. The Tyczyn Judenrat will issue detailed instructions for the relocation of the Jews. Any Jew or Jewish family disobeying this order will be subject to severe punishment, including death."

Manek read the order, his face pale and disbelieving. I took his hand, and he gripped my fingers tightly. We stood in silence, unwilling to leave and face our parents with the alarming new order. A group crowded around us to read the order. Someone said that the expulsion notice was posted everywhere, nailed to trees, telephone poles, and even the doors of many Jewish homes throughout Tyczyn. This was banishment from the town where generations of Jews had lived. Manek and I crossed the street and walked into our home to tell our parents what we now faced.

My parents were awake. My mother was starting a fire in the little stove to boil water for my father's substitute coffee. We sat down with them at the table, and our voices trembled as we told them about the new decree. My mother held her face in her hands and wept. My father turned to us with despair and resignation in his eyes. He needed to get more information about the German order. Manek left with my father, and I locked the front door behind them. I went back to the kitchen. My mother sat at the table with an open gray box. She was looking at our family photographs and the letters that she and my father had exchanged before they were married. I sat with her, and we cried together.

Manek came home. He had learned that all the Jews in Tyczyn, except for the very old and sick, would have to assemble the next morning at the Judenrat office. We would be given further instructions for the move to the Rzeszów ghetto. My father returned and joined us in the kitchen. He had spoken to several Jewish people in town. There was chaos among the Jews as the worst of our fears came true. He asked us to start thinking about what we should take with us to the ghetto. We would need to keep clean and warm and be able to cook our food. My mother said, "This is our home. If we have to leave, who knows if we will ever come back? How can this be happening to us?" My father went over to my mother and held her in his arms. He turned to Manek and me and said, "We will get through this together, and one day we will come home."

The next morning at ten o'clock the Jews of Tyczyn stood by the stone steps leading up to the Tuchman building and waited for instructions from the Judenrat. Our group grew until hundreds of us stood together. The door to the Judenrat office opened, and a heavyset German in an SS uniform came out. Two subdued members of the Judenrat followed him. The German gave a short, barking speech that I could not understand. My brother translated for me in a whisper, saying that we were going to the ghetto for our own benefit. It would be easier to control disease, distribute food, and assign work in the ghetto.

After the SS officer spoke, a member of the Judenrat told us in German, Polish, and Yiddish the specifics of our relocation to the Rzeszów ghetto. In four days, at eight o'clock in the morning, every Jew in Tyczyn must be packed and ready to leave. We would be allowed to take our valuables and as much clothing and bedding as we could carry. Farmers would transport us to the Rzeszów ghetto in their wagons. Taking or selling our furniture was forbidden. One wagon would be allotted for every three or four families. The Rzeszów Judenrat would conduct a registration and assign living quarters once we arrived in the ghetto. The SS man stepped forward. He told us that we would be under police escort. Any Jew found in Tyczyn after our departure would be shot on the spot. We were ordered to return to our homes and prepare for the move. We walked to our home, which would be ours for only another four days.

We sat at the kitchen table, and my father tried to make sense of our situation. We had no choice but to accept the German order to leave our home and move to the ghetto. Father had spoken to two Polish friends, who offered to hide our family for a few weeks. We were far from the front lines, and military rescue was thousands of miles away in distant Russia, Africa, England, and America. If we were hidden for just a few weeks, we would soon be without any place to hide from the Germans. A lone child or woman might be able to blend in with the Polish population, but that was impossible for an entire Jewish family. Because only Jewish men were circumcised, identifying us was easy.

My mother felt that it made no sense to risk our lives to avoid the ghetto. She wished that we could conceal our Jewish identity but knew that it was impossible. She did not believe that the Germans would move us to the ghetto to kill us but rather to take our homes and put us to work for them. She hoped that being near our relatives, including my uncle Kalman and our cousins, the Birmans and Kahanes, might help us find shelter, food, and work. Each of us turned to the painful task of deciding what to take and what to leave behind.

Manek and I went up into the attic to find our old suitcases. My mother was sewing pillowcases into backpacks. During the night my father had stayed awake and agonized over what we should take to the ghetto. He told us to select our sturdiest clothes and roomiest shoes, suitable for summer and winter. He wanted each of us to carry a blanket, pillow, some sheets, towels, a toothbrush, and soap. My mother collected a few cooking and eating utensils and any last valuables that we could hide in our clothing. She packed our small supply of beans and barley. They would not spoil easily and did not take up much space. My father told us to dress in double sets of clothing in case our suitcases were taken from us. We would have to leave behind for the looters that were sure to descend upon our house all the furniture, pots, and china, books and sheet music, clothing and toys, all the memories and heirlooms.

I opened the drawers in my bedroom chest and took out a few shirts and pants, underwear, a sweater, summer and winter jackets, my favorite green cap, the socks that my mother had mended over the past months, and my new brown shoes made from my mother's old ice skates. Everything was worn and tattered and would not hold up for long. I fingered the books and notebooks that filled my shelves, my collection of stamps and coins, my old pocketknife, a sling that I had made from rubber bands, and a forked willow branch. I looked over the souvenirs of vacations and trips to visit relatives along with photographs from school and family gatherings. I had photographs of my parents and Manek, of my grandmother and uncles, of the Tamars in Vienna and New York, of my Polish friends in school, and of me, swimming in the river and playing in the snow. I looked at the images that told of my life from a baby to a young boy. I chose three photographs to take with me. One was of my parents, before I was born. Another was of Manek on his bicycle, his blond hair blowing in the wind, his eyes and mouth full of laughter. The last was a photo of my whole family standing happily together on a street in Tyczyn. I wrapped the three photos in a sheet of notebook paper and put them in my pocket.

I showed my father what I had selected to take to the ghetto. He asked me to bring two more shirts and another pair of pants. I might be able to trade them for food. He gave me a small suitcase and one of the backpacks that my mother had sewn. He told me to pack the essentials in the backpack in case they took my suitcase away and to leave space for food and small utensils that my mother would divide among us. We would tie our bedding into bundles on the morning of our departure.

I finished packing and went outside. It was a beautiful sunny spring day in 1942. Soon the trees would bud, and the gardens would bloom with the flowers that my mother had carefully planted. In two days we would leave all this behind. We would walk away with our doors unlocked for anyone to enter. Strangers would claim our home, sleep in our beds, and eat off our dishes.

I woke the next morning, my last day in my house and in Tyczyn. We had to make good use of the little time that we had so that we could sell as many of our possessions as possible to buy food for the trip; we also wanted to say goodbye to the people we had known all our lives.

It was impossible to sell any of our belongings. All the buyers knew that the Jews would have to leave everything behind in one more day. My mother made a deal with the Polish man who had become our landlord and was to take over our house after we left. He was concerned that the authorities might confiscate the good furniture left in Jewish homes and offered to give my mother a small amount of food if he could take our furniture that very night. Mother agreed because we needed food much more than furniture. My parents wanted to find a Polish friend to keep a few papers, photographs, and family heirlooms until the end of the war. My father asked Mr. Gliwa, Tadek's father, to do this great favor. Mr. Gliwa agreed, and they arranged that I would secretly bring these things to the Gliwas' house after dark.

Late that afternoon we said goodbye to our Polish neighbors. I sought out some of my old Polish friends. We shook hands like men, and they told me to take care of myself. I wished them luck too and promised to come back one day. In my heart I knew that I would not return. Manek spent the last hours with Ruth. They promised to find each other in the Rzeszów ghetto.

After dark I left the house with the small gray box of family photos, letters, and school diplomas. I carried a small linen bag that held our silver Sabbath candlesticks. I made my way swiftly and quietly through backyards and gardens and came to the Gliwas' house. Mr. Gliwa sat on the back porch in the dark, waiting for me. He took the box and the linen bag and told me that he would keep them safe until we returned. I thanked him and ran home. When I got back, Polish men were carrying our furniture outside and loading it into a wagon. They had dumped the contents of our drawers, cabinets, and wardrobes onto the floor. My mother wiped tears from her eyes as the workers carried out the bedroom furniture that her parents had given her when she got married. We slept on the floor that last night in Tyczyn. Our suitcases and backpacks were packed and ready for our morning departure. Through the long dark night I heard my mother crying.

We were up at dawn. We washed our faces and brushed our teeth. We dressed in double sets of clothing and tied up our bedding. My mother boiled the last bit of substitute coffee that she had saved for this day and cut up a small piece of bread for our last meal. I heard voices coming from the street outside. I went to the window and saw large farm wagons parked outside. Each was pulled by two horses and driven by a farmer seated on a narrow bench. The Tyczyn Jews, carrying bundles and bedrolls, lined up along the street. Polish police carrying rifles supervised the departure. One police officer stood at the doorway of a Jewish neighbor and called the people out into the street. Polish neighbors stood on the sidewalk, watching the expulsion of the Jews.

We helped each other put on our backpacks, picked up our suitcases and bundles, and walked out the door, down the stairs, and into the street. I turned back for a last look at my home and saw my mother's face wet with tears.

We joined the other Jewish families lined up in the street. We exchanged no greetings. Everyone was shaken and upset. The Polish police went into the Jewish homes to make sure no one had tried to stay behind. A German SS man came, spoke with the Polish police officer, and then began to shout orders at us. He said that we should load the belongings of four families on each wagon and that all Jews except for invalids would have to walk. We loaded our things on a wagon and stood like mourners behind a hearse. The order to depart was given. The drivers snapped the reins, and the wagons slowly started moving and we followed. Our Polish neighbors watched from the side-walks, darkened doorways, and windows.

The procession of Jews went past the post office, turned left in front of the Tyczyn convent, and stopped next to a grassy mount with three large wooden crosses that the Catholics used for services on Easter Sunday. We stood there behind the wagons for nearly an hour. From the market square other wagons appeared, loaded with bundles and followed by weary Jewish families. Our group joined with the wagons coming down the main street from the market square. All the Tyczyn Jews were formed into one long and ragged column guarded by armed German and Polish police. We moved past the Tyczyn poorhouse, over the Hermanuwka Stream Bridge, and onto the main road that led to Rzeszów. The Poles watched as we were driven from the town that we had shared for so many years. I searched their faces for sympathy and pity but met only curious glances and hateful glares. I knew that the Poles had not organized our expulsion and that it was beyond their power to stop it, even if they wanted to. They could have shown support, voiced objections, or waved goodbye. They did and said nothing.

The sun was high, and the day was getting warm. We walked and sometimes almost ran to keep up with the pace set by the horses. Most of the German police were now riding in military trucks, one at the front and another at the back of our column. Others patrolled our march on motorcycles. Polish police rode on bicycles on the sides of the road. Parents clung to their children and struggled to carry the heavy bundles with precious food that they did not trust to the wagons. A few old people and small children begged to ride on the wagons. I kept my eyes to the ground, and I heard their pleading met with shouts and blows. The air was filled with the sounds of mothers and children weeping.

The parents of two little children were helping an old woman who could not keep up. Manek took the boy's hand and talked to him as they walked. Soon the boy became tired, and Manek picked him up and carried him. I took the girl's hand and made sure that she did not fall behind or stray from our group. The skinny little girl, dirty and weary, held my hand tightly. She kept her eyes on her parents, and every few minutes cried out, "Papa, Mommy, don't leave me! Don't let me get lost!" She added in a frightened voice, "Papa, Mommy, I am afraid, I am afraid, I want to go home." Her parents looked at their children in painful desperation as they struggled to help the old woman. I held the little girl's hand and tried to comfort her by repeating her parents' soothing words. I could do nothing but keep walking toward the ghetto, hand in hand with another frightened Jewish child.

We crossed the bridge over the Stryj River. The road to Rzeszów passed through the village of Biała. Many Ukrainians lived here and now stood along the road, watching us pass. Young men who had joined the Nazi Party wore green uniforms with red Nazi armbands that bore a swastika. The Ukrainians hooted and shouted at us. Some started throwing stones and cheered when one of the Jews was hit. The guards and police laughed along with the bystanders and stopped the stoning only after some Polish farmers complained that their horses were being hit.

We came to the outskirts of Rzeszów. We passed the Rzeszów Jewish cemetery, turned left on Lwowska Street, crossed the bridge over the Wisłok River, and came to Freedom Square. Our column of wagons and Jews stopped in front of the movie house. I had gone there many times. On Galezowskiego Street we came to the entrance and gate to the Rzeszów ghetto. German and Polish police stood guard with rifles. I handed the little girl back to her mother. Manek guided the boy to his father. The German police that escorted us from Tyczyn began to shout: "Damned Jews, get your bags off the wagons! Fast! Only what you can carry! Run into the ghetto! Fast! Fast!"

We rushed in a frenzy to find our bundles, trying to duck the blows of the Germans' truncheons. My father, mother, Manek, and I grabbed our suitcases and bedrolls and ran toward the ghetto gate.

◆ 7 ◆

We passed through the gate and into the Jewish ghetto. The wretchedness of life was evident everywhere. Crowds of people, desperate beggars, and starving and sickly children were pleading for food. The Tyczyn Jewish parents were desperately calling for their children, from whom they had been separated during the rush into the ghetto. Jewish orderlies appeared, in civilian clothing and dark blue police caps, and moved us away from the gate. Judenrat volunteers told us that little housing was available.

In the midst of the confusion we heard a voice calling, "Henryk! Andzia! Boys! Here! Here!" We looked around to see who was calling us and to our great relief spotted Uncle Kalman. I had not seen him in two years. He looked thin and haggard. He made his way through the crowd and into my father's arms. Kalman had heard that the Tyczyn Jews were being brought to the ghetto today. He and his wife lived in a small bedroom in an apartment that they shared with the Kahane family, near Szpitalna Street. The ghetto had no vacant rooms, and they offered to share their room with us. We were lucky, for most of the others would have to find shelter in a hallway or beneath a staircase. My parents were grateful and thanked Kalman. He helped us carry our bundles and suitcases, and we followed him through the ghetto to our new home.

Misery was abundant. Entire families wandered the streets seeking shelter. Parents huddled in doorways with crying children, unsure of where to go or who to turn to for help. Uncle Kalman told us that the ghetto had become horribly overcrowded during the last few weeks. The ghetto population had doubled as the Germans forced in thousands of Jews from surrounding towns and villages. These new, desperate Jews overwhelmed the orphanages, informal schools, and soup kitchens that the Judenrat had set up initially.

We arrived at the old rundown building where Kalman had lived since he was forced into the ghetto late the previous year. He took us into the room that my family would share with him and his wife, Blima. It would barely be large enough for the six of us to lie down in. Two other Jewish families were living in the apartment. They greeted us with a look of knowing hopelessness. Their children were thin and sickly, dressed in ragged clothing. They sat on the floor among the disarray of their belongings. We were so fortunate to have found a place to live. In the ghetto just having a door and sharing a small kitchen and a toilet were luxuries.

We placed our suitcases and backpacks in the corner of the room and sat down on mattresses on the floor. Father and Kalman talked about the reasons that the Germans had brought more Jews into the overcrowded ghetto. Kalman was worried about the German insistence that Jews do productive work or be sent to forced labor. It would be vital for Father, Manek, and me to find jobs right away. Kalman hoped to find something for my father at the Public Services Organization where he worked. He would try to help us, but we each would have to start looking for work immediately. The Rzeszów Judenrat would conduct a registration in the next few days for all new people in the ghetto. Kalman advised Manek and me to claim that we had technical skills and experience. Manek had worked as a bicycle mechanic, and I had worked in the locksmith shop as an apprentice. We would list these as our vocations.

My mother asked about the dangers in the ghetto streets. Kalman warned us to stay clear of patrolling Gestapo and SS men. It was safer to be out on the ghetto streets during the day than at night. Kalman told us how the Germans came to the ghetto late at night and killed Jews during the nightly forays. Aunt Blima added, "I know you are frightened, but we will survive this. You must be exhausted from your march from Tyczyn." She turned to my mother and said, "Andzia, let us prepare something to eat, and then you should all get some rest."

After a small bowl of soup and piece of bread, my parents went to another room to talk with the Kahanes. I undressed and lay down on the mattress that I would share with Manek. I wanted to sleep and push away the horrible reality of this day. I remembered my bedroom that I had left that morning. Now six of us were cramped in this tiny room, like the poorest of the poor. I was thankful that Kalman had taken us in, but this did not diminish my unhappiness at seeing my parents reduced to sleeping on torn mattresses spread on the dirty floor.

During the next few days I went with Manek to find his old friends from his Rzeszów high school. They talked with Manek about finding safe work, the jobs inside or outside the ghetto for the German military, businesses, or railroad. They gave Manek a list of factories and workshops to approach. We would also need to check with the German Labor Office every day for job listings. Manek's friends promised to try to help us find work. We were determined to find jobs and a way to help our parents.

We went to the few factories and workshops operating in the ghetto and to the Labor Office, but no jobs were available and no one was hiring. In the evenings we tried to sound optimistic when we told our parents about our prospects. Uncle Kalman had been able to find clerical work for my father.

I learned my way around the old streets and alleys in the ghetto. I watched as families still struggled to find safe shelter away from the murderous Germans. The ghetto did not have enough rooms for everyone. The streets were crowded with people looking for work or trying to sell and trade their last possessions. Poor, desperate, and hungry families wandered aimlessly, looking for help. Little children, swollen with hunger, lay on rags on the sidewalks and on their mothers' laps. Beggars pleaded for bread. Often, great alarm would spread with the news that a German patrol was coming down the street. Everyone would run frantically and try to hide in hallways and courtyards. The sick and dying lay in the streets, unable to stand and run from the approaching mob of Germans.

A Jew named Ojserowicz drove a wooden funeral wagon pulled by an old, wasted horse through the ghetto streets. Ojserowicz had the miserable job of collecting the dead from the houses and the gutters, where death found them alone and forsaken. He loaded them into the wagon and took them to be buried in mass graves dug in the Jewish cemetery outside the ghetto. Many times I passed the funeral wagon when it was filled with bodies. Some were shrouded in old sheets or half dressed, with their bare feet sticking out from under the heap. The funeral wagon was covered with a tarp before it left the ghetto. Great care was taken not to offend the sensitivities of the Germans and Poles in Rzeszów.

A week after we came to the ghetto, the Judenrat conducted a registration of all newly arrived Jewish men aged fourteen to sixty. I went with my father and Manek. It was held in the Rzeszów synagogue, once impressive and beautiful but now reduced to a desecrated and plundered shell. Thousands of Jewish men were there. We stood in long lines for hours. At the registration table we were asked our name, age, address in the ghetto, and vocation. Manek said he was a trained mechanic, and I said that I had been an apprentice locksmith. A Judenrat clerk wrote down the information. An SS man examined our Kennkarten, and then we were allowed to leave.

My father returned to his clerical job at the Public Services Organization. Manek went to see his friends to ask if they knew of any work. I went to the Labor Office to check on whether any jobs had been posted. On my way I unexpectedly came upon the Jewish Tennis Club, which I had visited before the war. I stopped and looked through the old fence. The hedges had died or had been cut down for firewood. The grounds were neglected and in shambles. The tennis courts were covered with flimsy shacks and lean-tos. People huddled around small fires to keep warm and to cook over. Old men and women sat on broken chairs, boxes, and the ground. A small group of children, thin and dressed in ragged clothes, played a game that I remembered from my childhood. They passed around a small rubber ball, singing, "I have a silver ball, to whom should I give it next?" They ran in circles, laughing and playing with an abandon that only innocent children could hold onto in this terrible place.

Manek and I had still not found work. Our food supply was growing smaller every day, and we were hungry all the time. Sleep was the
only escape from our daily misery. My mother cooked beans, and we
shared a meager loaf of rough black bread. One night I lay on the mattress and fell asleep to the soothing sound of the quiet conversation of
my parents, Uncle Kalman, and Aunt Blima.

Shouting voices woke me. I sat up and saw that the others in the
room were awake. Out in the street someone was screaming in Yiddish,
"Jews! Have mercy! Open the gate! Jews! Or they will kill me! Jews!
Take pity on my wife and my children! Unlock the gate!" "What is happening?" my mother asked. Kalman put a finger to his lips. "Shhh!" he
whispered. "There is nothing anyone can do for him. It is horrible but
the Germans will kill him anyway." Outside the screaming and the crying grew louder. Kalman continued in a whisper. "The damned Germans do this every week. They come to the ghetto to kill Jews and have
their fun. They break into apartments and shoot a few people, husbands
in front of wives and mothers in front of their children. Then they pick
out a Jew from that building and drag him to another building with a
locked gate and make him beg for his life." He was interrupted by the
noise of loud banging and pistol shots. The awful, heartbreaking pleading went on: "Jews! Have pity! Open up!" Kalman went on to tell us,
"No one can save that poor Jew. If we open our gate, the Germans will
shoot him, come in, and start shooting some of us, and then drag one of
us to another building to scream and plead for mercy. If no one opens a
gate tonight, the Germans may break in on their own or maybe just get
bored and leave the ghetto. They will always kill the last Jew that they
torment. We cannot save that poor Jew tonight. We can only pray that
they do not come into our building and that it is not our turn next."

I peered at the dark figures outside. The Jew was on his knees
before a group of uniformed Germans. Some Germans rattled the
locked gate of a building across the street. Others kicked the kneeling
and crying Jew. I lay on my mattress, trembling with hate and with fear.
I pulled my blanket over my head, and held my hands over my ears. I
could still hear the cries of the Jewish man. A few minutes later I heard
a gunshot, then silence.

The German restrictions and violence intensified every day. They demanded that the Jews pay an exorbitant sum of money as a special tax. When we could not raise the money on time, they executed a number of Jewish leaders as the penalty. The Germans came into the ghetto on the pretext of looking for Jews who had violated any of the many regulations. They arrested and beat Jews and killed them on the street. Soon the SS patrols abandoned all pretext and randomly shot and killed Jews for no apparent reason. We were trapped in a maze of violence, poverty, and hunger. The funeral wagon driven by Ojserowicz came through the ghetto many times each day to carry away the growing number of dead.

The number of German and Ukrainian soldiers guarding the ghetto walls was greatly increased. A barbed wire fence was built to separate a small section of the ghetto from the rest of the ghetto. The fenced-off area was called the small ghetto. We feared that the Germans were planning something bad. We heard rumors that the Germans would send all younger Jews to forced-labor camps in the forests or mines. We heard that the Germans were planning to sterilize the Jewish men. The most dreadful rumor was that the Germans were preparing to massacre every Jew in the ghetto. We were desperate to find a way to save ourselves but were without the means, plans, or help to survive outside the ghetto walls. We were trapped.

Two Judenrat orderlies came to the door of our apartment and asked to speak with Manek. An orderly said. "You are listed on the Tyczyn Judenrat roster as an orderly. We need orderlies, and we are here to tell you to report to the Judenrat office tonight for duty." Manek answered, "I never worked as an orderly, and I do not want to be one now." One of the Judenrat orderlies said, "Why not? It is a safe job with extra rations and other privileges. Besides, you do not have a choice. You are ordered to report at five o'clock for duty. You will need your identification and orderly cap." The orderlies left. Manek was upset, and my parents tried to calm him. My mother suggested that he get some sleep before he had to leave. He wanted to stay up and talk with my father. At four o'clock my mother gave him some cooked beans to eat, and then he left for the Judenrat office.

He did not come home until late the next morning. My father waited up all night. Manek looked exhausted and distraught. He said, "This has been the worst night of my life." He had been sent outside the ghetto to Gestapo headquarters twice to collect the corpses of Jewish men and women. He stayed at the Judenrat building until the office opened in the morning, and then he argued with the superiors until they let him quit. Manek wanted to lie down for a few hours and then go to the Labor Office for other work.

Manek and I walked to the Labor Office. He told me that he and another orderly had been sent to Gestapo headquarters on Jagiellońska Street in Rzeszów. They had brought a wooden two-wheeled handcart. After a while they were led to an underground concrete chamber to pick up the naked, bloody, and wounded bodies of several Jewish men and women. The Germans were desecrating the bodies. They stepped on them and dragged them across the dirty floor of the torture and execution cell. Manek saw a German use the long hair of a dead girl to wipe the blood from his boots. Manek and the other orderly loaded the bodies on the handcart and took them back to the ghetto for Ojserowicz to bury.

Manek and I got to the Labor Office where hundreds of people stood waiting for jobs to be posted and announced. We saw several Jews from Tyczyn, including Moses Verständig, Moishe Ziment, Mola Tuchman, Leon Horn, and Motek Hoffstetter and his younger brother. Through the windows we could see much commotion inside the Labor Office.

Four Germans in their brown SA (Sturmabteilung) uniforms (these were the storm troopers better known as the Brownshirts) came out of the Labor Office. We stopped talking and waited for them to speak. The Germans pointed to certain young Jewish men and demanded their Kennkarten. They examined them and then returned some and threw the others into a box held by an orderly. A murmur swept through the crowd of Jews. "What does this mean? Is it good or bad if they keep your Kennkarte?" No one knew. Some Jews pushed forward to get their Kennkarten examined. Others pulled back with uncertainty. A German demanded the Kennkarte from Hoffstetter's younger brother. We Tyczyn Jews knew that his parents had arranged for his Kennkarte to contain a false statement that he had a bad heart. They hoped that it would give him some protection from being assigned to hard labor. The German looked over Hoffstetter's Kennkarte and said as he threw it back at him with a sneer, "You did not want to work before, so go to the devil now!" That was the clue for us, that having our Kennkarte rejected was bad.

The crowd pushed forward as Jews fought to offer their Kennkarte to the Germans. The Germans started yelling and kicking us back. Other Germans went out into the street to force the Jews back. The German chief of the office came out and stood on the steps above the crowd and shouted and cursed at the Jews. Manek and I were near the front and were trying to back away from the Germans' kicks and shoves. The people trying to get their Kennkarte accepted pushed us forward. I held on to Manek so we would not get separated. In the midst of the shoving crowd Manek froze. He stared with disbelief at the chief of the Labor Office. He whispered to me, "That German chief was my high school shop teacher."

The chief of the Labor Office recognized Manek. He pointed at him and shouted, "Manek, give me your Kennkarte!" Manek handed both his and my Kennkarten to the German. The German took the two cards and threw them into the box. We pushed back through the frantic crowd. The Germans went back inside the building.

Manek and I returned to our apartment and told our parents, Uncle Kalman, and Aunt Blima what had happened. We were unsure what the Germans were planning and concerned that Manek had handed over my Kennkarte with his. The Jewish men whose papers were accepted were in their twenties and thirties, and I was only fourteen. Manek went to lie down, and the adults moved into the tiny kitchen to talk. I tried to sleep but stayed awake worrying about the consequences of what had happened that day.

The next morning a Judenrat orderly came to our door. He pulled both our Kennkarten out of a large envelope and handed them back to us. They each had a round stamp in red ink on the front, just below our photographs. The letters around the stamp said "Gestapo," and the stamp featured the symbol of a spread-winged bird perched on a swastika. We asked the orderly what the stamp meant. He shrugged his shoulders, turned, and left. We found out that some people whose Kennkarte was stamped had safe jobs, while others did not work at all. We were not sure why anyone had been chosen and what we had actually been selected for. We were worried that my brother and I had stamps and that our parents did not.

8

A few days later the Gestapo and German District Administration issued an order for the resettlement of Rzeszów Jews to the East. The lengthy notice, printed in German and Polish, was posted throughout the ghetto. The order stated that in one week all Jews in the ghetto, with the exception of those with the special stamp on their Kennkarte and their immediate families, would be resettled to German-occupied Ukraine. They would live and work on a large collective farm that the Russians had abandoned. The order stated that everyone would have work, more living space, and food, all of which were lacking in the ghetto. It listed the clothing that people would need for the new climate. Travel would take three days, and each family should take along food.

The ghetto was divided into four sections. The small ghetto, which we lived in, was designated as section 1. On the first day of the relocation the Jews with the special stamps and their direct dependents would be moved into the small ghetto, and all other Jews without the stamps had to leave the small ghetto for the *Umschlagplatz*, the assembly area, in the large ghetto. From the assembly area they would be taken to the trains. The Jews in the three other ghetto sections would be relocated over the next six days. The order defined direct dependents as a legal spouse and minor children. Immediate execution was the punishment for violating the order.

The resettlement gave us a reason for the Gestapo stamp. Many members of the Judenrat had been given stamps to stay in the ghetto.

Some Jews felt that this must mean that staying in the ghetto would be safest. Others believed that the Ukrainian farm could only be better than the ghetto.

My brother and I had the special stamp and would remain in the ghetto, while my parents would be deported. My father and Uncle Kalman desperately tried to obtain special stamps for themselves, my mother, and Aunt Blima. They went to everyone who had any influence, pleading for help. Days passed without success. I could not imagine being separated from them. I wanted to be with them in the ghetto or the Ukraine. I told them that I would not stay behind without them. My father promised that he would keep trying to get the stamp and stay in the ghetto.

The deportation would begin the next day. My father and Uncle Kalman left at dawn to try to get the special Gestapo stamp. My mother, Manek, and I anxiously waited in our little room for Father's return. I silently prayed for good news. My father returned late in the afternoon. He looked unhappy and defeated. I was the first to ask, "Daddy, what happened? Did you get the stamp?" "No," he said quietly. "Kalman and I have talked to everyone we know. We have tried everything, and we could not get the stamp." I looked at my mother. She was leaning against the wall, hiding her face as she wept. "Andzia, we have to get ready for the transport," my father said gently. "I will get ready too," I said. "I'm not staying here without you." "No, Lucek, no," my father said. "Your mother and I have talked about this. We have decided that it is better for you to stay here with Manek." I begged them, "Please, do not leave me behind. I am afraid to stay here without you."

I was frightened and crying. My mother put her arms around me and kissed my hair. "Do not cry, Lucek, please do not cry. We want you to stay because we love you. You will be safer here. Manek will look after you. There are Poles outside the ghetto that might help you. Be brave. I promise we will find you as soon as the war ends." I pleaded with my parents, but they would not change their minds. Manek said nothing as I begged them to take me with them. He put his hand on my shoulder and said, "We have to listen to Daddy and Mama. Do not be afraid. I promise that I will take care of you." He turned to Mother. "I promise you, with my life, that I will take care of him." Mother, Manek, and I held on to each other and wept. I looked over at my father. He looked forlorn and unhappy. For the first time in my life I saw tears on my father's face. I went to him, and he took me in his arms. My face was wet with tears, and my heart was full of sorrow. "Do not cry, Daddy, please do not cry. I will stay if you want me to."

Uncle Kalman and Aunt Blima came into the room. They could not get the stamps on their Kennkarten. My father told them that we had decided that it would be safer for Manek and me to stay behind in the ghetto. My aunt and uncle told us that they loved us. They said that we had been a part of their lives since we were little and that they would miss us and think of us every minute of every day. They promised that one day we would be together again. My mother and my aunt stood together crying.

My father got out the backpacks that they had brought from Tyczyn and started to pack their few clothes and belongings for the trip to the Ukraine. My mother was still crying as she put my father's medicine into his coat pocket and packed the few photos and letters that she had carried from Tyczyn. Manek and I stood in the corner of the room and watched them pack. I wanted to stop them, to stop time and keep them from leaving.

The resettlement order stated that they should take along food for three days of travel. We had very little food, and my mother and aunt wanted to leave most of it behind for Manek and me. We insisted that they take everything they could use. Manek argued that we would be able to get other food in the ghetto. We only had a half loaf of bread. My mother and aunt divided it between them. It was not enough bread for more than one day. They decided to cook a small pot of barley, potatoes, and beans to take with them. Mother and Aunt Blima divided their time between packing and cooking. Father, Kalman, Manek, and I looked over the things that they had packed and tried to decide what else they should take along.

We heard a timid knock on the door. Mother and Blima came out of the kitchen, and Manek opened the door. Esther, the shy girl from the family that lived near the Tyczyn synagogue, stood there. She was older now, emaciated but still beautiful. She stepped into our room and turned to my mother. "Mrs. Salzman," she said. "You remember me from Tyczyn?" My mother nodded and said, "Yes, Esther. Of course, I remember you." "Mrs. Salzman," Esther continued. "My family is preparing for tomorrow's train ride to the Ukraine. We are supposed to take along food for three days, but we have no food at all." She lowered her eyes and asked, "Can you spare some food for us, Mrs. Salzman? We have nothing." We felt her desperation as if it were our own. "We do not have much ourselves, Esther," my mother said to her. "But if you have a way to cook, I can give you some barley, beans, and a few potatoes. Cook it tonight and take it along." My mother went into the kitchen, came back with a small paper bag of vegetables, and handed it to Esther. "Thank you again," said Esther. "This is what we were hoping for. May God bless you." Esther was crying with relief.

This was the night before my parents' departure. We had only a few hours left to be together. It was almost time to say goodbye, to store in my heart their voices, their touch, their faces, and the feeling of their love. We stayed awake the entire night. We spent each moment embracing, kissing, crying, and holding each other. We tried to comfort each other, promised to send messages as soon as possible, and made plans to find each other after the war. We recalled the special moments and experiences of our lives. Father reminisced with Uncle Kalman about their years as boys in Lańcut and as law students at the University of Kraków. Father recalled the day that he met my mother, and she remembered the first love letter that he wrote to her. Manek told of how he taught me to swim and to ride my bicycle. We remembered our last vacation before the war, when we spent a month in the Carpathian resort village of Piwniczna. We spoke of the past as if it could somehow blot out the heartbreak and sorrow of this night in 1942. After a while we had no more words. My mother held me and rocked me in her arms. My heart broke that night from the great sadness and pain. Never had I imagined that such a terrible night was possible.

Our despair worsened as morning came. We dressed, and soon it was time for my parents to leave, time for our very last goodbye. My father gave Manek and me a slip of paper with the address of Uncle

Julius and Aunt Pauline in New York. "Keep and memorize this address," he told us. "When the war is over, we will find each other by writing to Julius and Pauline." His voice was filled with great emotion. "My boys, be brave. Take care of one another. I give you my blessings. May God protect you. I love you both, and I will miss you." My mother embraced Manek and said, "You are my big, beautiful son. I love you. Promise me that you will take care of yourself and watch over Lucek. I hope and pray that I will see the two of you again soon." "I promise, Mother, I promise," Manek answered. "Do not worry about us. Take care of yourself and Daddy. We will live for the day when we can see you again."

My mother turned to me. She held me and covered me with kisses. We were both crying. She lifted up my chin and looked into my eyes. She said, "Goodbye, my dear child. I love you. I will miss you. I will keep you in my heart and think of you every day. Take care of yourself and live. And if it should happen that you will have to grow up without us, remember that we want you to grow up and become a good person, that we want you to become a mensch." I cried and held on to them. "I promise, I promise," I kept repeating. "Daddy and Mama, I do not want you to go! Please do not go!"

It was time for them to leave. Uncle Kalman and Aunt Blima said goodbye to us. My parents put on their backpacks, and together we went out into the street. Judenrat orderlies standing outside told us that only people going to the assembly area were allowed on the streets. They ordered Manek and me back into our building and motioned for my parents to move on. We quickly embraced our parents. As we parted, I clutched my mother's hand until my father gently and firmly pulled her away. Manek and I huddled in the doorway and watched our parents walk away. They kept looking back, and we waved and stretched our arms toward each other as if to touch one more time. Soon we lost sight of them. They were gone.

Hundreds of people crowded the street, carrying bundles and walking to the assembly area. They crossed paths with those Jews who had the Gestapo stamp and were moving into the small ghetto. By late morning the shift of people between the two ghettos was finished, and the gate was closed and guarded. A few of the Jews who came into the small ghetto had their wives and children with them. Manek looked at the families moving into the small ghetto. He hoped that there might be a way to use the stamps on our Kennkarten to keep our parents from being deported. The resettlement order stipulated that only the wives and small children of the men with the special stamp would be permitted to stay in the ghetto. The order did not allow parents or other relatives to remain. Manek and I left our building and went looking for any Judenrat officials with whom we could plead to help our parents stay in the ghetto. Other Jews in our building saw us leaving and warned us not to go out. They shouted that it was dangerous and foolish for us to go. The SS were everywhere. They were searching for Jews who did not have the Gestapo stamp and were hiding in the small ghetto to avoid deportation.

Manek and I left our building and ran through the empty streets of the small ghetto. We headed toward the gate that separated us from the large ghetto. Two Judenrat orderlies were posted on our side of the gate, and several armed SS men guarded it from the other side. The two orderlies were surprised to see us. Manek knew one of them and explained what we were trying to do. The orderly told us that the Germans would not allow our parents to stay in the ghetto just because we had stamps on our Kennkarten. Manek insisted that we try everything to bring our parents back. The orderly told us that he and other orderlies also had stamps on their Kennkarten but could not keep their own parents from being deported. We both argued with the orderlies and pleaded for their help. The SS heard us arguing and started to move toward the gate. The orderlies saw the SS coming and began shouting at us to go back to our rooms. One of the SS asked who we were and why we were on the street. We turned and ran through the empty streets toward our building.

As we came around a corner, we came face to face with two SS soldiers. They shouted, "Halt! Halt, you damned swine Jews! Show us your Kennkarten!" Manek and I stopped running. We pulled out our Kennkarten and held them up so the two SS soldiers could see the red Gestapo stamps. They glanced at our Kennkarten and started hitting us with their rubber truncheons. They hit me on the head, and I heard Manek yelling, "Run! Run!" Manek and I ran with the two SS men after us, cursing and swinging their rubber truncheons. I felt the painful blow of the truncheon on my back. As we ran past one of the buildings, two young women opened the gate and stuck their heads out. I saw the shock on the women's faces when they saw the two SS men. The SS stopped and turned on the women. Manek and I ran to our building, up the stairs, and into our empty room. We changed our clothing to avoid being recognized in case the SS men came searching for us.

Manek and I sat on the mattresses on the floor. I could hear other people moving into our building. We spent hours sitting despondently in our room. In the late afternoon we heard the whistle of a departing train. "They're leaving now," Manek said sadly. He turned toward the wall, and I could see him shaking as he cried. I sat next to him and cried too. At this moment we felt helpless and alone, overcome with despair greater than our broken hearts could take.

That night the SS searched the small ghetto for Jews without the special stamps. Manek and I stayed in our room, dressed and awake. We heard the Germans in our building, shouting and banging on doors. They burst into our room many times. They checked our Kenn-karten and made us stand facing the wall with our arms raised. They searched our room and the apartment for any Jews trying to hide. From outside the building we heard the Germans shouting and firing guns. By morning the Germans had left the small ghetto. We could still hear cries and gunshots coming from the large ghetto. We looked out the window and saw that some of the Jews were leaving their building, and we cautiously ventured out into the streets.

Manek wanted to go to look for Ruth in the small ghetto. He had seen her before the deportation, while she was still hoping to get the special stamp. He asked me if he could leave me alone for a short time. I told him to go find Ruth. I stayed in the room for a while and then went outside. I cautiously made my way through the empty streets, looking for anyone who might know what was happening in the large ghetto. I asked a few people, but no one knew. The streets of the small ghetto were littered with clothing, broken suitcases, torn pillows, and blankets. Bodies lay in the streets, people who had been murdered by the Germans the night before.

I soon found myself standing at the Jewish Tennis Club. Everything was in complete disarray. Furniture, bedding, clothing, books, pots, and the things that people had treasured and protected only a few days earlier were strewn among the empty buildings and shacks. The cooking fires were out. The people were all gone, and there was only silence.

I spotted a child's shoe. One small scuffed shoe with round decorative holes cut in the leather strap that buttoned across the top. It could have belonged to a little boy or girl. I looked for the matching shoe but did not see it. There must be a child somewhere with only one shoe. I ran back to my room. Manek was there, waiting for me. He had not found Ruth.

A few days passed. I worried about my parents constantly. Inside the heavily guarded and sealed small ghetto we were isolated from the outside world. The Germans had left us alone. I spent most of the time with my brother, inside our small room. The little food that we had was almost gone. The shouts and sounds of gunfire that had reached us from the large ghetto stopped. I was told that the last Jews in the large ghetto had been deported the day before.

Early one morning I was roused by loud and angry German commands coming from the street. The Germans were banging on the doors and windows. I jumped up from the mattress and threw on my clothes. Manek was dressing too. The Germans were inside our building. "Out! Out! Quickly! All you damned Jews out on the street! Quickly! Anyone still inside in five minutes will be shot! Out! Do not take anything with you, only your Kennkarte!" They were screaming and shouting. I could hear people running in the hallway and down the stairs. Manek opened the door. I followed him down the stairs, and we ran out into the street. Many Jews from our building were already there. Others, especially those with wives and children, were still running out, driven by the curses and the blows of the Germans.

The SS and Ukrainian guards were on the street with a few Judenrat orderlies. The Germans and Ukrainians screamed at us to get into rows and to go quickly to the assembly area in the large ghetto. I thought that we must be going to the assembly area to be deported. I was devastated that my parents had gone without me, and now I would end up being deported anyway. What if I ended up in some other place and my parents could never find me? I held on to Manek's arm as we ran. Word spread that we were not being deported but that this was another SS search for Jews without the special stamp. Someone called our roundup a selection.

Armed SS men and Ukrainian guards surrounded us. We came into the large ghetto. The streets were littered with open suitcases, pots and plates, clothing, torn mattresses, pillows and bedding. The windows of the old buildings were broken, and the doors to the vacant buildings stood open. Small fires burned on the street and filled the air with foul smoke. We ran in a terrified silence. We came to the assembly area. It was once the Jewish cemetery, but the headstones were gone. Now it was just an empty rutted square. One corner was roped off and guarded by Ukrainians. The Gestapo and SS men cursed and hit us with their truncheons as they separated the Jewish families from the single individuals. The Germans kept hitting and kicking us as we came into the square. One German got up on a chair and fired his gun into the air. The beating and kicking stopped. He ordered us to squat down on the ground and not move or talk. I stayed close to Manek, with the other Jews without families. The Germans walked among us and kicked anyone who spoke or blocked their way. I kept my eyes lowered to the ground, hoping not to be singled out. I wondered if they had done this to my parents.

We were ordered to stand up a row at a time and move in single lines to tables set up across the middle of the square. We were shoved into lines, and I panicked when I realized that I had gotten separated from Manek. I saw him standing in another line ahead of me. He did not dare to turn his head to look for me. At the tables the Germans were questioning the Jews and examining their Kennkarte. Each family was brought up to the tables to be questioned. As I moved closer, I saw that the Germans were shouting at some Jews to jump up and down and squat. Most people were sent past the row of tables to squat down on the ground. Others had their Kennkarte taken and torn up, and they were taken to the roped-off area in the far corner of the assembly square. They were mostly older men who could not jump fast enough or high enough. Others were taken to the roped-off area for no apparent reason. I saw people pleading with the Germans to go with the others who had been sent past the tables. They were beaten and dragged to the roped-off area. A few people broke away from the Germans and tried to run to the group past the tables. They were caught and dragged to the old cemetery wall. The Germans threw them to the ground and shot them. I prayed silently in my broken Yiddish. "God, Dear God, you are all powerful and merciful. Save us." As I prayed, I wondered if maybe in this place, on this day, prayers did not matter. I was in hell. I had just learned what a selection was.

It was Manek's turn to be questioned by the Germans. I watched in anguish. The interview seemed to last forever. Because I was standing behind him, I could not hear what was being said or see the expression on his face. Suddenly, he ran to the squatting group of Jews and sat down, facing me. His eyes, full of fear and hope, were on me. I understood his concern. I was fourteen, and it appeared that I was the youngest person in the group of Jews. I stood as tall as I could and threw back my shoulders. The SS officer motioned at me to move up to the desk. He took my Kennkarte from me, glanced over it, and then looked up at me. He stood and walked around the desk. He thumped me on the back of my head with his wooden club, handed me back my Kennkarte, and motioned for me to pass. I walked, stiff with fear, and quickly squatted next to Manek. Our fingers touched. We said nothing. My heart was pounding furiously in my chest.

I had a clear view of the selection process. The Germans continued to motion the nervous Jews forward, examine their Kennkarte, ask questions, and make some people squat and jump. When they appeared to be too old or feeble, the Germans stood up from their desks to curse and strike at them with their truncheons and clubs. They sent most young Jews to join our group. The others were marched, bruised and bloody, to the roped-off corner of the assembly area. After a while the selection of the Jews without families was finished. I sat on the ground,

terrified to move or make a sound. I watched as the Germans continued the selection of the Jewish families.

The process was slow and extremely violent. The Germans brutally
questioned everyone, husbands, wives, and even young children. With
the assistance of the Judenrat orderlies, they examined Kennkarten
and other papers and documents. The Germans seemed to be chal-
lenging the marriage and birth certificates. A few families were allowed
to pass the row of tables. Some were challenged and told to stand aside.
Those men were explaining and pleading; their wives and children
were crying. Entire families were sent to the roped-off area. Some
women and children were violently separated from their men. A few
men argued with the Germans and refused to part from their families.
They were brutally beaten. I watched as one man continued to object
and tried to hold on to his wife. He was thrown to the ground and shot.
The assembly area was covered with dead parents and children. I
turned to look away but could not escape the shouts, cries, and shots
that filled the air.

I saw a familiar Jewish man and woman holding on to each other
and pleading with the Germans to let them stay together. The Germans
were screaming and beating them, but they refused to separate. Horrified, I realized that it was my cousin Stefa and her husband. She was
crying and struggling, clinging to her husband, and refusing the Germans' orders. An SS officer approached them and aimed his gun at
their heads. He fired twice quickly, and they fell to the ground. I lowered my head and closed my eyes.

The selection was over. A few large German military trucks arrived.
The Judenrat orderlies collected all the bodies and loaded them into
the back of a truck. The Jews in the roped-off area were forced to climb
onto the other trucks. The Judenrat orderlies tried to help the women
climb up and then lifted their small children up to them. When the
Jews had been loaded, the trucks started up and drove off. We sat
silently on the ground under the hot summer sun and waited. I was
exhausted and thirsty. My legs were cramping from sitting for hours in
a stooped position. At midafternoon an SS sergeant spoke to the Judenrat orderlies. The orderlies told us that the search of the small ghetto

was finished and we should return to our rooms. They said that at seven o'clock the next morning any Jews who had previously worked for German companies, the German military, or the railroad were to assemble at the ghetto gate on Baldachówka Street to be taken to work. Jews who did not have jobs before the deportation had to appear the next morning at the Labor Office for work assignments.

We were marched back to the small ghetto.

❖ 9 ❖

Manek and I went to the Labor Office early the next morning to get our work assignments. I was afraid that I might be sent to work in a forest or a mine. I had heard that the work there was very hard and that the supervisors and guards were brutal. More than anything, I hoped that Manek and I would be assigned to the same work group and that we would stay together.

A few hundred Jews were already standing in front of the Labor Office when we arrived. We waited with them for a listing of work assignments. Nothing happened for hours. We stood outside the closed door, too fearful to knock and too fearful to leave. At about noon a German officer stepped out and told us to stay there until the Labor Office posted lists of work assignments. He went back into the office and shut the door. In the afternoon he came back and handed several typewritten sheets to the Judenrat orderlies, who posted them on the Labor Office wall. We crowded around the lists searching for our names. Manek found our names on the same list. He pointed them out to me, and I was relieved that we would be working together. Our names were on a list with about a hundred people assigned to work at the Daimler-Benz Flugmotorenwerk, the Daimler-Benz Airplane Engine Plant, located on the outskirts of Rzeszów. The list was titled "Technical and Metalworking Specialists," and the names were divided into two groups. My name was included in a group of about sixty, listed under "Construction and Production," and Manek's name was included in a smaller group designated as "Repair." The Daimler-Benz list included orders that everyone appear at the gate on Baldachówka Street at seven o'clock the next morning. There was a warning that anyone failing to appear would be severely punished. I knew eight Jews on the "Construction and Production" list from Tyczyn.

Manek told me that Daimler-Benz was a major German company that manufactured the Mercedes-Benz cars. He did not know what the Flugmotorenwerk did and what our work would be. He asked some of the Rzeszów Jews if they knew about the work to which we had been assigned. One had worked at the Daimler-Benz factory before the deportation and told us that it was a large complex built before the war by the Polish government. He thought that we would be doing construction and excavation. The work would be hard and dirty, but the Polish overseers had treated them better than the Germans had.

Manek and I returned to our room in the late afternoon. Manek tried to assure me that the work at the Daimler-Benz factory should not be very hard and that I would be able to make use of what I had learned in the locksmith shop. I was glad that we would be working together in the same factory. We were drawing closer together as we tried to fill the loving roles of our parents. We decided to cook some of our few vegetables. It would be a meager evening meal, but we had nothing else. Manek wanted to go out to find out if there was any information or messages from the Jews deported to the Ukraine. I would watch the small pot of soup, while he went in search of news. The cooking and the smell of the food brought back memories of my mother's cooking and her fussing over our meals. I missed her so very much. I was glad that Manek and I were together and taking care of each other. When he came back, he told me that he had spoken to many people. Everyone was anxiously awaiting any word from the deported. There had been nothing yet. Manek thought that it was still too early for letters to have reached us. He expected that we would hear from our parents soon. He had asked around about Ruth, but no one had seen her since the deportation.

The next morning before seven o'clock, Manek and I joined the people standing at the Baldachówka Street gate. Jewish clerks from the Labor Office were assembling the men and the few women into work groups. A Labor Office employee called for the workers assigned to the Flugmotorenwerk to follow him. Manek and I and others followed him to an area in front of the gate. We were separated into two groups, one with those assigned to construction and production and the other with those assigned to repair.

I was separated from Manek. The ghetto gate was opened, and the work groups began to march out under armed guard. Manek's group left before mine, escorted by armed soldiers of the Luftwaffe, the German air force. A few minutes later my group of about sixty men was ordered to march out through the ghetto gate. We were surrounded by rifle-carrying Germans in dark gray uniforms who led us through the back streets of Rzeszów. They were part of the Daimler-Benz Flugmotorenwerk Werkschutz, or German factory police force, and they insisted that we march in a military formation. They yelled, kicked, and hit to get us in step. We were not trained to march, and it took some time of skipping and shifting before the Germans were satisfied. A German kicked me, and I struggled to keep up with the others. The Poles on the sidewalks stood and laughed at the sight of straggly Jews being taught by the Germans how to march like soldiers.

We marched under this brutal supervision for nearly an hour and finally arrived at the entrance to the Flugmotorenwerk factory. A German factory police officer came out of the guardhouse, opened the tall iron gates, and raised the barrier that blocked the entry. We were marched inside and brought to a small paved area next to a low brick building. A guard asked whether any of us spoke German. A few people cautiously raised their hands. The guard pointed to a young Jewish man standing near the front and said that he was to be the "senior Jew" of our group. I knew that his first name was Peter and that he had been deported from Germany to Rzeszów a few years before the war. He spoke German and Polish fluently. The guards gave orders to Peter, who translated the German into Polish for us. The Germans refused to look at us while they spoke, as if addressing us was offensive. We were commanded to stand and wait for the construction supervisor to arrive and assign us work for the day.

We stood quietly and tried to take in the surroundings of the Flug-motorenwerk complex. All around and as far as I could see were brick buildings and manufacturing halls. The buildings were bordered by grassy lawns and connected by narrow streets and sidewalks. Trucks and tractors drove in every direction. Hundreds of civilian workers were arriving for the morning shift on foot or bicycle. Other groups of civilian workers were leaving through the entry gate. The German guards were checking the identification papers of the workers entering and leaving the factory grounds. It was an immense factory, and I lost hope of finding Manek among the workers.

A tall German officer in an SA uniform and a civilian in a brown suit arrived to inspect us. We stood silently and kept our eyes to the ground. The German looked at us with contempt and spoke German in a harsh tone: "Jews, here we manufacture engines for the German air force. You are here because you supposedly have metalworking skills. We will find out if this is true when we put you to work. If you have deceived us, you will be more than sorry. Today you will be working construction." He pointed to the civilian and said, "The engineer will tell you what to do." The German turned and walked away.

The civilian engineer spoke to us in fluent Polish. "I am in charge of the Platzmeisterai. That is the department responsible for the maintenance of the factory grounds and for construction. I do not know when you will be sent to work in the manufacturing facility. For now, you will dig a drainage ditch at a construction site on the west side of the factory. You will work from morning until evening and then be taken back to the ghetto. At noon you will be fed." The engineer spotted a Rzeszów Jew who had worked there before the deportation. "You worked here before. Where are the other Jews that worked with you here? Where is Shapiro? Ungar?" He mentioned other names. "They were resettled to a Ukrainian farm with everyone else from the ghetto," the Rzeszów Jew answered. "They could not get permission to stay." The engineer looked surprised but said nothing. He walked over to the German factory police officer still guarding us and spoke to him quietly in German. He came back and said in Polish, "The factory grounds are surrounded by guarded walls." He turned to Peter. "You are responsible for bringing the work group back to this area after work. The factory police will meet you here and take you back to the ghetto. Now, follow me!"

We followed him past the office building, manufacturing halls, and several large warehouses. We came to the construction site at the far corner of the factory complex near some railroad tracks. A long drainage ditch had been started. The engineer spoke to an older man in dirty work clothes and muddy rubber boots. The man must have been the foreman. He quickly assigned us to different jobs. He gave picks and shovels to some and ordered them into the muddy pit to dig and fill the wheelbarrows. I was ordered to push a wooden wheelbarrow. I brought it into the ditch, and the men filled it with mud and rocks. Then I pushed the heavy load along a narrow wooden plank and emptied it on a mound about fifty yards away. The Polish foreman stood on the edge of the ditch and waved a wooden club as he yelled, "Hey, Jews and Jewboys! Work harder and faster! I will teach you how to work! Faster! Faster!" Bringing the empty wheelbarrow back to the ditch was easy, but pushing it full and heavy out of the ditch and up the incline without rolling it off the narrow wooden planks was difficult. The day passed slowly, and the work was almost beyond my strength and endurance.

A man arrived with a kettle of soup and box full of metal bowls. We were ordered to line up and were each given a bowl of watery soup. He told us that starting the next day, some of us would have to bring the kettle from the kitchen to the work site and bring it back afterward. He took back the metal bowls and told us that we had to bring our own bowls from the ghetto. I went back to pushing the heavy, muddy wheelbarrow. I whispered to the workers in the pit to load fewer big rocks. Without answering, they began to load less dirt and rocks into the wheelbarrow. It did not take long for the Polish foreman to notice. He began yelling that we were lazy parasites and bloodsuckers and climbed down into the ditch to make sure that the wheelbarrows were filled quickly and fully. Again I had trouble pushing it up the steep incline and keeping it from rolling off the slippery and narrow wooden planks. I could barely stand by the end of the day when the foreman halted our work.

Peter led us back toward the gate where we had assembled that morning. Everyone was covered with mud and completely worn out from the long day of hard labor. We formed a marching column and tried to get in step. Peter spoke loudly and in a defiant voice, "Walk. Do not march. We are slaves, not soldiers. And stay on the sidewalk. Screw the Germans." We walked back toward the paved area next to the bicycle stands. Civilian workers stared at our filthy group and our Jewish armbands. I desperately looked in all directions for Manek. As we walked between two buildings, I heard him call, "Lucek! Lucek!" I turned toward his voice and saw him. He was waving to me from a ground floor window. I slowed down and called back to him, "Manek, we are going back to the ghetto! Are you all right?" He called back to me, "I am fine! My group will go back soon. Wait for me in our room!"

The German factory police made us line up in a military formation and gave the order to march. One guard called out, "Links, zwei, drei, vier!" (Left, two, three, four!) We got into step. I was dizzy with hunger and exhaustion. My legs were heavy with pain, but I forced myself to move in step with the others. After a long and difficult march we came back to the gates of the ghetto. The German factory police told us to be at the gate by seven o'clock the next morning to return to work.

I returned to our room to wait for Manek. I fell to the mattress in my muddy clothes and was overcome with depression and desperation. How would I make it through another day? Manek arrived a short while later. He wanted to know everything that had happened that day. I told him about the engineer and Peter and the ditch we were digging. I did not tell him how hard the work was and how exhausted and discouraged I had become. He told me that his group was working in a large shop where airplane engines were overhauled and repaired. He was not working for Daimler-Benz but for a German air force repair unit. The German air force supervisors and the Polish mechanics had treated them decently. He told me not to worry about him. Manek had gotten a piece of bread from one of the Polish workers and saved it. We ate it together with the little cold soup that was left from the previous day. I was too tired to talk or stay awake. I undressed and lay down on my mattress and quickly fell asleep.

The next morning Manek and I dragged ourselves off the mattresses, quietly dressed, and headed out to walk to the ghetto gate on Baldachówka Street. I had found a metal pot in our kitchen that I would bring for my noon meal. It was a white enamel pot with a hinged lid. I joined my work group at the ghetto gate and marched under the escort of the German factory police, back to the Flugmotorenwerk factory. We were again sent back to the drainage ditch. The Polish foreman handed me a shovel and sent me into the ditch to dig and load the wheelbarrows. It was hard and muddy work but not as difficult as pushing the wheelbarrow. I felt sorry for the workers struggling with the harder job that I had had the day before.

I watched for the order for someone from our group to fetch the kettle from the kitchen. We had worked for hours, and the sun was high overhead when the foreman called that it was time for lunch. I climbed out of the ditch and said, "Mister Foreman, I will do it. Please, Mister Foreman. I would like to go to get the food." He looked at me with scorn and said, "Get back to work, Jewboy. I will tell you when you should do something." The foreman picked two other young Jews and sent them up the street to the kitchen. I slid back into the ditch. After a meager noon meal and short break, I was back in the ditch, digging and shoveling mud and rocks into the wheelbarrows.

My days went on this way, without change. Each morning at dawn I left the ghetto and marched with my group to the Flugmotorenwerk factory. The work in the ditch became more difficult as the ditch grew deeper. Groups of uniformed German officials came to inspect our work. Their approach drove our foreman into a frenzy of yelling and hitting us with his stick. Every time the Germans were in sight, he made us work faster and forced the workers to run with the wheelbarrows. I had gotten to know some of the others in my group. Motek Hoffstetter, Moishe Ziment, Moses Verständig, and Mola Tuchman were all from Tyczyn. There were two teenagers from Rzeszów, Julek Reich and Julek Schipper. They were both older than I and became my close friends.

Every night I returned to the ghetto tired and muddy and waited alone in the room for Manek to return. I was lonely and terribly unhappy. Working silently all day gave me the opportunity to think about my parents. I was glad when Manek returned each evening. I did not want to think about how I would survive if something happened to him. We ate our meager rations, and we were still and always hungry. We stayed in our room in the evenings. We worried that no one had received any messages or news from the deported Jews. We tried to come up with all kinds of explanations. Surely, a letter from our parents would come soon.

At the Flugmotorenwerk I continued working in the drainage ditch. Finally, one afternoon the ditch seemed to be finished. The engineer came to inspect. He spoke to the foreman, who told us that the job was finished and that there was other work for us. The next morning, when we came to the factory, the engineer was waiting for us by the bicycle stands. He told us that twenty men from our group would be assigned to work in the metals warehouse. The warehouse supervisor arrived and selected twenty of the strongest-looking men for his work detail. I was not chosen. Peter was told to lead the rest of us back to the construction site.

As we were about to leave, the engineer ordered me to approach him. "Boy, do you know how to use a broom? I mean, to work as a street sweeper?" he asked. I knew enough to claim to be able to do any job, especially one that did not seem too hard. "Yes, Mister Engineer, I know how to sweep the streets," I answered. I was left behind and told to wait for a supervisor to come and get me. I waited alone for a long time. A German factory police officer walked by and stopped to question me. "What are you doing here, Jew?" I tried to explain that the engineer had told me to wait there. The officer did not believe me. "I think you are here to steal a bicycle!" he shouted. I tried to convince the German that I was telling the truth, but he would not listen. "Come with me," he ordered as he unfastened his holster and took out his gun.

Just then a young man in work clothes approached us. "Ah, Mister Wachman," he said to the police officer in Polish, "where are you taking my Jewboy? He will be working for the Platzmeisterai, cleaning the streets. The engineer asked me to show him what to do." The officer answered in Polish: "To hell, you cannot have Jews standing about the factory grounds without informing the police." The Pole said, "The engineer is just now telephoning Herr Gross, the police chief." The officer returned his gun to his holster, shook his head in disgust, and walked away.

The young Pole winked at me. He looked like a farm boy and spoke Polish with a rural accent. He took a bicycle from the rack, got on, and told me to follow him. He rode slowly, and I followed him past the metals warehouse, past the building where Manek worked, along the railroad tracks, almost to the factory's outer walls. We stopped at a small stucco building with three doors and no windows. The smell was horrible.

The young Pole pointed to the doors of the building. He explained that behind one was where they kept wastepaper that I would collect every morning from the offices. Another led to the storeroom for garbage and the manure that I would sweep up every day from the factory's streets. And in the room behind the last door were the brooms, shovels, and two trash cans for paper, garbage, and manure. He told me to get the wastepaper trash can. I got the trash can and pushed its squeaky metal wheels, following the bicycle. He took me to different buildings, including the factory's headquarters and the police station, where full baskets of trash were left outside the doors. I emptied each basket, and we started back. On the way he pointed out the main streets of the factory that I would have to keep very clean and sweep at least twice each day. The other streets I could clean less often but at least every second day. He told me to go to the kitchen by the construction site each day for some food.

In the ghetto, life was getting more difficult. The Germans placed new and harsh demands on the Judenrat and prowled the streets and alleys of the small ghetto, beating and arresting the Jews. The food rations were reduced, and we were always hungry. The Germans reduced the size of the ghetto, and the crowding and congestion worsened. More people moved into our building and apartment. Two young Jewish men, both working for the Ostbahn railroad, shared the small room with Manek and me. There was still no news from anyone who had been deported.

At the factory I collected wastepaper and office trash every morning and spent the afternoons sweeping the streets and picking up garbage. Most factory transportation was by motorized vehicles, but horses were also used. They left mounds of manure, and my job was to clean up after them. My work was filthy and degrading but did offer some advantages. I worked alone and without supervision. Even though I had to work all the time and was constantly on the move, I could stop for a short rest, get a drink of water, or go to the toilet. I was also getting more food. Two young Polish women working as the cook's helpers took a liking to me. If no Germans were in sight, they allowed me to eat at the little table in the back of the kitchen. Sometimes they refilled my pot with soup to save for later. Franek, the cook, saw what they were doing but said nothing. Often, I rolled my garbage can to the building where Manek worked and pretended to sweep the area under his window. Before long Manek would notice and come to the window. I shared my extra soup with him, and we spoke quietly for a few minutes. His Luftwaffe supervisors and Polish coworkers knew about our meetings but did not stop us. Manek told me that they joked that he should throw some trash outside the window or the authorities would notice that it was the cleanest part of the factory complex and become suspicious. In the evening, after I stored my brooms, shovels, and trash cans, I walked to the bicycle stands to march with the other Jewish workers back to the ghetto.

One evening at the bicycle stands, as I waited I noticed that Peter was absent. I asked the others where he was. They looked around to make sure that no Germans were close by, and then one told me what had happened. That morning one of the German factory police had shouted at Peter and began to beat him with a stick. Peter grabbed the stick and held on to it to stop the beating. He argued with the policeman in German, and after a while the policeman left. Soon after the noon meal the policeman returned in a car with two Gestapo men. They beat Peter with rubber truncheons, threw him into the back of the car, and drove away. That afternoon some Polish bricklayers told the Jews that the Germans had shot Peter just outside the factory gate. The Jews who told me this spoke of Peter with a deep sadness but also with admiration.

They spoke of his courage. I remembered a discussion with Manek about the meaning of courage. Peter had been strong and unafraid. Now he was dead. Was he courageous, or had he wasted his life? He died and nothing had changed. I knew that I would give up my honor, that I did not want to become a martyr but wanted to live to see my family.

A few days later I was sweeping the gutters near the metals warehouse when I noticed a new group of civilians working at the far end of the factory. I rolled my garbage can closer and saw that the factory police were guarding the people. They were all young men wearing Jewish armbands. I moved closer, wanting to find out who they were. A factory police officer ordered me to back away. I moved and then stopped, pretending to sweep a section of the street. I turned my right side toward them so they would see my Jewish armband. A few nodded discreetly to me. They lifted large pieces of wood from the railroad cars and carried them through a gate in the factory wall. The factory police officer who had ordered me to leave looked back at me. I put my broom and shovel in the garbage can and moved away.

That noon in the kitchen I asked Franek if he knew about these workers. He told me that they were new Jewish workers brought here from Dębica and Przemyśl a week earlier to build barracks for the Jews. I got some soup and went to Manek's window. As he ate, I told him what I had seen and heard from the Poles in the kitchen. He had not heard that any Jews had been brought into the factory or that a camp was being built. That evening, as we were waiting for the factory police to escort us back to the ghetto, I told my Jewish friends about this news. They had seen the new group from a distance. They thought that it was less expensive and simpler for Daimler-Benz to continue bringing us from the ghetto. Motek Hoffstetter thought that if we were moved into a factory camp, at least the police here, miserable as they were, were less dangerous than the SS that had been terrorizing the ghetto. That night Manek said that he thought that it was unlikely that we would be moved out of the ghetto. He was concerned that if we were, we might not receive any letters from our parents.

One Saturday evening after work my group gathered at the bicycle stands, tired and eager to get back to the ghetto. The factory police arranged us into the usual marching formation but did not give the command to march. A tall German SA officer and Gross, the fat German commander of the factory police, came up to us. Gross told us that we would not be going back to the ghetto, that as of this day we were transferred to the camp at the factory. The SA man told us that we were inmates of the Reichshof Jewish work camp and that anyone attempting to escape would be shot. The factory police gave us an order to move out, but instead of leading us toward the main gate, they led us in the opposite direction, across the length of the factory and to a guarded black iron gate in the factory's outer wall. I desperately looked for Manek and his work group from the repair shop, but they were nowhere in sight. We reached the black iron gate and marched through. I was now a camp prisoner and separated from my brother.

❖ 10 ❖

Inside the camp were rows of wooden barracks surrounded by double barbed wire fences. Armed guards patrolled a walkway between the fences. Other Jews were lined up in long rows between the barracks. I looked in all directions for Manek but did not see him. We were ordered to halt, and a tall Jewish orderly lined us up in rows of three. One German counted us, and then he left the camp with the other factory police. The Jewish orderly went along the rows asking for first and family names, which he wrote down in a notebook. He came to me, took down my name, and said, "You look too young to be here." "No, sir," I answered. "I am old and I am strong." He went on to the next person. When he finished, he told us to line up at a supply room door to get a blanket and then to find a place to sleep in Barracks Number 2. Others rushed to the supply room to get blankets and be first to find a good place to sleep. I approached the orderly and told him that my brother was in the group of Jews from the Rzeszów ghetto that worked in the Flugmotorenwerk engine repair shop. I asked him if that group would be brought to the camp. He told me that we were the only Rzeszów Jews being transferred to the camp. No arrangements had been made to bring in any other Jews from Rzeszów. I was devastated and felt terribly alone. A Tyczyn Jew from my group saw me standing there. He shook me and told me to get a blanket and find a place to sleep. He had heard that we would be given soup. I went to the supply room and was handed a small rough blanket.

With the blanket rolled up under my arm, I went to Barracks Number 2. Inside were wall-to-wall long, shelflike wooden platforms. I realized that we were to sleep on these and that I had to find a space to claim. The lower platform was full, with rolled-up blankets and clothing. I placed one foot on the edge of the lower platform, lifted myself up, and saw no empty spaces on the top. I moved along the narrow aisles, peering into the dark windowless barracks. Men were sitting on the bunks, standing in the crowded narrow aisles, talking, and holding their metal bowls, waiting for soup. The men from my Rzeszów work group were here along with many others.

I was almost to the end of the barracks, when a man in his early forties called down to me from the upper platform that there was still a space left. A crude wooden, three-rung ladder was attached to the lower and upper shelves. I climbed up next to some straw and rolled-up blankets. The man told me that he and a fellow from Dębica were also sharing the top bunk. He told me that his name was Katzenfliegel and asked my age. I told him that I was fourteen. He sighed and told me that somewhere he had a son who was also fourteen. He asked about my family, and I told him that the Germans had sent my parents to the Ukraine to work on a farm there. I told him about Manek, that he worked in the factory, and that I was hoping that he would be moved into the camp.

Katzenfliegel did not say anything more. I put my blanket down and sat on the bunk. My space had no straw, but I did not care. I was miserable and worried. The only clothing that I had with me was what I had worn to work that morning: summer pants, a short-sleeved shirt, a thin blue windbreaker, and my cloth cap. The other things that I had brought from Tyczyn to the Rzeszów ghetto, warmer clothing, underwear, and my family's pictures, were all back in the ghetto. I had nothing. I wanted to ask Katzenfliegel if I would be able to get a towel or a toothbrush, to find out where I could wash. He sat with his eyes closed, and I did not want to disturb him. I was worried that the orderly and Katzenfliegel had noticed how young I was. I decided that I had to lie about my age and say that I was seventeen. I would have to become invisible by standing in the back rows of formations or by staying in the middle of the ranks when we were marched to the factory and back. I was tired, but I did not dare go to sleep. Soup was still to be distributed that evening.

I looked around the barracks and at the men. I saw Motek, the two Juleks, and a number of Rzeszów Jews from my group. I realized that all the Jews without caps had no hair. Their heads had been shaved. They looked like prison inmates. I turned to Katzenfliegel. His eyes were now open, and he was looking at me. He wore a hat. I asked him if they had cut his hair. He told me that they had shaved his head and that tomorrow the rest of us would get our heads shaved as well. I wondered how Manek would ever be able to recognize me without my thick black hair. He went on to tell me that the Germans would paint big yellow stars on the front and back of our clothing so that everyone in the factory would know if any of the Jews tried to escape.

Later that evening, after eating a bowl of thin vegetable soup, I climbed up to my place on the sleeping shelf and tried to sleep. I worried about Manek and whether he knew what had happened to me. I longed to be back with him in our ghetto room. All around me men were tossing and moaning, speaking in whispers, and praying. I covered myself with the rough blanket, kept my bowl by my feet, and drifted off into a restless sleep on the hard wooden planks.

We were awakened at dawn with shouts to get up. We ran out into the yard where we lined up to receive a small portion of grainy dark bread and a ladle of substitute coffee in our bowls. We ate quickly and were ordered to line up in front of Barracks Number 1. Three men stood by stools with hair clippers. My turn came quickly, and after a few zips of the clippers, my hair was gone. I ran my hands over my scalp and pulled my cap over my head. I looked around at the others and fought the knowledge that I looked like them, like a prisoner. I walked back into the barracks and climbed up to my space on the upper shelf. I felt violated and ugly. At least I would now blend in with the others. Katzenfliegel had said that it did not matter if we had our hair.

We were left alone in the barracks until the afternoon, when we were ordered outside for another roll call. The prisoners had to line up in rows in the yard behind the barracks. Men were waiting with paintbrushes and buckets of yellow paint. I was standing toward the middle of the group and could see what was going on. Each prisoner stood still while a stencil of a large Jewish star was held against the front and back of his jacket. A large older man sitting on a high chair used a large paintbrush and bright yellow paint to sloppily brush the stenciled star on the prisoner's clothing. He shouted insults at the Jews as he marked each one. A camp orderly checked the prisoner's name in a notebook and then sent him to another line. Two young men used stencils to paint the word *Jude* and a three-digit number with black paint on the yellow star. The prisoners were shoved about, and the paint splattered all over their clothing. A young prisoner standing next to me told me that the young painters were named Zimmerman and that they were Jewish brothers from a village close to Przemyśl. They worked in the factory carpentry and paint shop. The older fat man was the boss of that shop. He was a Volksdeutscher.

The young man next to me introduced himself as Emil Ringel. He looked a few years older than I. He was thin and haggard but spoke in a gentle voice. He was from Przemyśl and was now living in Barracks Number 3. I told him my name, that I was from Rzeszów, and that I had been moved into the camp only the day before. He extended his hand to shake mine. I had made a friend. He asked my age, and I did not hesitate when I told him that I was seventeen. He looked surprised but said nothing.

Before long it was my turn to be painted. As the young Zimmerman held the stencil to the right side of my chest, the Volksdeutscher dipped his brush in the small can that he held and roughly painted a yellow Star of David on my blue jacket. He shoved the small can at me and used his brush to point to a large bucket of yellow paint on a table. He ordered me to fill it with more paint. I took the can from his hand and walked the few steps to the table with the paint bucket. There was no ladle so I dipped the can into the bucket, filled it about three-quarters full and brought it back to the painter. He took it from me and ordered me to take off my cap. As soon as I did, he poured the can of yellow paint on top of my head. The paint ran down my face, into my eyes, my ears, and down the front and back of my jacket. My eyes were burning, and I was blinded with the paint. I tried to wipe it from my eyes and my mouth with my hands, which were soon covered with paint. The German ordered me to turn around. I turned and felt someone press a stencil against my back and the brush painting a second yellow star. He shouted at me to move on. Someone took me by my arm and led me away. A man asked my name and then told me that my number would be *222*. I could feel someone painting on my chest and back again. The hand under my arm led me farther away. Someone gave me a piece of paper to wipe the paint from my eyes and face. He pushed wads of paper into my hands, and I tried to clear my eyes. When I could open them a little, I saw that one of the Zimmerman brothers was helping me.

"Why? Why did he do this to me?" I asked. "The paint bucket has a little spigot on the other side, and he wanted you to get the paint that way," he answered, "not to dip it from the top." "And for this he is killing me?" I cried. I was covered and splattered with yellow oil paint. My eyes were burning, and I could not stop crying. "What do you expect from those damned Germans?" Zimmerman whispered. "You know, this paint will not come off with water, not even with hot water, even if we had any. After we finish here today, the German will go home. Help us carry our stuff back to the shop. We have turpentine, and we will get some of this paint off you. It will not ever come off your clothing, and it may not come off your head, but we will get it out of your eyes. You will still look like a yellow devil, but at least you will be able to see. The turpentine will burn like hell, but that is the only way to get this stuff off." He took me to the camp washroom and told me to wait for him to come get me after the Germans left.

I cried burning tears of pain and shame as the others saw me there, painted yellow. Some brought me wet rags and more paper to wipe off the paint, but nothing really worked. Some tried to comfort and reassure me but I did not believe that I could be saved. I was trying to survive by hiding my age. Now I was a marked ugly scarecrow covered with thick yellow paint. I stood there with my eyes closed, afraid and without hope. I longed for my parents and my brother.

I stayed in the washroom for a long while, and then the two Zimmerman brothers came for me. They told me to carry some of their equipment so that the factory police at the gate would believe that I worked in the paint shop. "The way you look, it will be easy to convince them that you are a painter," the other Zimmerman said. "Come. Cheer up. We will help you." I walked with the brothers and carried a small bucket of brushes and rolled-up stencils. Through my half-closed eyes I looked down at the front of my jacket. There was a yellow Star of David with the word *Jude* and the number *222* painted on it in black. The Zimmermans worked for a long time to scrub the paint off my head. When they were finished, the skin on my face and neck was raw. There was still yellow paint on my head, covering my hands and behind my ears. But my face was nearly clean, and I could open my eyes and see.

Back in the barracks the others said nothing about the incident or my appearance. I wanted neither to talk about it nor to be pitied. We lined up outside for our evening meal of a meager piece of bread and some watery cabbage soup. We returned to the barracks, and I climbed up to the top of my sleeping shelf and covered myself with the blanket. Even though I was exhausted, I could not fall asleep. The horror of the day washed over me, and I felt that I would die. I tossed and turned on the hard shelf, and the others, sleeping next to me, mumbled and complained. I waited for the morning and longed to see Manek at his window. I worried that he would be upset by my shaved and painted appearance. I wondered what I could say to calm him. I knew that I would not tell him what they had done to me.

After the roll call at dawn the camp prisoners were assembled into rows and marched to work. Some went to the production hall, others to the metal warehouse or the construction site. The Zimmerman brothers went unescorted to the paint and carpentry shop. A police officer stopped me at the gate. He was a mean and ugly man with an aquiline profile whom we would later nickname "the Hawk." He looked at my stained clothing and hands and asked in disgust, "Where are you going, dirty Jew?" I told him that I was the street sweeper. He spoke briefly to another guard and then waved me through the gate. The guards all laughed as I passed them. I hurried by to avoid any more trouble.

I wanted to finish the morning work quickly so that I could go to Manek. I nearly ran to the storage building to get the trash can and then to the various offices to collect the trash. I ran back to the storage building to dump the full trash cans. With my broom, shovel, and garbage can I went to Manek's building, praying that he would be at the window. I did not care that my clothing and running with the squeaky trash can might attract attention. I needed to see Manek and tell him that I was still here and to make sure that nothing had happened to him. I turned the corner and saw Manek leaning out the window, waving and calling out to me. I rushed to the window and reached up to him. He leaned out as far as he could and for a moment our fingers touched. "Lucek, Lucek!" he shouted. "I was so worried when you did not come back to the ghetto. I ran everywhere to look for you and asked everyone if they knew what happened to your work group. I found out that they kept your group in the camp, and I worried about you all night." "I am all right, Manek," I answered. "They kept us here in a camp on the factory grounds. We are living in a barracks right outside the factory wall. It is not so terrible. The worst thing is that we are separated." Manek had noticed the yellow paint on my clothing, hands, and ears. "My God, Lucek, what happened to you?" "It is nothing, just an accident with paint." I tried to reassure him. "Do not worry, I am not hurt."

Manek did not believe me. "I am worried about you. I promised Mama and Daddy to look after you. You are my little brother, and I love you." "I know," I replied, "I love you too." He asked me to take off my cap. I could hear someone inside call him. "Oh, Lucek. They cut off your hair, didn't they? I am so sorry," he said. He must have seen the misery on my face. "It does not matter, it is not important," I said as I tried to convince him. He asked me to come back in the afternoon. I asked him to bring some of my things to work with him. I needed some clothing, my toothbrush, and towel and also wanted the envelope with photographs and the New York address. Someone again called his name. "I have to go," Manek said. He disappeared from the window. At noon I went to the kitchen to get some soup. Franek, the cook, laughed at my appearance but the Polish women felt sorry for me. They gave me a little extra soup and a piece of crusty Polish bread. Later I took the soup and the bread to Manek's building, and when he appeared, I offered to share the food with him. He seemed moved that I, now a camp prisoner, was still thinking of him and wanting to share my meager portion. He insisted that I was still a growing boy and should eat everything myself. At my urging, Manek took a small corner of my bread and the two of us ate together in silence. He told me that the conditions in the ghetto had not changed, and I told him about the barracks and some people in the camp. I told him that I had made a friend. I told him about Julek Reich, Julek Schipper, and Emil Ringel. I did not tell him about how terribly lonely I was or that I missed him more than ever. He promised to bring my things to work the next day. Soon he had to go back to work and I to my sweeping. Our fingers touched again, and we parted.

When I saw Manek the next day, he had brought me the photographs and the few pieces of clothing that I had left in the ghetto. I asked him to keep some of it at his workplace and said that I would sneak it into the camp one piece at a time over the next few days. Manek gave me a small can of paint remover that he had found in his workshop. I used it over a few days and slowly and painfully removed most of the paint from my skin.

I saw Manek for a few minutes almost every day. We were careful to keep our visits brief, and I kept working below the window in case a guard came along. Several times I would scurry away to avoid being caught taking an unauthorized break. Manek was always encouraging and affectionate. But when I saw him a few days later, he seemed subdued and upset. I was alarmed and asked him to tell me what had happened. I feared terrible news about our parents. Manek shook his head sadly and told me that something awful had happened in the ghetto two days before. He asked me whether I remembered the few hundred men who had stayed in the small ghetto with their wives and children. While all the men were working outside the ghetto on Friday, the Germans had rounded up all the mothers and children and deported them. The men had found out when they returned to the ghetto after work. The husbands and fathers screamed and cried for hours. Many people were suspicious about the whole resettlement story. Why would the Germans send mothers and little children to work on some farm in the Ukraine?

My life was filled with endless hunger and constant abuse. Every few days the engineer from the Platzmeisterai or other Polish workers would come looking for me to complain about work that I had done or to give me especially difficult and dirty jobs. My clothes and shoes stank of manure and rotten garbage. I could not wash the smell out of my clothing and attracted the attention and insults from the patrolling factory police. They would stop to question me and then dismiss me with a kick from their heavy boots. After a while I realized that certain guards kept after me and that they enjoyed frightening, cursing, and kicking me. I desperately looked forward to seeing Manek. We tried to encourage each other, and seeing him even for a moment made me feel better and less alone. We did not mention it, but we were both worried because we had had no news from our parents. I pressed Manek to tell me what people in the ghetto were saying. He had heard rumors that Jews were dying in the east and that their bodies were being used to make soap. Other stories said that some Jews in the ghetto had received postcards from the Ukraine and that the resettled families were well. We tried to come up with reasons why our parents had not been able to send postcards to us. Each time we parted, we promised to meet the next day and hoped that we would have news from our parents.

My life was difficult. Each morning we were awakened with shouts and driven outside to stand and wait for the putrid substitute coffee. We had nothing to eat unless we saved a little bread from the evening meal. At night, after the prisoners were counted, we were given a bowl of watery cabbage or turnip soup and a small chunk of coarse bread. I slept on the hard wooden shelf, in a tight space between other men. I had to keep watch over my bowl, because I would get in trouble if I had to get another one. My clothing was dirty and shabby. Our bunks were infested with every imaginable bedbug. I used the cold water in the camp to rinse my hands and face but had no way to clean my body. Luckily, I did not yet need to shave. Other Jewish prisoners had to struggle with a few shared rusty razors. If they showed any signs of a beard, they exposed themselves to abuse by Germans who tortured them as religious Jews. The factory police were mean and abusive. They hit us with their clubs and truncheons and kicked us if we did not march in step or remove our caps quickly enough in their presence. The guard we called "the Hawk" was especially violent and hit us with his rifle every time we came within striking distance. I dreaded going to the factory when the Hawk or other brutal guards were on duty. I was beaten and kicked as I passed through the gates.

A special kinship arose among the Jews in the camp. Our very suffering, our longing for our families, whose fate and whereabouts were unknown, made us reach out to one another for companionship and support. A few Jews tried not to share our fate. Alfred, a young Jew from Germany, was designated as the senior prisoner. He was arrogant and treated the rest of us with meanness bordering on brutality. I came face to face with him in the camp one evening, after my first week when he came to my barracks. The prisoners greeted him by name, and when he came to me, I did too. He turned to me and without a word slapped me across my face. I looked at him with pain and bewilderment. He slapped me again and shouted for me to take off my cap when I spoke to him. I removed my cap, and he walked away.

With the coming of autumn the days were cooler, and it rained a lot. I still swept the streets and picked up the wet manure and garbage. I was cold and soaking wet most of the time. My throat hurt, and I coughed constantly. Manek worried about my health. The rain was relentless, and the camp had no physician or medicine. Manek brought me a piece of oilcloth from the ghetto, which I fashioned into a cape to keep some of the rain off my back. I was getting sicker and running a high fever. The others in the barracks saw that I was ill and tried to help me. Katzenfliegel insisted that I use his blanket at night to keep warm. Another young man in my barracks, an observant Jew whom we nicknamed "Yossel," got me a small packet of white powder that helped me to feel a little better.

A few days later everyone in the camp was assembled in a formation and counted by the German factory police. Alfred announced that starting on the next Monday, all Jews working for the factory's Platzmeisterai would begin working inside the large production hall, where airplane engines were built. I would be working inside and be out of the rain, away from the garbage and manure. I knew from people who worked in the production hall that it was dry, warm, and orderly. The work would be hard but not exhausting. I realized with alarm that this might make it impossible for me to see Manek. I would have to take risks to see my brother or lose him as well.

During the evening I spent hours in the camp washroom trying to wash the stink from my clothing and shoes. It was hopeless. I did not have other shoes and had to wear my tattered blue windbreaker with the yellow star, which marked me as a Jewish prisoner. I threw away my old pants and shirt and switched to the clothing that Manek had brought me from the ghetto.

✦ 11 ✦

Very early on that Monday morning in the fall of 1942, I lined up with the men who worked in the production hall. A guard marched us to the back entrance of the large building. I was excited to see that the entrance was near the building where Manek worked and just across a narrow grassy area from his window. Inside the building a Polish foreman met the Rzeszów Jews and led us to a corner that was filled with rows of work tables and high stools. This was the Parts Finishing Shop.

We were given rags and steel files and ordered to clean, file, and polish machined metal parts of airplane engines. The foreman instructed us and checked our work. He was critical and rejected many pieces as not acceptable and demanded that we work faster. The metal pieces were dirty, oily, and had sharp edges; soon, my hands were black with dirty oil and full of small bleeding scratches and cuts. The foreman's shouts and our awkwardness amused the Polish workers. The work was familiar to me from my days in the locksmith shop of Mr. Gorzelec. The foreman yelled and complained but did not strike or even physically threaten us. After a few hours he lost interest in us and talked to the Polish women working at the polishing machines. A German supervisor wearing a white laboratory coat came into the area, silently inspected our work, and left.

An hour or two passed. I was glad to be working there. I was inside, out of the rain and winter winds. The work was easy, and I was sitting down. My cold would get better. This was much better than sweeping the streets and collecting garbage. I had to find a way to leave the build-

ing for a few minutes to see Manek. His window was so close to the
back entrance of the production hall that it gave me the confidence to
find a way.

We had to ask the foreman for permission to go to the toilet. He
usually responded by saying, "Yes, you better go. I do not want you to
shit here! But come back right away!" He told us that the only toilet in
the building that Jews and no one else could use was located right next
to the door that we used to enter the building. I noticed that some men
came back from the toilet right away, but others stayed away for as long
as fifteen or twenty minutes. The foreman did not seem to care. He was
busy with the young Polish women.

This was the chance for me to go out to see Manek. I asked the
foreman for permission to go to the toilet. He waved his approval. I
walked quickly through the enormous building, past row upon row of
noisy lathes, drill presses, and other machines. Many people were bus-
ily working at their machines, pushing carts, carrying boxes, and walking in all directions. No one paid any attention to me. In a minute I was
at the rear exit. It was not guarded. I could see through the glass pane
in the door that it was drizzling outside. Just across the wet strip of
grass was Manek's window. A door right next to the rear exit had a
large sign on it in German and Polish: "Jewish Toilet." I went in. Some
Jewish men stood talking by the sinks. They did not seem concerned
about the time. I looked around and, as I expected, in one corner stood
a bucket, a mop, and a broom, just what I needed. I took the broom
and walked out. The men took no notice. Broom in hand, I walked out
the rear door. No one stopped me. I could feel my heart beating in my
chest. I crossed the patch of grass and came to Manek's window. It was
closed. I gently knocked on the glass with the broomstick. A face
appeared behind the rain-streaked glass and disappeared again. In a
moment the window swung open and out leaned my brother. He was
happy to hear of my new work inside the production hall. He said that
he still had no news from our parents. It had been more than two
months since the deportation. I knew that I had to hurry back before I
was discovered. I waved to him and ran back to the production hall. I
put the broom back into the Jewish bathroom and shook the rain from

my cap. In a minute I was back at my workbench. No one asked any questions. I had found the courage and the way to see my brother.

I continued scraping, polishing, and filing the oily iron and aluminum components piled on the workbench. At noon the work in the shop stopped. The Polish civilian workers gathered in the corner to eat food that they had brought in lunch boxes. A Jewish prisoner accompanied by a Jewish orderly pushed a cart into our shop. They gave each of us a slice of dark bread and a cup of warm, weak substitute coffee. The small piece of bread did not satisfy my terrible hunger. I wanted to save some for later to share with Manek, but I could not resist eating it all. I devoured it in seconds. Afterward I was still hungry and felt guilty that I had not saved any. Our break ended, and we were ordered back to work. After the twelve-hour shift we assembled at the rear door of the hall and marched back to the camp. The Hawk was on duty at the gate, but I was in the middle of the large group of prisoners, and someone else got the beating.

My job in the production hall settled into a routine. I worked for twelve hours at the Parts Finishing Shop and managed to see Manek for a few minutes almost every day. A group of Jewish workers from the ghetto was brought in every day to take over the construction work that my group had done. Some Jews in the metal warehouse had contact with them, and they became a link to the ghetto and the world outside.

The Jewish orderlies announced that we would start working day and night shifts. We were divided into two groups. The day shift worked from six in the morning until six in the evening and the night shift from six in the evening until six in the morning. We would switch from day to night shift every week during the Sunday afternoon break. I was assigned to start working on the day shift. I would get to see Manek only every second week. That week I saw Manek four times. I told him that I would be working the day shift every other week and starting the night shift on Monday. It would be hard to go a week without seeing each other, but we had no choice.

On Monday I started the night shift. The guards left us in the barracks until noon. After that we were ordered to scrub the barracks floor, build a latrine, dig ditches, and build shelves in the camp supply room. I worked in the supply room, carrying large boards and hammering nails. Late in the afternoon we stopped working and lined up for the evening meal of watery soup and a slice of bread. I was already tired and sore from the day's work, and the prospect of starting a twelve-hour night shift was grim. It was nearly six when we were marched to the production hall.

Inside, the lights were on, and the shift change caused great confusion. We were ordered to our jobs and warned to be there before the six o'clock whistle. I realized that Manek would be marching back to the ghetto right now, and I dreaded the long night before me. A tall man in a white lab coat walked hurriedly ahead of me. I saw a white envelope fall out of his coat pocket and fall to the floor. I picked it up and ran after him. "Mister! Mister! This fell out of your pocket!" I called to the man as I ran after him. He stopped, turned, and saw me with the envelope. He felt his coat pocket. I handed him the envelope, and he took it and looked surprised as he said, "Thank you." I turned to run to my workspace before the six o'clock whistle.

I had been working at my bench for about an hour, when one of the Jews working beside me whispered loud enough for everyone to hear: "Lucek, you jerk, it was a pay envelope you returned to the German supervisor. There was money in it. You should have kept it and used it to buy things from the Poles. Bread, socks, whatever." The others at the bench chimed in. They shook their heads and whispered, "Returning money to a German. Stupid, you have much to learn." I listened to them, concerned that I had done something foolish. I had returned the envelope automatically. I never gave any thought to what was in it and never considered keeping it. One worker said, "The supervisor may have lost some of his money when he dropped the envelope. If there is any money missing, he will blame you." I was worried. The others tried to reassure me. "Do not worry. Even if he lost some money, he will not recognize you." Another hour passed and nothing happened. The incident with the envelope was forgotten.

Sometime before midnight two German factory policemen came into the Parts Finishing Shop. They looked around and called out: "We are looking for the young Jew that found the supervisor's pay envelope. Tell us who it is, or there will be trouble!" I was terrified and kept silent. The Germans kept shouting and demanding that the culprit step forward. From the corner of the shop an arm, a finger, pointed at me and said that I was the one. A police officer tapped me on the shoulder and ordered me to follow him. I got up and walked behind him with the other police at my side. Heads turned and watched as the two Germans led me out of the finishing shop. They marched me the length of the hall to a row of glass-enclosed offices. I could see the tall German supervisor waiting for me.

The police opened the door to the supervisor's office, led me in, and announced that I was the Jew who had picked up his envelope. The supervisor thanked the police and asked me to come in. The police closed the door and left. The supervisor turned to me and smiled. He thanked me for returning his pay envelope. He said that I had done a fine and a decent thing and that he was surprised to get it back. I wanted to say something that was appropriate but could only mumble my thanks. The supervisor sat down behind his desk and motioned for me to sit down in a chair. He asked me questions about which department I worked in and what work I did before I came to the camp. He asked my age. I told him that I was seventeen and that I had worked as an apprentice to a locksmith. He asked about my father. I felt nervous answering his questions. I knew enough not to tell him that my father was a Jewish lawyer, so without hesitating I replied that my father was a locksmith.

He opened a desk drawer and took out some sandwiches wrapped in white paper. Yellow cheese on buttered dark bread. He handed me one of the sandwiches, unwrapped the other, and began eating. I unwrapped my sandwich and took a small bite. It was unbelievably wonderful. I was too nervous to eat. I wrapped the sandwich back up and asked if I could save it for later. He did not say anything and continued eating. I sat there in silence, unsure whether to leave or wait for him to dismiss me. He finished eating and told me to return to my work. I thanked him for the sandwich, which I stuck in my pocket as I backed out the door. In a few minutes I was back in the Parts Finishing

Shop. Everyone was surprised to see me return. They wanted to know what had happened to me. "Nothing," I said. I unwrapped the sandwich and started eating. Yellow cheese on buttered dark bread. I had forgotten what food tasted like. No one bothered me as I ate it; the other prisoners knew that a fight among us under the watchful eyes of the guards would result in severe punishment.

I stayed close to the other Rzeszów men living in the factory camp. I met some other prisoners from the nearby towns of Dębica and Przemyśl. Many were still distraught about being taken from their families. The crowded camp, hunger, brutality of the guards, constant exhaustion, and frequent illnesses left us all depressed and bad-tempered. When we argued, the peacemakers reminded us that we needed each other to survive.

The holiday of Rosh Hashanah came. I was working the night shift that week. During the day we worked our extra jobs before we received our evening rations and rushed to the factory for the six o'clock whistle. There was no way for us to observe the holiday. In the factory on Erev Rosh Hashanah, we were sad and forlorn. I thought about the wonderful holidays that I had celebrated with my family and wondered where my parents and my brother were that night.

In the barracks the next morning some men gathered in the corner to pray. We had no prayer books; they chanted the prayers from memory. I recognized some melodies and words. I went and stood among the praying men, hoping that their words would carry my pleas to the heavens. The prayers ended, and I climbed up to my place on the upper shelf. I was tired from the long night, but I could not sleep. In a few hours the camp orderlies would wake us.

I worked the day shift the following week. On the night that Yom Kippur was to begin, we marched back to the camp in tense silence. We ate our evening meal quickly and returned to the barracks. Many men had already moved to the corner to pray. A few stood by the door to watch for any Germans. I stood with the men in the corner. Outside, shadows fell across the camp as the sun was setting. A young man from Dębica turned to face east and began to chant the Kol Nidre, the beautiful ancient prayer that asks for forgiveness from God. I remembered sitting by my father's side in the old gray stone synagogue in Tyczyn and hearing this mournful chant. The men began to recite the Shema, our declaration of faith to our one God. All around me, the prisoners were weeping and holding on to each other. Two Jewish camp orderlies, Walter and Jurek, were praying, crying, and asking for forgiveness. I remembered my father saying to me, "On this day, it shall be written, who shall live and who shall die. Who shall prosper and who shall be brought down. This is the day to confess our transgressions and pray for forgiveness." I prayed for my parents and my brother. The night was filled with great weeping and lamentations. It felt as if this was the world's last minyan.

The next day, after I had worked less than an hour at the Parts Finishing Shop, I asked permission to use the toilet. I wanted to see Manek. I got the broom from the Jewish toilet and casually walked out the rear door of the production hall. Manek was at the window. I held the broom as if to sweep and slowly continued across the patch of grass separating our two buildings. I reached Manek and swept under the window as we exchanged greetings and wishes for a better year. I did not speak of my great sadness or ask if he had heard from our parents. It was as painful for me to ask as for him to have to tell me that there was still no news.

I looked up at his face and saw that he had changed. He had lost a lot of weight. His eyes were sad and serious. I wished that I could reach up to him and embrace him, but I kept my hands on the broom. I remembered the tears and misery of the night before and felt restored just by standing and gazing at him. Manek reached behind him and then leaned out the window. He was holding an egg in his hand. He told me that he had bought two eggs from a Polish worker. He offered me the egg, but I did not move to take it. I explained that it was Yom Kippur and that today I would fast. Manek looked at me with disbelief and urged me to eat the egg so that I would not starve. He had eaten the other one already and told me that to stay healthy we were supposed to eat on Yom Kippur. He promised me that we would fast on every Yom Kippur after the war.

I took the egg and put it in my pocket. I had forgotten how an egg felt. We said goodbye and promised to meet again soon. He left the window, and I walked back to the production hall. Later, when no one was looking, I peeled and ate the egg. It tasted delicious. It brought back fresh memories of home. The adults fasted, and even though I was a child and allowed to eat, I fasted with my parents and my brother until sundown. I recalled breaking the fast in our kitchen. My mother would make egg sandwiches on fresh rolls. As I finished the egg, I promised God that if I survived the war, I would fast every Yom Kippur and remember my first Yom Kippur as a prisoner in a German concentration camp.

Not long after Yom Kippur, I was assigned to operate a lathe in the manufacturing area of the production hall. After brief training by the Polish foreman, I was ordered to demonstrate to an older, bald-headed German that I was qualified to work as a lathe operator. The German approved of my work, and I was left at the machine to make wide brass rings that would be used inside an airplane engine. I had to produce a certain number of rings per hour, and Polish and German inspectors would periodically check my work. I started to work on my own, and after a few mistakes I was able to make the rings quickly enough to meet the quota. I was lucky to be transferred to a job where I worked alone and was less likely to be harassed by a Polish foreman or the German guards. I was now a lathe operator and more valuable to the Germans than as a locksmith's apprentice.

When I worked the day shift, I was able to see Manek at his window once or sometimes even twice on the same day. We still had heard nothing from our parents or any of the Jews sent to the farm in the Ukraine. In the ghetto the Germans still bullied, beat, and executed Jews. Neither Manek nor I had any extra food to share. Our visits were especially emotional on Saturdays before I changed to the night shift. We knew that we would not see each other for an entire week.

One Friday in early November 1942 the temperature dropped, and strong winds foretold the coming Polish winter. I saw Manek at his window late in the afternoon. He was worried that I did not have any warm clothing and promised to find a sweater or coat for me in the ghetto. He tried to calmly tell me that some Jewish workers in his group had heard that the airplane engine repair operation might be moved closer to the German-Russian front. Manek did not think that they would move it anytime soon, if at all. We both knew that his move would pull us apart for the rest of the war. We promised to meet again on Saturday before I started working the night shift again. I began to walk back to the production hall but after a few steps turned back toward Manek's window. He was still at the window. "I love you, Manek. I will see you tomorrow," I said. "I love you too, little brother. Be well," he answered.

On Saturday I went to see Manek twice, but he did not come to the window. This had happened a few times in the past when he had worked in another part of the building. I was disappointed but not alarmed. The next day the weather was cold and rainy. In the afternoon I was assigned to a group that had to unload coal from railroad cars. I was cold, tired, and hungry and felt desperate to be inside, out of the rain and away from the guards.

On Monday they took us back to the railroad siding to shovel coal. We were marched back to the barracks late in the afternoon, with just enough time to wash the coal dust from our faces and to quickly eat our rations before we were taken to the production hall for the night shift. At the production hall I met some day-shift Jews who were preparing to march back to the camp. Two from Tyczyn approached me. They had heard from the Jews who still came from the ghetto that the Germans had staged a deportation on Saturday morning. Hundreds of Jews were deported, among them Manek's group.

"Oh, my God! Oh, my God! All of them were sent away? Manek too?" I cried out. "Yes, we're sorry but yes," they answered. "They were assembled at the ghetto gate just as if they were going to work. They were surrounded by the SS and marched to the train station. They are all gone." My brother was taken away, just like my parents.

All around me in the factory people were shouting orders. The day-shift workers were lined up for the march back to camp. The night-shift workers took their places at the machines. I stood by the back door, not moving toward my lathe. A German guard shouted at me, and I did not understand what he was saying. He shoved me roughly toward the manufacturing area. I walked in a daze toward the lathe. I leaned on the machine, incapable of getting started. I thought about Manek's face. I had seen him just last Friday afternoon. The Polish fore- man came over and asked if I was sick. I shook my head. He saw that something was wrong. He whispered that I should turn on the lathe and start making the brass rings. He said that if the Germans saw me just standing and not working, they would accuse me of sabotage, and then both of us would be in trouble. I did not answer him or move to turn on the machine. He began to shout at me to turn on the lathe and start working. Slowly, I began to work. I was making the brass rings that would become a part of a German airplane engine. I made a ring and then another. I worked intently and mechanically while panic and worry raced through my mind. I worked bent over the lathe, dreading daybreak when my shift would be over and I would have to face my loss without the distraction of work.

Hours passed. It must have been after five in the morning. Already Tuesday. Some Polish workers on the day shift started coming in. I kept working. "Salzman?" a strange voice asked from behind. I turned and saw a Polish civilian standing close to me, vaguely familiar but still a stranger. "Salzman?" he asked again. "Yes," I answered. The stranger handed me a folded little piece of paper and warned me to be careful. He walked away. I stood holding the paper in my hand. I looked up and down the rows of lathes and other machines and saw that no one was watching me. I looked at the folded paper in my hand. It was a small square of white paper with thin blue lines, like paper from a notebook. Everyone was working, and no one seemed to be watching me. I unfolded the paper inside the palm of my hand and read the short pencil-written note:

> Dear brother, I escaped from the train. I am safe. It is not safe
> to write more. Will try to contact you again soon. Destroy
> this note.
>   Love, Manek

I felt a flood of relief. Happiness replaced the despair and fear that had consumed me through the night. I wanted to shout and dance, to share my good news, but I knew to keep quiet. I read the note again and again. My brother had defied the Germans, and they did not get him. He had escaped. Not only was he brave but also his love for me was so fierce that he had found a way to let me know that he was safe. I was overwhelmed and tears of joy rolled down my cheeks. The note had to be kept a secret. I bent over my lathe and pretended that I had a cold as I wiped my eyes.

The night shift was ending, and the Jewish prisoners of the day shift arrived. The Jewish prisoner who worked at my lathe during the day came toward me. He must have heard about the latest deportation from the ghetto and my brother's being taken. He told me to have faith, that they would live and return to find us. I thanked him and held the note in my fist as I ran to the toilet. Inside a stall I reread Manek's note. He asked that I destroy it, and I understood that it was dangerous for us both if the Germans discovered it. I kissed the note that had been held in my brother's hand, tore it into little pieces, and flushed them into the toilet. I kept the tiny corner that said "Love, Manek" and put it in my pocket. I joined the formation of night workers and marched back to the camp in the cold gray morning.

· 12 ·

As long as Manek had been nearby and I could see him, even for a few minutes, I was not alone. He had helped me to face the horror of the camp and shared the worry and despair about our parents. We supported each other with our hopes and by sharing the silence when we ran out of words.

I worked at the lathe, hoping that the stranger who brought the note from my brother would return. One night, several months after I got the note from Manek, another stranger, a middle-aged Polish civilian, stopped at my lathe and asked if I was Lucek Salzman. I nodded my head quietly, trying not to attract attention. He handed me a small piece of folded paper and quickly walked away. I knew that it was a note from Manek. I looked around to see if anyone was watching me. I let a few torturous minutes pass, and then I carefully unfolded the paper in the palm of my hand. Inside were two folded twenty-złoty bills and a short message written in pencil:

> Beloved little brother, I am well and think about you. I am in the forest with friends. Take good care of yourself. Hope the money helps. Will contact you again soon.
>   Love, Manek

Manek was still alive and able to contact me! I had not been forgotten, and even though he was far away, I still had a brother. Bent over the noisy lathe, I read the note many times. I placed the paper money inside my shirt and then tore the note into tiny pieces. During the next few days I used the money that Manek had sent me to buy, through a Jewish prisoner in contact with a Polish worker, half a loaf of crusty bread and two pairs of used socks. I needed the socks, for it was late December and winter had come. The night shifts were long and exhausting. At the lathe I was left alone to meet my quota. In the production hall I was shielded from the cold, snow, and ice. I knew that I was lucky. Many Jews had died out in the cold, sick from the conditions and starvation, beaten by the brutal guards and police.

Every few weeks different strangers approached me and slipped me notes from Manek. The notes included small amounts of money and were brief and without names or specifics. He wrote that he was well, that he thought about and missed me, and that he hoped that I was well too. Reading between the lines, I assumed that Manek had joined the Polish Resistance and was fighting in the forests near Rzeszów. I worked at the factory bent over the lathe, always hopeful that a messenger would appear with a note from my brother.

The German factory managers wanted us to be reasonably clean and free of any vermin. Every few Sundays the factory police marched us through the back streets of Rzeszów to a prewar Polish army barracks for showers. We undressed, and our clothing was disinfected with hot steam. Even the showers were used to torment us. While we were showering, the water would be turned to freezing cold or scalding hot temperatures. We still welcomed the opportunity to wash and scrub our bodies even though we would be filthy again in a day. On those rare Sundays we did not work. We were allowed outside the camp for a few precious hours.

Our Sunday marches to the showers took us through the streets of Rzeszów. Many Poles were home or on their way to church. The German factory police marched us in military step with kicks and punches. They ordered us to sing as we marched. Some prisoners who had served in the Polish army before the war started singing old Polish marching songs. The rest of us hummed and mouthed the words to make it appear that we were singing too. The Poles on the streets found the sight of Jews marching in step and trying to sing old Polish military songs comical. Some stood on the sidewalk and shouted insults at us. The Polish children shouted, "Filthy Jews! Go to the devil! Dirty Jews to Palestine!" The Poles shouted while we sang at the top of our voices. The Germans were amused that the Poles mocked and cursed us.

I fell ill with a cold and constant cough. I forced myself to keep working in the factory and at the extra jobs to which I was assigned. With no medicine or time to rest I got much worse and developed a high fever and sharp pains in my chest. I felt so sick that I considered staying in my bunk and telling the orderlies that I could not work. Other prisoners were lying on the wooden bunks, feverish and ill, unable to go to work. I did not think that the Germans would tolerate sick Jews who could not work. On the next Sunday afternoon the Germans conducted a selection in the camp. A Daimler-Benz official, an SA officer named Lafferenz, supervised the selection. All the prisoners were lined up in rows out in the assembly area and physically examined and questioned by the German police. I copied the people who rubbed their faces with snow to turn their cheeks red to hide their sickly complexions. A German looked me over and moved on to inspect others. When the selection was finished, the prisoners who seemed ill or feeble, and all the men lying sick in the barracks, were loaded into a truck and driven away. We feared that they would be killed.

Until the selection many of us believed that the work that we did made us valuable and brought us some degree of safety. The selection showed us that any Jew who could not work would disappear. I heard rumors of a planned escape from the camp. I talked with my friends Schipper, Reich, Ringel, Wachs, and Hafferflock about the possibility of escape. We had no money, weapons, or friends on the outside to whom we could run. Our clothes were painted front and back with large yellow Jewish stars. We would never be able to escape the Germans.

One night two young men dug a tunnel under the wire fence, escaped, and ran into the woods. The guards discovered their tunnel and sounded an alarm. The police set off into the woods with hunting dogs. We were forced to line up, and they counted us repeatedly while the guards shouted at us and hit us. We stood outside, cold and beaten for hours, until the Polish police brought the escapees back. The two young Jews were unrecognizable. Their clothing was torn, and they were nearly naked. Their hands were tied behind them with ropes. Their bodies and their faces were swollen and bloody.

They were locked in a small storage shed. The guards did not stop us from speaking to them through a small window. One was bleeding from his mouth, and his face was so swollen that he could not speak. The other told us that they had not gotten far from the camp when some Polish farmers spotted them. The Poles chased them through the fields and the woods. The farmers caught them, tied them up, and beat them. The Polish police came and took them back to camp. After a while the Germans ordered us away from the shed. The Gestapo came and took them away. The next day a Polish worker in the factory told us that the two Jews were shot right outside the factory gate.

It was now 1943. My birthday came and passed like any other day. I was fifteen. With the coming of winter the small group of Jewish workers no longer came each day from the ghetto. I was cut off from any news about my parents. The prisoners began to look to each other as family. I clung to a few teenage boys in camp with whom I had become close, including Julek Reich, Julek Schipper, and Emil Ringel. Julek Reich was a supportive friend, always full of energy and self-confidence. He was not intimidated by the Germans and was always ready to try anything and, when we needed it, to cheer us with a story or a song. Julek Schipper was serious, considerate, and as loyal as one could wish a friend to be. He was troubled about being alone, without his parents and his sisters. In this way he was most like me. Emil Ringel was from Przemyśl. He was decent and kind. He had a smile for everyone and was optimistic under the most difficult circumstances. I had other friends—Hafferflock, Wachs, and Rypp, all good young men.

A new director took over the Reichshof Daimler-Benz Flugmotorenwerk. His name was Werner Romstedt. I saw him walking through the production hall, observing and asking questions. One Sunday afternoon he came to inspect the camp. The factory police and the Jewish camp orderlies were nervous as they showed him around. After Herr Romstedt arrived, Jewish workers had to meet higher production quotas. The new quotas affected the amount of food that Daimler-Benz issued to the camp kitchen. No matter how hard we worked, we often ended up getting less food.

A large group of Jewish prisoners was brought to the Reichshof camp from Rawa-Ruska, a town about seventy miles east of Rzeszów. Most of these prisoners were in their twenties and thirties. They were assigned to a barracks with the Jewish prisoners from Przemyśl. I saw them line up for the roll call and for their first meal in camp. They seemed different. Despite their gaunt appearance, something about them gave an impression of toughness. They were dressed in torn Russian army uniforms. I wanted to speak to them. I heard that they had been sent to our camp from the east and hoped that they had some information about the Jews deported to the Ukraine.

The night after the Rawa-Ruska Jews arrived in the camp, my friend Katzenfliegel told me that he was going to see the new prisoners and ask whether they knew anything about the Jewish families resettled from the ghettos of Rzeszów, Przemyśl, and Dębica. It was forbidden for prisoners to walk from barracks to barracks after dark. I warned him to be careful, and he slipped out the door. A few minutes later Katzenfliegel came running back. Something was very wrong. "What's the matter? What happened?" I asked. Katzenfliegel was so upset that he could not speak. Others gathered about him. They pressed him for news. Finally, he spoke. "The Rawa-Ruska Jews are fools and liars! Yes! Yes, they are liars!" The prisoners standing around asked, "Why? What did they say?" Katzenfliegel answered in a choked voice. "They say that we are stupid to believe the Germans. They say that we have been deceived, that there never was any Ukrainian farm. They say that all our people, all our families, were sent to Belzec, a camp near Rawa-Ruska, where everyone was killed with poison gas." We listened in stunned silence. Katzenfliegel continued in a strange mournful singsong. "They say that all our loved ones have been dead since last July. They say that we should stop asking stupid questions and start saying Kaddish." His face was wet with tears, and he sobbed as he spoke in that anguished singsong. "The Rawa-Ruska Jews must be fools and liars. What they say cannot be true! Oh, my God. My God! What has happened to my family, my wife and my beautiful boys? My family. My Sara. My babies!"

I listened to him in horror. I heard someone shouting, "No! No! It cannot be! They are lying! He is crazy!" No one wanted to believe the terrible things that he was telling us. Katzenfliegel climbed to his sleeping shelf and pulled his blanket over his head. I could hear him crying. Some men wanted to run to the newcomers' barracks and hear what they had to say. I followed them to the door. Motek Hoffstetter stopped us. He said that only three men should go, lest the Germans catch us. Motek picked two other men, and they left our barracks. I thought about Katzenfliegel's terrible words as we waited for them to return. A terrible dread rose up in my throat. We crowded around the door.

Motek was the first to return to the barracks. He looked solemn and grim. The two others from our barracks and two men from Rawa-Ruska were with him. "Friends," Motek said quietly. "I am terribly sorry, but the news is bad. I brought two of our new friends to tell you what they have told us." Motek turned to the two strangers. One spoke: "*Chaverim*, friends. It is worse than anything one can imagine. I have to tell you what I must. You must know the truth. There is no other way. God forgive me. All your families, all our families, everyone deported from this area was taken directly to Belzec. Our Jewish men, women, and children were stripped naked, beaten, and killed with poison gas." A cry rose up in the barracks. The stranger from Rawa-Ruska went on. "They are all dead, all gone." He was quiet for a moment. His face was streaked with tears, and as he wept, his shoulders shook with sorrow. I knew in my heart that the terrible things that he was saying were true. He went on. "I cannot accept it, either. I hate to even speak these words. My parents, my brothers and sisters, my wife, and my beautiful children." His voice broke; he covered his face with his hands and wept.

The other stranger put his arm around his shoulder and turned to us. "What my friend told you is true," he said. "We heard it from the Polish railroad workers in the last camp. We heard it from the Poles who talked to the Ukrainian guards who worked at Belzec. And from the one Jew that escaped Belzec. The truth cannot be denied. There is nothing we can do but say Kaddish." A somber voice called us to prayer. I stood with the other men: "Yit-gadal ve-yit-kadash shmei raba, b'alma . . ."

My parents were dead. They were beaten and murdered, and I was not with them to comfort them or save them. I felt guilty and heartbroken. I left the group of weeping and praying men and climbed onto my sleeping shelf. I lay down next to silent Katzenfliegel. I pushed my face into the straw and shut my eyes tight. I could not keep out the image of my father, naked, beaten, and bloody. His frail shoulders, his stifled cries. My mother, her body exposed to the mockery and whips of the Germans. Her eyes when she understood what was being done to them. Oh, God, my father torn from my mother, each of them alone at the end, suffocated by the poison gas. My heart ached. If only I could have been there to cover their nakedness, to tell them that I loved them, to take away their pain. My uncle Kalman and aunt Blima and all the Jews of Tyczyn—the Tuchmans, the Goldmans, the Krugers, the Rabs, and the beautiful shy Esther who came to us to beg for food. The little Jewish children driven into the killing chamber, crying out with their last breath for their parents. And my parents! Oh, God, my parents! I knew that in their last moments they had called out for Manek and me. Where was Manek tonight, when I needed him more than ever? When I needed to know that he was still alive.

It was a night never to be forgotten. A night filled with pain and sorrow. A night forever marked by the death of my parents. A night where the pain of their suffering was burned into my soul. I whispered into the darkness. "My dear father, my beautiful mother, I miss you, I love you, I am so sorry for what has been done to you." I turned to God, the God I always knew as merciful and loving. "My God, where were you? Where were you when you should have saved my parents?"

The terrible news spread to the other barracks. Weeping and lamentation echoed throughout the camp. The morning wake-up whistle blew. We dressed and lined up for the march to work. There were no greetings, and no one spoke. Everyone in the camp, including the orderlies, was red-eyed and mournful. In the production hall I could not concentrate on the lathe. The Polish foreman noticed that something was wrong. He must have seen the pain in my eyes, for he left me alone for the rest of that day. I prayed for another message from my brother. None came. I stood at the lathe, motionless, thinking of my parents, remembering our parting, my insisting that I go with them, and their making me stay behind in the ghetto. Did they know what awaited them? How I had argued with them. They gave me up to save me.

That evening in the camp only a few people went to collect their evening meal. In my barracks everyone was silent. My friends Julek Schipper and Julek Reich sat next to me on a wooden bench. We sat like that, silent and unhappy, for a long time. Then Julek Reich stood up and started singing a sad Yiddish song.

Shtein, tayere shtein du bist ein moel my mein Mamyniu gevein,
Dos ganze leben vot ich aveg-gegeben ob, dich my Mamyniu, noch
   ein mal zu sein.
[Stone, dear gravestone, at one time you were my dear mother.
The rest of my life would I give away to see you, my mother, one
   more time.]

I had never heard that song before. It touched my heart, and I joined Julek in singing. The others joined in, and we sang it over and over again. Then we cried and embraced. We were orphans. The terrible story was true. We had fought every day to stay alive. Now we wondered what and who was left to live for.

I worked both the day and night shifts in the production hall. I tried to avoid the terrible visions of Belzec. The images stayed with me during my waking hours and came to me in my dreams. Then, after a few weeks a strange numbness came over me. The horror of Belzec seemed to define my life and my destiny. I felt that nothing in my life mattered anymore and that all the terrible things that I had gone through had somehow been my due. Only thoughts of Manek gave me hope. I needed to hear from him. I looked to every passing stranger with the fervent hope that he might be the one that would bring me the message that I longed for. One night a Polish worker whom I had seen before in the production hall stopped by my lathe. He whispered to me that he knew about me from others and believed that he could trust me. I was disappointed that he did not bring me a note from Manek. He continued to whisper and told me that he was a member of a resistance group in the factory and asked if I was willing to help. I said that I was. He told me that the rings I was making were critical to the flow of oil inside the airplane engines. If I operated the lathe faster than the speed specified, the rings would have tiny grooves on their surface. The oil would clog, and the engine would overheat. I did not give any thought to the danger of getting involved on the say-so of a stranger and told him that I would do it. For months I made defective oil rings. I could see the small grooves, but no one else noticed, and the rings passed inspection. I had a sense of purpose. Slowly, I started to recover from my despair.

A few days later another Polish man approached me at the lathe. I expected more instructions from the resistance group. After asking me my name, he handed me a familiar folded piece of white paper. A stone fell off my heart. I unfolded the note. Manek was safe and well. He thought of me and missed me. He asked me to take care of myself and promised to write soon. He included three twenty-złoty banknotes. I was filled with relief. I had a brother. He was alive. We would one day be together again. My parents were dead, but I still had someone to survive for, someone who needed me to survive for him. I was alone in the camp but not in the world.

It must have been March. The trees outside the barbed wire fence showed the new buds that signaled the coming of spring. Three young Jewish brothers from Barracks Number 1 were executed. I knew them well. They had been very protective of each other and friendly with others. They were the only brothers in the camp besides the Zimmermans, and we all had known and envied them. I heard that one brother had argued with Alfred, the senior orderly. The other two brothers joined the argument, and Alfred called the factory police. They were brought before Lafferenz, the SA officer. I was told that he shot them all.

In the spring of 1943 we heard from Poles in the factory that the Germans had suffered major defeats on the Volga River in Russia and in northern Africa. I did not even know that the Germans were in

Africa. Many were overjoyed at the news and felt that the Germans' chain of victory was breaking and that defeat would come within a year. I felt no joy. I was hungry and afraid. The Volga and North Africa were far away, and a year was longer than I might survive. The guards were brutal, and selections continued as our numbers dwindled. Each day posed new challenges, risks, and dangers.

One Sunday Itzok Rypp, Motek Hoffstetter, and I were told that we would now have to work every Sunday for the factory police. We would be under their constant supervision and exposed to more frequent beatings. My job was to clean the police quarters and help maintain the air-raid shelters throughout the factory. I had to unload truckloads of sand and carry the heavy bags to the air-raid shelters, where they would be used to douse fires. One day I was unloading sand from a truck when Lafferenz, the German SA man, came by and decided that we were not working hard enough. He started whipping us with a leather whip. My heart was full of hatred and rage. I started singing under my breath as I felt the whip on my back and heard it turned against my companions:

I przyjdzie jeszcze dzien zaplaty, Sendziamy wtedy bedziemy my . . .
[The day of payback will still come; we will be the judges then . . .]

"Are you crazy? Shut up! Shut up!" Motek Hoffstetter, who was next to me, whispered angrily. "He will recognize the melody!" I stopped singing, upset at my stupidity. The melody was the communist "Internationale." I do not know where I learned the song or what possessed me to sing at such a time.

A group of sixty Jewish prisoners arrived at the Reichshof camp from another labor camp in the town of Nowy Sacz. The prisoners looked to be in much better physical condition than we were. Our original group had been in the camp for more than a year. Our clothes were torn and filthy. I had worn through all the clothes that Manek had sneaked into the camp from the ghetto. I was wearing pants that were split open in the back and worn through at the knees. I had tried to stitch them several times, but the fabric was so thin that it shredded. I still wore my old blue windbreaker, which kept me neither warm nor dry. The jacket had been repeatedly steamed for de-lousing, and the seams had worn out. The Jewish stars once painted with yellow paint were barely visible. I still wore the brown ice-skating boots that had belonged to my mother. I tried to patch the soles with scraps of cardboard, which I tied over the boots with string. When it rained, my socks were soaking wet, and in the winter they froze to my feet. I felt dirty all the time and longed for a hot bath and clean clothes. One day an SS truck delivered crates of used clothes and shoes to the camp. The orderlies announced that we would each receive a jacket, a shirt, a pair of pants, and shoes.

On Sunday I rushed to get a place at the head of the line to get our clothes and shoes. I feared that if I did not get up front, they might run out before my turn came, which was sometimes the case with our food rations. I entered the storage room and was told I should hurry and pick out my size. The clothing was obviously used but most looked to be in good condition. I grabbed a short warm overcoat, a long-sleeved shirt, and a pair of brown pants. I moved into another room where hundreds of shoes and boots spilled out of two big wooden crates. The shoes were all mixed together. They had not been tied or kept together in pairs. I knew that these shoes must have been taken from Jews killed by the Germans in a camp. The others in the room stood with me; no one was willing to start digging through the shoes. One young Jewish prisoner picked up a black shoe and started digging in the pile for its mate. He turned to us and said that we all knew where these shoes came from. These shoes and clothes would be our salvation. The Jews who died would help us live by the gift of their shoes. I started digging through the pile. I found a black left boot and a similar right boot. It seemed to be the same size and color but a different style. I quickly put them on and left my old boots in the pile.

It was September again. One factory manager kept a calendar hanging on his office wall. We tried to keep track of each day, which was difficult because each day was as miserable as the one before and the one to follow. One day I was at the lathe, thinking of Manek and

Lucjan "Lucek" Salzman (George Salton) as a baby with his mother, Anna Salzman, in Tyczyn, Poland, 1928. An unknown person stands in the background.

Left to right: Anna, Manek, Henry, and Lucjan Salzman in 1928. One of the only surviving images of the Salzman family from before the war.

Manek Salzman, the older brother of Lucjan Salzman. He was six years older than Lucjan and survived the Holocaust but was killed in 1946 in Poland, never to be reunited with his younger brother. Date unknown.

Watercolor by Lucjan Salzman (George Salton), painted in 1946 at the Neustadt displaced persons camp in Lübeck, Germany. The image depicts the liquidation of the Rzeszów ghetto in 1942. United States Holocaust Memorial Museum Collection, gift of George Salton.

Watercolor by Lucjan Salzman (George Salton), painted in 1946 at the Neustadt displaced persons camp in Lübeck, Germany. Surrounded by Nazis and onlookers, a young Jewish man kneels before an execution pit. United States Holocaust Memorial Museum Collection, gift of George Salton.

Pencil sketch by George Salton, drawn in 2008, depicting slave labor in a Daimler-Benz factory concentration camp in Reichshof, Poland, 1942–1943.

Pencil sketch by George Salton, drawn in 2008, depicting prisoners working on the stone quarry in the Flossenbürg concentration camp, Germany, 1944. Salton is the farthest prisoner on the left, number 16019.

Pencil sketch by George Salton, drawn in 2008, depicting prisoners unloading from the boxcars as they arrive at a new concentration camp, 1944–1945.

Pencil sketch by George Salton, drawn in 2008, depicting a winter roll call in the Watenstedt concentration camp, Germany, 1945.

Pencil sketch by George Salton, drawn in 2008, depicting concentration camp prisoners waiting for soup, Germany, 1944. Salton, number 16019, can be seen among the prisoners on the right.

Pencil sketch by George Salton, drawn in 1999, of a concentration camp prisoner.

Prisoner list from the internment (number) book of Flossenbürg concentration camp, in Germany. Lucian Salzmann (alternate spelling), prisoner number 16019, with name highlighted. From the Arolsen Archives.

Prisoner list from the number books of Natzweiler (Struthof) concentration camp, in France. Luzian Salzmann (alternate spelling), prisoner number 33339, with name highlighted. From the Arolsen Archives.

Liberation from Wöbbelin concentration camp, May 2, 1945. *Third from left*, Lucjan Salzman; *first from left*, Lucjan's friend Emil Ringel. Photograph from *The Devils in Baggy Pants*, combat record of the 504th Parachute Infantry Regiment.

International Tracing Service file card regarding Lucjan Salzman (George Salton) that lists his concentration camps, prisoner numbers, and information on his departure to the United States in 1947. From the Arolsen Archives.

Top row, left to right: Moishe Ziment, Itzok Rypp, Motek Hoffstetter, and Tobias Nussen. *Bottom, left to right*: personal diary, displaced persons camp pass of Lucian Salzman (alternate spelling), and his personal calendar. Items from Salzman's time in the Neustadt displaced persons camp, Lübeck, Germany, 1945–1947.

Lucian Salzman (alternate spelling), Hebrew Immigrant Aid Society identity card noting his sponsorship (required for immigration to the United States) and immigration status: departing on September 22, 1947, from Bremen, Germany, on the USS *Marine Flasher*, and arriving on October 2, 1947, to New York City.

Lucjan Salzman aboard the USS *Marine Flasher*, September–October 1947.

George Salton, serving in the U.S. Army Signal Corps at Fort Monmouth, New Jersey, 1951–1953.

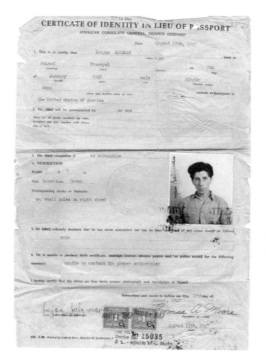

Lucjan Salzman Certificate of Identity in Lieu of Passport, from the American Consulate, Munich, Germany, 1947. Required for those with no identification or birth certificates.

Ruth and George Salton
at their wedding,
March 29, 1953,
New York City.

George Salton graduating
with a bachelor's degree
in physics from Syracuse
University in 1960, with
Ruth Salton in background
and, *from left to right*,
children Alan, Anna,
and Henry.

praying for another message. Two months had passed since I received a note from him. A Polish worker approached me and asked my name. He gave me a small folded note from my brother. I bent over the lathe and read:

> Dear Lucek, Hope you are well. I am sorry that I am to enter an activity and will not be able to write to you again. I will love and miss you always. Do not let bad news defeat you. When this is over, remember to write to America. We will find each other and be together. Take care of yourself. Destroy this note.
>   I love you, Manek

I knew that I would not hear from Manek until after the war. I tried to memorize his words and promises. If we never saw each other again, this would be my last moment with him, holding the paper that he had held in his hands. I kissed the note, tore it up, and dropped it into the pile of brass shavings under my lathe. I looked over at the calendar on the wall. It was September 3, 1943.

◆ 13 ◆

In September the SS took command of the camp operation. Oberscharführer Oester became the commander, and a troop of Ukrainians was brought in to serve as guards. Oester was the former deputy to Schupke, the German commander of the Rzeszów ghetto. Oester inspected the prisoners, barracks, and washroom at random. He carried a heavy truncheon and struck at anyone within his reach. He would punish an entire barracks for the slightest reason. He denied us our meals and made us stand in roll call for hours in the worst weather. He liked to point his pistol at our heads and threaten to shoot us. He instructed the orderlies to mistreat us, or they would be replaced. Oester had a sick fascination with animals. He had a large vicious dog that he treated with care and affection. He brought six large geese into the camp and kept them in a small shack that the prisoners built next to the washroom. Every afternoon some Jewish men were sent to clean the goose shack and feed the geese by stuffing chunks of dough down their throats. The wild geese fought being force-fed. They bit at our hands. Oester and the guards loved to watch us feed the geese and especially to see us bitten and pecked at. He had prisoners plant a large vegetable garden just inside the factory gate. We grew tomatoes and other vegetables for the kitchen to use for the Germans' meals. What torture for us prisoners to tend to the tomato plants that we were forbidden to eat under threat of execution.

One afternoon I was picked with two other prisoners to clean the goose shack and feed the geese. Oester came by to inspect our cleaning and watch us feed his animals. He left after a few minutes, and we were spared his antics. Not long after, I heard two gunshots. I looked toward the sound of the shots, which came from the entry to the camp. Four prisoners were carrying a limp body toward the washroom. I saw that the dead man was Katzenfliegel. I was told that Oester had killed him in the tomato garden. Oester claimed that he saw Katzenfliegel urinating there. Katzenfliegel tried to deny that he done such a thing. Oester stepped around him and shot him twice in the back of the head.

The Ukrainians were happy to be our guards. They were often drunk, which made them eager to shoot at the Jewish prisoners. It was dangerous to be outside the barracks after dark, even though we were permitted to walk to the latrine. I had to go to the latrine one night. It was between the barracks and the double barbed wire fence. I was running toward the latrine when a drunken voice called out for me to halt. The guard yelled at me to fall to the ground. I dropped down, hoping he could not see me in the dark. "Fall down! Stand up! Fall down! Stay there. Your mother is a whore, you Jewish swine!" The Ukrainian was shouting. "Trying to escape, you filthy Jew! But I caught you!" I heard the click of his rifle bolt. I jumped up and ran into the black night toward the rows of barracks. He fired his rifle. I kept running from the shouting and gunshots and made it to my barracks. The camp lights were flashed on, and soon the guards were shouting and firing more rifle shots. I climbed onto my shelf and covered myself with my blanket. The other prisoners were awakened by the commotion. No guards came into our barracks, and after a while the shouting stopped and I went to sleep. At roll call the next morning Oester announced that the guards had stopped an escape attempt. He told us that from then on, he would shoot prisoners if anyone managed to escape or even attempted to.

In our barracks Oester instituted a new system to prevent escape attempts. Two prisoners were assigned to a two-hour shift during which they had to stand by the door and make sure that all the prisoners were accounted for. At the end of each two-hour shift the next shift would count all the prisoners in the barracks to make sure that they were all there before they took over. If any prisoners were missing from the barracks, the shift that had been on guard would be shot. The prisoners lay on their bunks sleeping. We would walk up and down the narrow aisles and climb to the top sleeping shelves to count the prisoners.

One night a prisoner escaped. He dug under the fences and ran into the woods. A guard saw him and chased him with the other guards. They quickly caught and killed him. The next morning we were called out for roll call where they had laid his body. Oester pulled a young Jewish prisoner from our ranks and ordered him to lie down next to the dead man. The young man begged for his life. Oester hit him with his truncheon and kicked him until he was on the ground next to the body. The young prisoner tried to get up on his knees. Oester took out his pistol and quickly shot him in the back of his head. He fell to the ground. Oester returned his gun to his holster, smiled at us, and walked away.

Every day blended with the next, filled with hunger, sleepless nights, hard labor, and the constant threat of beatings, selections, and executions. On a Sunday afternoon I was assigned to a work group to clean the entry to the factory office building. Some prisoners were raking the grass and collecting leaves, while others washed the stone steps or polished the large wood doors. The Polish foreman told me to wash the large glass window above the front doors. He gave me a bucket of water and some rags and helped me raise a ladder. We stood the ladder on top of an iron grate built into the top step. I had climbed up and was washing the window when a German factory police officer came out the front door. The ladder blocked his way, and he had to squeeze around it. He looked up at me and gave the ladder a strong kick. The ladder toppled over, and I fell onto the stone steps. I felt a sharp pain and saw that my pant legs were torn, and my knees were bleeding heavily where I had landed on the sharp edges of the iron grate. The German kicked at the spilled bucket and rags and yelled at me to get back to work.

The other Jews helped me to sit on the steps. Even the Polish foreman seemed concerned. He told me that the window was clean enough and that I need not go up the ladder again. One Jewish man tore a cleaning rag into strips and wrapped them around my knees. He looked after the policeman who was walking away down the street and said in Yiddish, "The bastard should burn in hell." He turned to help me to stand and told me that the cuts did not look too bad. The others went back to work. I stood there, not sure what I should or could do. The foreman just ignored me. Another German factory police officer rode up on a bicycle. He was to take us to the railroad tracks to unload flatcars of coal. We followed him to the rail lines. I had trouble keeping up with the others. They saw that I was hurt and tried to walk slowly and even ignored the shouts of the policeman. At the railroad tracks we were given shovels and wheelbarrows to unload the third flatcar. Some of the others helped me to climb onto the rail car where I shoveled the coal into the wheelbarrows. My knees hurt terribly and then became numb. Blood had seeped through the dirty washrags. It took us hours to finish, and we were exhausted and black with coal dust. It was getting dark when we were marched back to camp.

We went to the camp washroom to wash the soot off our hands and faces. I untied the rags from around my knees and lowered my pants. The cuts were oozing blood and full of black coal dust. I could not raise my legs up into the common sink. I rinsed the dirty rags in water and tried to wash the black dust from the cuts. The coal washed off the surrounding skin, but the open wounds remained filled with blood and black coal dust.

Schipper had heard about my injury and came into the washroom looking for me. He looked at my knees and told me that I needed to go to see the camp doctor. I argued that I would be fine and that the cuts did not hurt badly. Schipper told me that if I did not get the cuts taken care of, they would probably get infected, and then I would have a serious problem. I pulled up my torn pants and limped after him. The camp doctor was not a physician. His name was Klein, and he had been a medical student in Italy before our imprisonment. He was kind and made no secret of his limited medical training. He had no medical supplies or medicines. He tried to patch up scrapes and advise those who became ill. He inspected my cuts and said that they would have to be cleaned out. He asked Schipper and another man to hold me down, while he cleaned the cuts with water and tufts of cotton. He brushed on a brown liquid that burned and made me cry out. When he was finished, he wrapped my knees with strips of white cloth.

Schipper helped me to get in line for the evening soup and bread and then helped me back to the barracks. I could not eat much. I wanted to lie down, but I could not climb up to my sleeping shelf. Schipper persuaded the man beneath me to change places with me for the night. I woke throughout the night in horrible pain. My right knee ached, but my left leg throbbed and felt hot and swollen. In the morning I could not bend my left knee. Someone went to speak to the doctor about me. The doctor sent word that he would register me as ill for the day and see me after the day shift had left for the factory. Several hours later I sat up and rolled myself off the bunk. The barracks was quiet, the day shift had left, and the night shift was sleeping. I leaned on the walls and bunks and tried to hop on my right leg. Outside I fell on the wet and slippery ground and had to crawl. Half-way across the roll call area I saw a young man from Nowy Sacz. He offered to help me. He bent down, picked me up, and carried me to the doctor's room.

The doctor looked at my swollen knee and tapped on my swollen left thigh with his fingers. He put a thermometer under my armpit and measured my temperature. He told me that my leg was surely infected. He sprinkled some powder on the cuts and told me to go back to my barracks and lie down. The Nowy Sacz prisoner carried me back to my barracks and put me on the lower sleeping shelf. He worked the night shift and promised to return the next day to carry me back to the doctor.

The next day the doctor was worried that I was still in pain and running a high fever. The cut on my right knee had started to heal. The cut on my left knee was also improving, but the swelling above the wound was getting larger and more painful. The doctor feared that the coal dust had traveled up from the cut. The area was infected and probably full of puss. He wanted to make an incision to drain it but warned me that if he made the wrong incision, I would never be able to bend my knee again. He decided to drain the wound to try to prevent the infection from spreading. I sat in a chair while several prisoners held me down. The doctor sat across from me with my swollen leg stretched onto his lap. He took a long metal knitting needle and pushed into the cut and under the skin until it reached the infection. I yelled and tried to jump and kick, but they held me down. The doctor pulled the knitting needle out of my leg and a stream of bloody puss came out. I screamed as he pressed and squeezed on my leg. He used the knitting needle to push some gauze deep into the opening. I was too faint and exhausted to protest. The doctor cut the gauze and left a small piece sticking out of the cut. He would change the gauze again the next day.

My friend carried me back to my barracks and into my sleeping place. Later, a night-shift worker brought me water and a little piece of bread that he had saved from the evening meal. I saw the doctor every day for the next week. As men held me down in the chair, the doctor pulled out the gauze, squeezed out more bloody puss, and used the same knitting needle to push a fresh strip of gauze into my leg. I screamed and cried every time. There was only a slight improvement. I was still running a fever and in terrible pain, which was relieved only if I lay down and kept completely still. I spent most of the time lying in my sleeping place. I knew that on any given day the factory management allowed only three Jews out of the four hundred in the camp to be excused from work because of sickness. My being sick and unable to work allowed only two other sick people to stay in camp and forced some others who were sick to work. The doctor told me that he would try to keep me in camp for a while longer. The worst danger was that the Germans kept records of the Jews who were ill and unable to work for an extended time, and these prisoners would frequently disappear. The Germans did not want Jews in the camp who could not work. I knew that my illness put me in danger.

I had been sick for three weeks, when a Ukrainian guard and an orderly came into the barracks. They called my name. I had no time to hide. The orderly saw me, and they came over and ordered me to dress and go with them. The orderly helped me pull my pants on over my stiff left leg and helped me to get on my shoes. The other prisoners watched sadly as I was taken away. I was led to the camp gate, where I saw a German military truck and several German factory police. I was hoisted onto the back of the truck, where I joined four other Jews who seemed to be very ill. Two more prisoners were brought from the camp and loaded onto the truck. Two policemen climbed on, and the truck started moving slowly through the factory streets. We stopped near the front entrance of the production hall. One police officer went into the building while we waited in the truck. I knew that I was in great danger, but there was nothing that I could do. A few Polish workers and some Germans walked by the truck and looked up at us. Suddenly, I saw the German supervisor whose pay envelope I had returned more than a year before. He recognized me. He walked over to the factory police officer and commanded him to release me. He shouted that I was one of his best workers, and he needed me back at work. The senior police officer looked at me and told the supervisor that he could have the Jew and ordered me to jump off the truck. The police officer asked my name, crossed it off a list, and turned away. I turned to thank the supervisor. He motioned for me to follow him. I moved a few steps, and he noticed my limp. He told me to return to the camp and that he would get me a new job assignment the next day. The tall German supervisor walked away. I started toward the camp, and I heard the truck's engine start and the truck drive away. I could not bear to turn and watch the truck drive away and see those Jews who knew that they were sentenced to die on this day. I limped back to the camp. I felt glad that I was saved, grateful to the German, but I felt terrible for the Jews who were still on the truck.

The Ukrainian guard at the gate stood and watched me limp toward the camp. He stopped me and asked what I was doing back. They hoped that they had seen the last of me. I answered that a factory supervisor had asked that I be returned to work to finish a special project. An orderly had approached and listened to my response. "Did they take your name off the transport list?" he asked. "Yes, I watched them scratch my name from the list," I replied. The guard murmured, "Sooner or later," and let me pass.

The prisoners in the barracks were shocked to see me. I was the first to ever return after a selection. They could not believe that such luck would come to a prisoner, that after a year the supervisor would recognize me among the other skeletal and shaven prisoners. Schipper said that this was a good sign and that all hope was not lost, that we might survive this camp. Someone began to sing an old Yiddish song: "Wo nemt men ein bissel Mazel?" (Where does one get a little luck?) I had come so close to death and had been able to walk away. The others smiled and sang along. I felt good that my return had lifted their spirits, but I still remembered the others who were not so fortunate.

In the morning a Jewish orderly came over to my bunk and told me that I was to report to the Precision Manufacturing Building after roll call. I had been assigned to work as a janitor. I assumed that the supervisor had arranged this. I thought about the work that I had done cleaning the streets and my fall from the ladder and hoped that I could do the work with my injured knees. I had never been inside the Precision Manufacturing Building. No Jews were working there. I walked over to the building and cautiously entered. An SS guard was sitting behind a desk. He asked my name and then turned and called over to a Polish worker to say that I was there. The Pole spoke as I walked behind him. He would be my boss, and my job was to clean the toilets and locker rooms. He noticed my limp, and I told him how the German had kicked the ladder out from under me and that I would do any work that he needed. He turned to me with a knowing glance. "Do not worry. Your work here will be easy, and your legs will get better."

Working as a janitor turned out to be an easy assignment. I swept and mopped the floors and washed the sinks and toilets twice a day. No factory police or guards watched or supervised me. I could work at a comfortable pace and even stand and rest in the bathrooms when I was cleaning them. The only problem was that I had to walk back to the camp at midday to get my meal. This was difficult at the start when my legs were still infected and sore. For many days I went without the meager bowl of watery soup. On a few occasions some Polish workers who ate in the locker room gave me some food left over from their lunch. Soon my legs were improving, and I made the daily walk for my own rations.

One day I was walking back to the camp to get my meal. The sun was bright, and the sky was a glorious blue. I was glad to be outside and away from the locker rooms and toilets for a short while. I turned onto the main street and walked toward the camp gate. I was surprised to see a carriage pulled by two horses coming down the street. A German officer sat in the carriage with some other people. I stepped behind a wooden pillar of a building to avoid any confrontation about being alone on the streets. I pressed back against the wall and watched as the carriage passed. Oester sat on the front seat, holding the reins and driving the two horses. He was smiling and talking over his shoulder to a young woman and two blond children. Oester called to the horses and stopped the carriage. He climbed down, tied the horses to a large tree, and helped the woman and children down from the carriage. He led them to a small grassy area, embraced the children, and headed toward the gate to the camp. The woman opened a blanket on the grass and sat down with the two children. I watched them laughing and playing. I stayed hidden, afraid that if I stepped out, someone might notice that I had been hiding. I knew that if I stayed here much longer, I would have to get back to work and forget about getting a meal.

Oester reappeared. The children saw him and ran to him. He smiled and lifted them into the carriage. The woman folded up the blanket and climbed onto the carriage. She picked up a straw hat from the seat and put it on. Oester climbed onto the front seat. He shook the reins, skillfully turned the carriage around, and drove away. I held my breath as the carriage passed, and I waited until the sound of the horses faded. I peeked out and saw that the carriage was gone, then hurried toward the camp. I was too hungry to return to work without getting some food. The guards posted at the gate knew that I came to the camp alone every day at this time and they let me pass.

In the camp groups of night-shift workers who normally would have been sleeping in the barracks were standing at the roll call area. I walked over to some men I knew and asked, "What has happened? Why was Oester here?" A prisoner whispered to me, "Two young boys from Nowy Sacz escaped today. In broad daylight they threw their blankets over the fences, climbed over the wire, and ran into the woods. The guards saw them and started chasing after them and shooting. They brought one back. He was dead. The other was beat up pretty bad but still alive. Oester showed up. They pulled us out from the barracks and made us line up and watch. Oester was kicking the corpse and started whipping the other boy, who was almost dead. The guards tied him up into a bundle and beat him with a shovel. They broke his legs and feet and smashed his face until he was a bloody ball. The boy was screaming so. He kept passing out, and Oester had the guards pour buckets of cold water on him, and when he came to, they started again. Then Oester just shot him in the head."

"Who were the two boys?" I asked. He told me their names. I must have seen them in camp but did not recognize their names. Groups of prisoners started walking around the back of the latrine. I followed them, and we came upon the bodies. The two boys lay face down in the mud. They were naked and covered with bruises and bloody gashes. They were so thin and white lying there on the muddy ground. Were they better off now, I wondered? Would we suffer this life and never see freedom? Would I end up like this or on a truck to be murdered? I was not ready to go back to the factory. Slowly, I walked to the far side of Barracks Number 5, the side just a few feet from the barbed wire fence. I could be alone here for a few moments. Death had ruined my mood and my appetite. I fantasized about making Oester suffer. I could not bear to think of him with his wife and children, riding in the carriage and having picnics. An afternoon of merriment and murder. I swore that one day revenge would be mine.

A woman appeared, walking on the dirt path just outside the barbed wire fence. She looked around nervously and looked to me as if to say something. I stood near the fence. She quickly asked, "Do you know the men from Nowy Sacz?" She named the two who had tried to escape. She must have been waiting for them outside the camp. "Yes," I answered. "Are they in camp?" she asked. I hesitated. "Yes, they were caught." She moved closer to the fence. "What happened to them?" I looked into her eyes. "They are dead." She started to cry and turned and ran into the woods. I went back to work. Word spread about the failed escape. The prisoners were saddened, while the guards mocked the boys' stupid attempt.

To add to our misery we got word from some Polish workers in the factory that all the Jews from the ghetto had been deported. Ten Jews had been kept behind and sent to our camp. Dr. Heller, a Rzeszów physician, was among them. I went to see him to ask about my left leg, which I could not bend at all. I told him my name, and he told me that my father and uncle Kalman were his friends. He examined my left leg and pressed the swollen lump above my knee. It was still infected. I asked him if I would ever be able to bend my left knee. He told me that I would have to force my knee to bend a little each day. He would try to get some supplies and would need to drain my knee. I trusted him and knew to follow his advice. There were still selections in the camp, and my limp was enough to single me out for execution. Every day I worked through horrible pain to bend my left knee. At night I raised my rigid leg up, hoping the weight of the leg would cause my knee to bend even a little. After a while my raised leg would become numb, but my knee still would not bend. After resting for a few minutes, I tried again. Nothing worked. I was desperate but determined not to give up.

· 14 ·

The SS scheduled another selection in the camp. A large number of guards came into the camp on a Sunday afternoon when the day and night shifts were in the barracks. We were crowded to one side of the roll call area, and then we were ordered to run in groups to the other side as fast as we could. Oester and some SS men watched and pointed out those who were last or did not run to their satisfaction. I was afraid that they would pull me out for my bad leg. I tried to hide in the middle of my group and to take off running as quickly as they shouted for us to go. Someone in my group whispered, "They are picking people for the grave."

Suddenly, the guards yelled for our group to go. I ran past the Germans like I was on stilts, with both legs extended and rigid so they would not notice that I had one bad knee. I ran fast, looking straight ahead, ignoring the terrible searing pain. The Germans did not pull out anyone from our group. I stood with the prisoners who had passed the selection. My legs were burning, and I felt like I was going to faint. My friends, who had worried that I would be selected, were happy and relieved to see me. We were ordered to return to the barracks. The orderly shut the barracks door, but we could still hear the prisoners who had not passed as they pleaded for another chance to run, a chance to stay alive. We could hear the guards shouting and hitting the prisoners. Soon all was quiet. We were safely inside but tormented that some of our friends, coworkers, and bunk mates would die. Next time it could be—no, it would be—some of us still here tonight.

I lay awake for most of the night. I had passed the selection, but I was overcome with a terrible sadness. My life had become a constant struggle, and in most instances I was helpless to control my fate. One stumble and I would be with the others, waiting for an undeserved death. My left leg was sore and stiff from my run in front of the Germans. I tried to hold it up to bring down some of the swelling. Today my bad leg had jeopardized my survival. Suddenly, I felt a burning pain in my knee. I looked down to see that it had bent.

I was assigned another job, in addition to working as a janitor. Every morning I went to the kitchen near the railroad sidings to light and tend the fires in four potbellied stoves. The kitchen workers cooked and served the meals to workers from the maintenance and storage buildings. The stoves had to be lit very early in order to heat the kitchen before the cook arrived. I went to the kitchen while it was still dark outside. I cleaned out the ashes from the night before, added firewood to the four stoves, lit the fires, and kept them burning until the cook's Polish helpers arrived. The job was difficult. Often, the wood was soaking wet and would not ignite, or the wind blew cold air into the iron stove's chimney pipes and snuffed out the fire. The chief cook would give me a cup of coffee and a piece of stale bread if the fires were roaring and the room was warm when he arrived. On the days that the fires would refuse to stay lit, he greeted me with the back of his hand and a torrent of insults.

The military barracks where the Ukrainian guards were quartered was close to the kitchen. The Ukrainians came in at all hours to drink coffee, eat, and flirt with the female Polish kitchen workers. They bragged about their influence with the Germans and the rewards that they expected. Sometimes they would boast about the ways that they had caught, tortured, and murdered Jews. They talked about the ghettos they had guarded and liquidated and how they had forced the Jews onto the cattle trains that would take the Jews to special camps. They tried to outdo each other with stories of Jewish men they had humiliated and the thousands of naked Jewish women they had seen. When they realized that a Jewish boy was in the kitchen, they made me listen to horrific tales of murder.

One guard in particular liked to tell me with great pride of the Jews he had disposed of. He spoke Polish and made many references to "Holy Mary, mother of God." In camp our nickname for him was "Holy Mary." He saw me tending the kitchen stoves almost every morning. Inevitably, he would call out, "Holy Mary, mother of God, you are still here, you stinking Jewboy?" At first I tried to pretend that I did not hear him, but he threatened to beat me if I did not answer him. Afterward I would remove my cap to tell him that I was still here. He liked to ask, "Holy Mary, mother of God, did you have a family in Jasło?" Or in Sanok or Tarnów or any of the towns in southern Poland. If I answered no, he would say, "Mother of God, you are lucky. Holy Mary, how we got rid of the stinking Jews in that town. The rabbis with their beards and side curls, the Jewish women and their round behinds. Mother of God, the women just wanted to screw us. But we took care of them all. Holy Mary, we took care of them. They are all rotting in the same ditch." If I told him, "Yes, I had family in that town," he would say, "Mother of God, not anymore, Jewboy." And he would continue with his story about rabbis and Jewish women, just like those he told when my answer was no. Terrible, sadistic, mocking stories sprinkled with references to "Holy Mary" and "mother of God." Stories that broke my heart.

One day someone made a large dent in a kitchen wall. The cook was enraged and tried to blame the workers for causing it. Secretly, I thought a guard had probably caused it during one of their drunken brawls. I was afraid that I would take the blame and punishment for the damage. I told the kitchen boss that if he got me a large piece of paper and some paint, I would paint a picture that he could use to cover the hole in the wall. The cook looked at me with doubt but got a large sheet of paper and a black carpenter's pencil. I quickly drew a picture of a Polish mountain man wearing a low round hat with a feather and a native costume. I drew an outline of tall craggy mountains behind him. The cook liked the drawing and attached it to the wall over the hole and told everyone how he had a talented Jewboy in his kitchen.

"Holy Mary" the Ukrainian seemed impressed with my drawing. He came into the kitchen the next morning while it was still empty and called me over to a corner table. He took out a small notebook and a pencil from his pocket. He handed them to me and said, "Holy Mary, mother of God, you know how to draw good, Jewboy." He pointed to the notebook. "Here, I want you to draw me a picture of two people screwing. And do it well. Or, mother of God, I will kill you!" I was terrified and dumbfounded. I had only a vague understanding of sex from the whisperings of the other boys back in Tyczyn. I had never touched a girl or seen one undressed. I had never seen pictures or drawings of people having sex. I quietly told him, "Please, I do not know how to draw that. Let me draw for you something else." He was furious. "Holy Mary, mother of God, do not lie to me!" he shouted. "I see from your picture that you know how to draw. And you sons-of-a-whore Jews are taught how to screw when you are five years old. Draw me a picture of people screwing, or I will kill you right here!"

I took the pencil, bent over the open notebook, and drew what I thought people having sex looked like. I tried to draw the man from his back, on his knees, reaching out to a reclining woman. His shoulders blocked her body and only her outstretched arms, shoulders, and legs were visible. I gave the notebook back to the Ukrainian. He looked at it and seemed very pleased. "Holy Mary, mother of God! This is good. Draw me another." I drew many pictures that were similar to the first. Soon he demanded more explicit drawings, things that were crude and disgusting and brought tears to my eyes. He saw my discomfort and demanded increasingly obscene pictures. He put the notebook and pencil back into his pocket. "You will get better, Jewboy," he told me and then left the kitchen. I made sure that the fires were burning in all the stoves and went on to the Precision Manufacturing Building to begin my second job washing floors, cleaning sinks, and scrubbing the toilets.

One day I recognized Toniek Roskiewicz from Tyczyn among the workers washing their hands in the locker room of the Precision Manufacturing Building. We had known each other for many years. He had been our neighbor, and his younger brother Jurek was one of my closest Polish friends. I had been in their house many times. I saw that he recognized me and walked over to speak to him. Toniek looked at me with indifference. At first he was silent, and then he asked me the dreadful question that Poles asked Jews they knew when they met them by chance. "Lucek, how come you are still alive?" His words stung, and my excitement at seeing him was gone. Everything had changed. I was a Jew, and our past connection mattered not. He offered no greeting and did not ask any questions about my family. He, who had more than once shared meals at our table. "Yes, Toniek, I am still living," I replied. He shrugged his shoulders, finished washing his hands, and left the washroom without looking back.

An SS guard was always stationed in the glass cubicle near the lobby of the Precision Manufacturing Building. Four young SS men, Volksdeutscher from Romania, took turns at the front office. I had to keep this area clean. After a few weeks the SS men came to know me and talked to me on occasion. One was friendly when no one else was around. He greeted me in the morning and spoke to me about the weather or my work or his family back in Romania. After a while I suspected that he did not know that I was Jewish and a prisoner of the factory camp. I was worried that he thought I was a Polish worker and how he would react if he found out that I was a Jew and thought I had tried to keep my true identity from him. One day he started to tell me about an anti-Jewish exhibit that the Germans had put up in Rzeszów. He asked me whether I had been to see it. I shook my head. He urged me to see it right away, as it proved that the Jews started the war, that the Jews have lice and spread typhus, and that all Aryans and Christians needed to fight the Jewish plague.

I knew that I would be in great danger when he discovered that I was a Jew and that I had tricked him into speaking with me as if I were a Christian. I had to get out of my job at the Precision Manufacturing Building. At noon the next day, instead of going to the camp for my meal, I slipped into the production hall and sought out my old Polish foreman. He was surprised to see me and seemed interested that I had recuperated from my injury and was ready to come back to work at the lathe. "Someone else is working at your old lathe," he said. "But we need a skilled metalworker to operate a complex drill press. I will tell the German supervisor to get you assigned back here."

I thanked him and assured him that I was experienced in operating a drill press. This was a lie, but I had learned that, to survive, truth was a luxury. I would not give up my chance at life to prove my honesty. That night I got off my bunk and went to speak with Walter, a Jewish camp orderly who gave out work assignments. I asked him to help me get work in the production hall. I told him that the Polish foreman had said that they needed me and that being the only Jew at my current work was dangerous. He promised to do whatever he could to get my job changed. A few nights later Walter sent another prisoner over to get me. He told me that I was ordered to return to work in the production hall. I was grateful and thanked him for helping me. On Monday I reported to the production hall to learn how to be a drill press operator. I had no regrets about leaving behind the filthy toilet bowls and sinks, the worry about the SS guard, and most of all the shame of having to draw "screwing" pictures for "Holy Mary."

In the early spring of 1944 a new group of about one hundred prisoners was brought to the Reichshof camp from another camp called Budzyń. Most prisoners were young German Jews who had been deported to the ghetto in Minsk from Germany many years before. They had been in several camps before being transferred to Reichshof, and they told horrible stories of the starvation, beatings, shootings, and mass killings that they had witnessed. They were in terrible physical shape, and I wondered how long they would survive in our camp, which now held nearly five hundred Jewish prisoners from all over Europe. Life in our camp became more difficult. Crowding, illness, long hard labor with meager rations, and the continuous selections whittled down our numbers. Despite Dr. Heller's medical skills and best intentions, many were dying.

I would stand and look out the barbed wire as the trees and flowers bloomed in their full spring glory. Just beyond the fence I watched Polish children playing in the woods. I was sixteen years old, and I had lost my youth, my home, my life, and my freedom. I had only the courage to face each day and could not imagine that I would live out my life in these miserable, inhuman conditions.

In the factory we overheard some Polish workers saying that the tide of war had turned and that the Germans were losing. The Western Allies, the Americans and the English, were advancing in Italy. The Russian army was pushing the Germans out of Russia and approaching the Polish border. I listened to these stories and tried to hold faith, but the whispers in the air were drowned out by the steady and immediate suffering. Oester in his SS uniform rampaged through the camp, while the Ukrainian guards kept up a constant vigil of brutality.

In the Flugmotorenwerk I became adept at my work on the large drill press. I worked alternating day and night shifts and then worked on crews to clean and sweep the factory buildings and streets and to load and unload railroad cars. The stories of the German losses continued, and in the late spring things in the factory started to change. There were power outages, which we heard the Polish Underground caused with their attacks. Soon, fewer Polish workers appeared each day in the factory. The German officers, supervisors, workers, and police became nervous and short-tempered. Rumors spread that the Russians were not far away. Then one day factory production stopped. There was panic, uncertainty, and confusion. The Germans ordered us to dismantle the heavy machinery for transfer out of the factory. No Polish workers returned, and the Germans forced the Jewish prisoners to take down the large and complex machines and move them on trolleys and trucks to the railroad tracks, where we loaded them onto freight cars. We had no cranes or large trucks, and the process was difficult and slow. The German factory police and supervisors drove us ruthlessly, hurrying, demanding, screaming, hitting, and kicking us. They were in a great hurry and acted as they never had before, frightened and nervous.

We worked continuously through the day and were sent back to camp for only a few hours to rest late at night. Our hopes were tempered with despair, for we knew that the Germans would kill us before they would give us up to the Russians. That night groups of Jewish prisoners from all the barracks gathered to discuss and argue about what we should do. The younger and healthier men, expecting that the Germans would shoot us all before the Russians arrived, wanted to plan an attack on the Ukrainian guards and escape into the woods. The older and weaker prisoners argued that if some prisoners escaped, all the rest in the camp, those too old and weak to run, would be killed. The younger prisoners vowed to help everyone escape. Still others argued that the Poles would turn us in or kill us themselves if we did miraculously make it out of the camp. They wanted to wait for the Russians to arrive. The arguments went on through the night. Another prisoner shook me from my sleep: "Lucek, do not fall asleep. What do you say? Should we run or wait?" I had no idea what to do. "I will do whatever everyone agrees on." "Hell, no!" he shouted at me. "That is not an answer! Tell us what you want to do!" I thought of the danger of running and the risk of staying. I thought of Manek, who took the risk and escaped. I knew the answer. "Escape. I am for escape," I insisted. "And I will do whatever I am asked to do." My answer did not settle the argument. Finally, we decided to delay any decision and action until the next night.

Early the next morning we were lined up outside and marched back to the factory to dismantle and load the remaining heavy machines onto the freight cars. The work was hard for our group of weak and malnourished prisoners, and the Germans were impatient with our progress and generous with the truncheons. No Polish workers were at the factory. By evening all the available freight cars were full, but we continued to haul machinery and equipment to the railroad tracks for the trains scheduled to arrive the next day. It was nearly midnight, and we were still working when word spread that an iron gate in the factory wall was open and that some prisoners were escaping. Groups of Jewish prisoners slid away from the work teams and ran into the darkness toward the open gate. I followed some men I was working with, and we ran through the darkness. Suddenly, we came upon a group of prisoners. They were standing and waving their arms at us. "Too late," they told us. "The gate is closed and guarded." I saw in the dim lamps by the gate that the factory police were standing there, smoking cigarettes and talking. We quickly turned back in the black night and hurried back to the railroad tracks.

We worked for several more hours and were finally ordered to line up for our march back to the barracks. Back in the camp we noticed that many armed Germans had reinforced the Ukrainian guards at the camp's gate and fences. We were exhausted and hungry, and our lost chance to escape was very distressing. The regular evening ration of bread was distributed, and we were told that in a few hours, we would be returning to work. I noticed that no one was eating or climbing into their bunks. Everyone wanted to know who had escaped and if they had gotten away. The word in the barracks was that about seventeen men had escaped before the open gate was discovered. Among the escapees were a few prisoners from Rzeszów and Tyczyn. We gathered, and a prisoner offered a prayer for their safety. We worried what the daylight roll call would bring when Oester realized that prisoners had escaped.

In the first light of the morning we were ordered outside for roll call. The new guards in German uniforms had the swarthy look of Mongols or Tartars. The Jewish prisoners from Budzyń believed that the new guards were turncoats, former Soviet soldiers captured by the Germans who had volunteered to serve in the German army. We stood nervously in rows while the guards counted us. After a while we realized that we were not being marched toward the factory for work. Some prisoners whispered nervously about our impending punishment, while others stood and trembled in silence. Oester arrived about an hour later. He spoke to the Jewish orderlies for a long time. He approached the roll call area and climbed up on a chair to address us. He told us that the Daimler-Benz Flugmotorenwerk in Reichshof was being closed and that we were to be sent to another camp. He said nothing about the missing prisoners and the escape. I feared that we were being tricked and that we were to be deported like the other Jews from the ghetto. I was bitterly disappointed that the Germans were moving us. The Russians must be on the way. If only they would come before we were taken away!

We were given our usual meager ration of moldy and stale brown bread. Some ate quickly to fill their empty stomachs, while some decided that it would be wise to save some bread for our uncertain journey. Lengthy and serious discussions took place about a palm-size chunk of bread. We were allowed back into the barracks to collect our filthy blankets and few belongings and then marched to the railroad tracks. Several empty freight cars were standing there. We were ordered to pile our blankets and belongings in a huge heap on the dirt path. We would have to load the remaining manufacturing machines that we had labored to dismantle and move the night before. Several hours later they told us to stop work, even though six boxcars still stood empty. Much of the machinery would be left behind to make room for the prisoners. In the midst of war and the approaching Russians, we were more important to the SS than the manufacturing machinery.

They ordered us to quickly gather our blankets and climb into the boxcars. We tried to help each other climb up, while the guards shouted and struck at anyone who moved too slowly. We were crowded inside the boxcars until there was not room for another prisoner; then the Germans slid the doors shut. We stood in the darkened car and listened as the rest of the prisoners were rounded up, and the other boxcar doors banged shut. I moved toward the side wall and found a tiny space on the floor where I dropped my blanket and sat down. I had a tattered extra shirt and two pairs of patched underwear that the escaped prisoners had left behind. I had my old chipped enamel soup bowl and my essential tin spoon. In my patched shirt pocket were my most important treasures: a few old photographs of my parents and Manek and the scrap of paper with the address of my uncle Julius and aunt Pauline in New York.

Before long the train started to move. I was overwhelmed with a premonition that we were being taken to a certain death. I thought of my parents, who had left Rzeszów in a train just like this and ended up murdered. I thought of my brother, who had escaped from a train and whom I was leaving behind. I vowed to survive to find my brother. Hours passed slowly, and we traveled in the cramped boxcar. Two small dirty windows were high up on the sides of the boxcar. Every so often a prisoner would climb onto another's back to peer out at the passing countryside. No one knew where we were headed, and they saw only military detachments traveling along the roads. We traveled through the day and into the night. We had no space to lie down and leaned against each other as we drifted in and out of an uncomfortable sleep. Someone found a bucket that had been left in the corner, and we passed it around as a latrine. Soon it was full, and we had no choice but to soil ourselves and the boxcar that we were trapped in. The air was stuffy and the stench unbearable.

Sometime during the next day the train came to a stop. A great panic spread through the car. We sat there for several hours until the doors were slid open and the glaring light of day broke the darkness. The Germans ordered us to empty our bucket and gave us some water in our bowls but no food. Soon they slammed the doors shut, and the train again began to lurch forward. After several more hours I lapsed into a miserable sleep. I awoke numb and disoriented. I did not feel my hunger or smell the stink of the latrine bucket. I did not feel the pressure of the men leaning against me. The passage of time was without beginning or end. I wondered if I might be dying. I felt only a terribly painful and unrelenting craving for water. Others in the boxcar were moaning and crying out for water.

Our boxcar had traveled for more than two days, and we had not stopped again for water or been given any food. Someone looking out the small window read the name of the station that we were passing: Kraków. I had been there before the war. It was only eighty miles west of Rzeszów, and a normal train trip would have taken only two hours. I was confused and angry and overcome with a desperate need for water and air.

· 15 ·

Our train came to a stop. We could hear the Germans shouting and their guard dogs barking. A prisoner climbed up to look out the window. He told us that the SS men were armed with machine guns. I began to awaken from my stupor. All I cared about was getting out of the boxcar to find some water and fill my lungs with air. I pulled on my worn mismatched boots and gathered my few belongings. The boxcar doors slid open with a deafening slam. The SS men outside pointed their guns at us and shouted: "Out! Out! Fast! Fast! Out, you damned Jews!" Their dogs barked menacingly and strained at their leashes. Stumbling over each other on our stiff legs, we jumped down from the boxcar. I jumped out and forced my way into the middle of the group of prisoners. We were ordered to quickly assemble into a column of fives and marched out of the station. We walked along a narrow street and crossed a desolate field. Soon we saw tall barbed wire fences around a large hilly area. Posted on the fences were warnings in black and red letters that said not to approach the fence or take photographs of the camp. We stood before the ominous iron gates. A senior SS officer and prisoners in striped prison clothing approached us. Inside the camp we were stopped and counted. The guards marched us to an open, sandy lot deep inside the camp. A few old tables and empty chairs were lined up at the edge of the lot. A man in a striped uniform was wearing a black armband with the word *Kapo* written across it in black letters. He spoke to us in Polish. "You are in the Płaszów concentration camp. Before anything else, you will be registered and taken to be de-loused." Some men pleaded with the Kapo for water, and he told us that we would get water after we had been registered. For a long time we stood in lines and nothing happened. We broke ranks and moved to stand with other prisoners we knew. I stood close to the two Juleks, Motek, and Emil.

The camp was enormous. The ground was sandy and barren of any grass. Barracks and huts were clumped together. Stone slabs were stacked in tall piles. In every direction prisoners were running and marching, digging in the hilly, uneven ground, carrying heavy stone slabs, pulling and pushing large wagons loaded with stones and boxes. No one stood still or even moved slowly. Many prisoners wore the striped uniforms. Others wore filthy civilian clothing. The prisoners' heads were shaved, and they looked weary and frightened. Many SS guards, both men and women in green-gray uniforms, were shouting, cursing, and striking the prisoners with long leather whips and wooden clubs. Above the shouts and curses of the SS guards was the sound of sporadic gunfire coming from all directions but mostly from a hill at the far end of the camp. Bodies of prisoners lay scattered on the ground.

A prisoner in our group began to whisper, "This was the cemetery of the Kraków Jews." Another prisoner spoke: "God, dear God, they are digging up graves." A group of women was pushing big clumsy wagons. Their heads were shaved, and they wore dirty threadbare prison dresses with the same stripes as the men. The SS cursed and drove them with their clubs and whips. These were the first Jewish women I had seen in two years, and it was horrible to see how brutally they were treated. From the hill at the far end of the camp came a long series of gunshots.

We stood about for hours, waiting for the registration to begin. A mean and impatient SS sergeant and the Kapo came to supervise the process. They ordered us to stand in a single line before tables where three clerks were seated. The Kapo had told us that we would get water after we were registered, and I pushed to get to the front of the long line. Already, close to forty prisoners were ahead of me. At the table I had to give my name and the number that I had been assigned at the Reichshof camp. The clerk checked my information against a typed list. We moved past the desk, and another clerk handed me a small band of white cloth with a stenciled number and Star of David formed from a center red triangle and three small yellow triangles. I was handed a needle and a small stretch of thread and told to quickly sew the cloth onto the left front of my jacket. I took my jacket off and sat on the sandy ground to sew the cloth on as fast as I could, still hoping drinking water would be given to me once I finished. I returned the needle to another clerk, who checked my sewing and wrote my name and my new Płaszów number on a list. I was registered in the Płaszów concentration camp as prisoner 25113.

I was told to wait with others who had been registered. I ran over to the group, hoping to get some water. There was no water. Julek Reich came over and whispered that he heard that the Płaszów prisoners were not allowed to own boots. Both of us wore old, unmatched boots from Reichshof. Julek had somehow gotten an old dull razor blade. He pulled off his boots and began to cut away the tops. He handed me the razor blade and I quickly cut off the top of my boots. He passed the razor to another man, and we left the shredded leather strips in the dirt.

We sat huddled in a group for hours until the last of the prisoners were registered. We were told to assemble in a column and then marched by the Kapo to a nearby cluster of buildings. Other Płaszów prisoners stood there waiting for us. The Kapo told us, "Here, your hair will be cut. You will be given a shower, and you and your clothes will be sprayed with louse-killing powder. Then you will go to your barracks." The Kapo had spoken to us in Polish and German. He quietly added in Yiddish, "Go quickly to the washroom building over there, and drink all the water you want. Line up and hurry. Do not give the German bastards an excuse to use their whips and guns on you."

We rushed to the doors of the washroom building and shoved our way in. Water ran from long pipes into washbasins. I stood under the pipes and let the water run into my mouth and all over me. I left the washroom building to face the de-lousing process. We lined up again and took turns having our heads shaved. We stripped off our clothes and left them in small bundles on the ground. We went back into the washroom and stood under the spigots to rinse our filthy bodies. We ran back outside and quickly dressed in the same dirty clothing. We stood still while a white powder was sprayed over us. SS soldiers armed with guns, whips, and clubs stood and watched the whole process. It was late in the day, and I was exhausted and hungry. We had not eaten in days, and I felt so weak that I could barely stand. We were lined up again and taken past a prisoner who tattooed the inside of our right forearm with a single jab of a mechanical needle. The needle left a small blue mark. He used only one needle to tattoo the whole group. When it was finally finished, it was already dark. The Kapo told us that prisoners moving about the camp after dark were shot on sight and that we would spend the night right there, out in the open near the washroom building. I was too tired to care. I lay down on the sandy dirt, rolled myself in my old blanket, and fell asleep.

The glaring sun woke me early the next day. The other Jewish prisoners began to stir, and we sat up and looked around. The camp was waking up. Groups of prisoners appeared, marched under the brutal and fierce shouts of the Germans and their barking dogs. The first gunshots of the day echoed through the camp. The Kapo stood nearby, conferring with the Jewish orderlies from the Reichshof camp. Alfred, Walter, Gryspan, and Reb came over and told us to stand up and form a column. We carried our bundles and blankets and were marched to two large barracks. The Kapo told us, "Go inside and find a place to leave your things. Be out in five minutes. You will get food, and then I will take you to work. Work hard—the SS will be in charge of you."

I found my friends, and we ran into the same barracks. It was a large, long room filled from end to end with roughly built wooden sleeping shelves three levels high. My friends and I found sleeping spaces on the top shelf and marked them with our blankets and our small bundles. We heard the Kapo and the Jewish orderlies outside shouting for us to come out quickly. A table had been set up outside, and we lined up for our first meal at Płaszów. I held my old soup bowl and spoon. We were given a ladle of warm substitute coffee and a slice of rough, dark bread. We were told to eat quickly, that it would soon be time to work. I wanted to save some of the horrible bread for later, but my hunger was stronger than my willpower. I ate and drank hastily, in a few bites and swallows. I was still hungry, thirsty, and filled with regret that I had not saved any bread.

A group of women prisoners came out of the next barracks. Their heads were shaved, and they looked like starving young boys. I was embarrassed to see that some women were dressed in short, loose prison robes that left much of their bodies exposed. They lined up for their rations and pushed their skinny bodies forward for the meager chunks of bread. A loud whistle blew throughout the camp. We were lined up and marched across the camp to an area where a group of prisoners was working. They were digging up the cemetery. We were divided into groups and assigned to different jobs. One group had to knock down the large and heavy gravestones and carry them to big piles, where other prisoners broke them up with large mallets. Prisoners were digging up the graves and filling wagons and wheelbarrows with the clumps of earth and human remains. Skulls and bones stuck out from the dirt. The SS were shouting, cursing, and hitting any prisoner who stopped for a second to wipe the sweat from his brow. Two SS guards were kicking a skull as if it were a soccer ball.

An SS guard started yelling at a prisoner who was struggling with a heavy wagon. Before the prisoner had a chance to turn around, the SS man pulled his gun out and shot him in the back of the head. The other prisoners kept working, carefully stepping around his body. It looked like digging in the deep graves was the safest place to avoid the vicious guards. I moved toward a group of workers who were getting shovels and jumping down into the graves. I took a shovel and jumped into a grave with two other prisoners. I shoveled out clumps of earth and bones. I imitated the other prisoners, who picked up the large bones and skulls with their hands and tossed them up from the graves. I tried not to look at the skulls in my hands. Some still had strands of hair. After a few hours I became numb to the horror and assigned the blame for this desecration to the Germans standing above me.

We worked until late in the day without stopping for a break. In the evening we were ordered to form columns and were marched by the Kapos back to our barracks. An old Płaszów prisoner told me as we marched back that Płaszów had nearly ten thousand prisoners. Almost all were Jewish, and the majority were from Kraków. A few German factories nearby used prisoners for labor. Those were the best jobs and impossible to get. The camp commander set an example for the guards by killing many Jews every day. I asked about the gunfire that came from the hill at the far end of the camp. He told me that it was Hujowa Hill, the place where the daily executions took place. "Who is being executed there?" I asked. The prisoner marching next to me answered without pausing, "Jews, who else?" "Why are they executing them? Don't they need us to work?" I asked. "Don't be stupid, boy, and do not ask stupid questions," he answered. "The Germans need no reason to kill Jews. Any Jews, all Jews. You and I are on the same list." He was irritated by my questions. I was annoyed with myself. My questions were stupid, and deep down I had already known the answers.

Something was strange about the women in the next barracks. They were in their late teens and early twenties and spoke a language that we could not identify. Their faces and bodies were not as skeletal or malnourished as the rest of us. But something was wrong with their eyes, as if they were in a daze. Their scanty prison robes barely covered their bodies, and their thighs and chests were often exposed. I tried not to look at them. I feared seeing their shame, but they seemed oblivious. The women shared our latrine, a small hut with a long wooden bench down the center with holes cut out for our eliminations. The men were embarrassed when the women were there, but the women did not seem to notice us. We asked the Kapo for a partition to separate us from the women. He laughed at our request, a bunch of filthy prisoners trying to preserve the dignity of Jewish women.

We decided to approach some women to find out who they were and what language they were speaking. Four women were walking by the barracks, and two other prisoners and I stepped in front of them. The women stopped and looked at us with empty sad eyes. Their faces showed alarm. "Where do you come from? Who are you?" we asked them, first in Polish and then in German. But they shrugged their shoulders, and one said something that we did not understand. Then one in our group asked them in Jewish, "Do you speak Jewish? Do you speak Yiddish?" They seemed to understand, and one, a very young girl, pointed at herself, nodded in the affirmative, and said, "Yiddish. Yiddish." We pointed at ourselves with both hands and replied, "Yes, yes, Yiddish." The girl said, "Moment," and quickly walked away. We waited with the other women for her to return.

The young girl came back with another older woman who looked about thirty. She spoke to us in a Yiddish that sounded closer to German than our Yiddish. "We are Jews from Hungary. Are you Jewish? Polish Jews?" she asked. "Yes, we are Polish Jews. And you, how long have you been in the camp?" we asked. "Three weeks ago we were in Hungary with our families. We were first sent to Auschwitz," she answered. "Auschwitz?" we asked. "Where is Auschwitz?" Her empty eyes filled with tears. She spoke in a somber voice of the deportation from their small town in Hungary. They traveled in boxcars for days. They arrived in Auschwitz, where they were taken off the trains. The SS soldiers separated the women and children from the men. The strong young women were separated from the older women, and mothers with children and infants, who were taken to the back of the camp. Her group was marched to a barracks where they had to undress and have their heads shaved. Numbers were tattooed on their forearms. They stayed completely nude for two days in front of the German soldiers. They begged a Kapo to tell them where their families had been taken. The Kapo told them that, except for them and a small group of young men, all the others were killed with poison gas and then their bodies were burned. The Kapo pointed to the oily, fiery smoke rising from the tall chimneys in the camp and told them that the horrible odor was the burning flesh of their families. Two day later they were issued the skimpy prison robes and wooden shoes and put on trains to Płaszów. Darkness fell on Płaszów as we walked back to our barracks.

I was exhausted from digging up graves. I lay on the hard wooden shelf and closed my eyes. The story of Auschwitz, the Hungarian Jewish men brutally separated from their women, and the mothers from their children reminded me of my own tragic parting from my parents. I imagined their staggered march to the gas chambers and the horror when they realized that they were being killed. In my mind Auschwitz became Belzec, and it was my parents, deceived, humiliated, and murdered with the gas. I cried for their cruel death and for me, abandoned. As the night wore on, I silently called out to my brother, somewhere in the night, to save me. He was my past and my future, my only reason to survive. I remembered his caring face and his last words so long ago. I tried to feel his presence. I believed that he was alive somewhere, but that night I was alone in the hell of Płaszów.

Every day I worked digging up the Jewish cemetery. Most of the time I was lucky to work down in the graves, but on a few occasions I was put to work pushing wheelbarrows or carrying the heavy gravestones. Not only was the work physically harder but I also suffered the blows from the SS whips and clubs. At the end of the day I was covered with painful bruises and welts. The SS would often go into a furious frenzy of beating and clubbing a prisoner until he was dead or close to it. If a prisoner could not get up to go back to work, the SS would just shoot him. It was frightening and painful to witness these beatings and not be able to act. We had to keep working. Even a look of disdain upon a prisoner's face would provoke the SS. The dead were carried away in the wheelbarrows with the skulls and skeletons.

In the evening we staggered back to the barracks to collapse on our bunks. I would search out my friends from Reichshof, making sure we had each lived to return to our corner of the barracks. One night, Julek Schipper, Emil Ringel, and Hafferflock looked distressed. No matter how bad it was, I needed to know what had caused their spirits to fall. Hafferflock was closest to me. I touched his arm. "What happened? Why are you all standing together like this?" I asked. He turned to me and his face was very sad. "The Germans killed Yossel today. They beat him to death. We were digging and came upon a body that was mostly decayed but still more than bones. Yossel approached a German to say something. The German started hitting Yossel with his wooden club. Another German took a shovel and joined in, and they kept hitting him until he was dead."

Although I had witnessed such killings, this was the first of my group to be murdered in the camp. Yossel was such a decent and helpful person. Among the best I had met in the camps and extremely religious. If his life would not be spared, then what was the hope for the rest of us? "After soup we will meet to say Kaddish," Hafferflock said. I nodded, even though I knew that I would not join them. In this place praying did not seem honest. There was no need for prayers if God had allowed the murder of Yossel. The terrible deeds committed here should have been enough to evoke God's mercy or his fury. What good would my prayers do?

A few days later our Kapo told us that we would be transferred to another concentration camp. We were upset and worried that we might be sent to Auschwitz, the terrible death camp that we had heard about. The Kapo relieved our panic when he later told us that we were being transferred to a camp in Wieliczka, a small town near Kraków. The prisoners there worked in the salt mines. We shared a cautious optimism that no camp could be as terrible as Płaszów. Later that afternoon we were marched to the assembly area by the main gate. A convoy of trucks was waiting. We were ordered to leave behind our blankets and bundles and to take only our soup bowls. I hid the slim packet with photographs and the New York address in my shirt pocket.

We climbed into the back of the trucks and sat down, holding our bowls on our laps. Several soldiers armed with machine guns climbed on the trucks to guard us. I looked through the slats on the side of the truck and saw that Dr. Heller and Reb, a Jewish orderly from Przemyśl, had not gotten on the trucks. They were standing silently on the side of the road. I had no idea what their separation meant. The trucks started up, and we slowly passed through the gate and drove away from Płaszów.

We rode in silence under the watchful eye of our German guards and arrived at Wieliczka after a few hours. We drove into the camp and stopped. The SS guards ordered us off the trucks. They screamed, "Get off! Fast! Quick! Off!" We jumped and stumbled off the trucks as quickly as we could. The guards climbed back on the trucks and drove out through the camp gate. An SS sergeant had watched us jump and scramble down from the trucks and ordered us to line up into rows of five. A Kapo counted us, and then the SS sergeant counted us again. The Kapo herded us through a narrow barbed wire gate that led into a small yard with two barracks that seemed to be separated from the rest of the camp by a barbed wire fence. Several hundred prisoners were crowded into the small area and stood milling around, trying to keep away from the fence, which was guarded by SS. The SS were hitting and kicking any prisoner who came within their reach. Every so often they fired their pistols into the air and began to shoot at the huddled groups of prisoners. The bodies of the dead and wounded lay in pools of blood, and we pushed and shoved each other to avoid the bullets. I managed to push my way in through the prisoners and felt the wall of the barracks. The doors were locked, and our only protection was the unfortunate prisoners who were between the SS and us. There was a great crying out as the SS shot at us and more and more bodies fell to the ground. An old prisoner crouched next to me. His eyes were closed, and he seemed to be waiting for whatever fate would bring.

The shooting stopped. Several Kapos came into our area to restore order. They shouted and hit some prisoners in an obvious attempt to impress the SS. A few prisoners were ordered to carry the bodies and lead the wounded and bleeding away.

We were lined up in the small yard, and after a long wait we were each given a little soup and a small chunk of coarse bread. The Kapos unlocked the barracks and told us to go in and find a place to sleep. Some prisoners said that they had arrived in Wieliczka within the last few days from camps in Radom and Stalowa Wola. They had heard rumors that we would be sent to another camp. One said that it was good to be sent out, for the Wieliczka prisoners working in the salt mines did not live very long. We climbed onto the hard wooden shelves, and after a short while the barracks were quiet, except for the moans of those unfortunate enough to be dreaming of their homes and families.

The Kapos came into the barracks at daybreak and ordered us out. We stumbled into the yard where the SS met us with clubs and whips. Again we tried to huddle and turn away from their beatings, but they forced us to stand in lines and randomly struck prisoners down. A group of SS guards surrounded us. The gate was opened, and the SS guards marched us through the camp, past the gate, and down a village road. As we marched at their frantic pace, they continued to hit us. Along the road Polish civilians came out of their houses to watch the spectacle of Jews being beaten and abused. Some laughed and mocked us and urged the SS on. The sky was blue, the sun was shining, and summer was in its full glory. Soon the streets were washed in our tears and blood.

We arrived at a small railroad siding. We were crowded into several boxcars and were given two metal buckets, one filled with water and an empty bucket to use as a latrine. The car doors were then slid shut. Inside we fell on each other in the darkness. Many hours passed, and our train stood still. It was extremely hot and difficult to breathe. I could hardly stand, and there was no room to sit. I knew that if I collapsed, I could be trampled. In the darkness I pressed against the bodies around me, seeking a wall of the boxcar. After a long time of pressing and pushing and being pushed back, my shoulder touched the wall. I leaned against it, taking some weight off my tired feet. I could hear the moans and complaints of the other prisoners. I felt a terrible hunger and a burning thirst. I started to feel as if I would pass out, and I slid down the wall until I was nearly sitting. I could not stretch out my legs, and I sat with my knees pressed up against my chest.

There was a loud banging and jerking movement as our boxcar began to move. All around me prisoners cursed as they fell against each other. Our car shook and swayed. The stench from the latrine buckets, the heat, and our thirst and hunger created a madhouse of misery. Prisoners were delirious as the hours and then days wore on. Two or three prisoners in the boxcar were still strong enough to stand and look out the small filthy window to try to determine in which direction our train was moving. They read out station names, and we knew that we were still in Poland, moving west from Kraków. We may have been traveling for two days, when suddenly, in the darkness of the boxcar, the prisoner at the window cried out, "My God, dear God! We are headed for Auschwitz!" Others tried to climb up and look out to see. "Yes," other voices cried out. "This is the way to Oświęcim, to Auschwitz." A strong voice called out, "There is only one thing left to do— say the Shema." The prisoners pulled each other up until we were all standing and leaning upon each other. I stood among the beaten, humiliated, and orphaned, the starving, forgotten, and forsaken, and we declared our faith to our God. I moved my parched lips and repeated the words: "Shema Yisrael, Adonai Elo-heinu, Adonai ehad!" (Hear, O Israel, the Lord our God, the Lord is One!)

I could feel that God was with us in the stinking crowded boxcar. Our prayers and unshaken faith had summoned him. God was here. It could not be otherwise. I stood in the dark moving train, reciting the Shema. I prayed silently from my heart that I might live. A prisoner near the window cried out, "Thank God! We have passed the turn to Oświęcim. We are not going to Auschwitz!" I slumped down against the wall. The train lumbered through the night, moving west, its wheels beating a steady rhythm on the rails.

Our trip lasted three days. Once, during a stop, the car doors were slid open, and an SS guard let us empty the overflowing latrine bucket and gave us more water. Then the doors were slammed shut, and we were again in the hot darkness. I stood and pushed myself desperately toward the bucket of water. I was too late. The precious water was gone. I hallucinated that I was drinking streams of clear cold water and at other times of drinking my urine or sucking blood from my veins. I drifted in and out of consciousness. The other prisoners were protesting and fighting off those who leaned and fell upon them. I lay in the sweat, tears, and filth of our group and gave in to an exhausted sleep that I felt sure would bring me to death. I awoke when another prisoner shook my shoulder to tell me that the train had again stopped. From outside came angry German voices and the ferocious snarling and barking of their dogs.

· 16 ·

The boxcar doors were pulled open. My legs were stiff and numb from the days and nights on the floor. I tried to pull myself up to stand as the Germans began to shout and violently pull the prisoners out of the boxcar. "Out! Fast, you pigs! You shit dogs! Out! Line up to be counted!" I stumbled out of the boxcar and fell to the ground. I struggled to stand on my unsteady legs. A few prisoners were still lying on the floor of the boxcar. They had died along the way.

Armed SS guards, with their vicious barking dogs, surrounded us. Several prisoners with Kapo armbands and black caps stood nearby. The white patches sewn to their jackets bore stenciled numbers and green triangles. The Kapos ordered us to quickly line up to be counted. I pushed deep into the group, trying to find a place in the middle of a row. I needed to clear my head and prepare for what I was to face. I looked around. We were at a small railroad station in a village surrounded by mountains. A sign on one of the buildings gave the German name of a town. On one high hill stood the ruins of a large, old stone castle. It was gutted and ruined but still looked ominous. We pleaded with the Kapos for water. They told us that we were on the way to the Flossenbürg concentration camp and would get plenty of water there. The Kapo spoke German. I knew that we must be in Germany, in the den of the beast.

After we were counted, the SS men marched us out of the station. We passed through a small village lined with large stone houses. Some villagers came out of their houses to watch. They were mostly old men and a few women and children. They stood silently and looked upon us with cold angry eyes. The SS guards cursed and yelled for us to march in step, and when we could not, they kicked at our ankles. An SS man kept repeating, "Jews. Yes, damned Jews. We never had Jews in Flossenbürg. We will have fun. Hah!" We marched on a narrow road that led up a mountain. Soon we could see the camp. It was nestled against the side of the rocky mountain, with the castle ruins towering above. We passed through the main gate and were halted in a large open yard in front of a two-story gray building. In every direction were barracks of all sizes and more large stone buildings. The camp was surrounded by high wire fences and tall, massive stone guard towers. Some prisoners fell down from exhaustion and struggled vainly to get up. The Kapos were shouting that we were to remain standing in ranks. After a while they gave up and let us stay on the ground. Other prisoners in striped uniforms brought us large buckets full of water. I jumped up, got in line, and held out my bowl, which they filled with water. I lifted the bowl to my lips and drank in gulps. An SS sergeant stood on the steps of the stone building. He said that Flossenbürg was an orderly and strict concentration camp where everyone had to work hard, where disobedience was swiftly and severely punished, and where cleanliness of persons, buildings, and the camp was of the utmost importance. Anyone caught with even one louse would be harshly punished. He told us that each of us would be given a shower before we would be sent to a barracks. He pointed to a Kapo and told us that he would be in charge of us.

The Kapo had a low four-digit number and a green triangle on his uniform. "You stinking pig-dogs must take a shower before I let you go to the barracks," the Kapo commanded and pointed to a door in the building. "The shower room is in here. I will send a hundred of you at a time to the showers, and I want you to be fast! Now, everyone stand up and line up in rows of five! Fast!" I got into line with the other prisoners. I had heard that the Germans tricked prisoners into the gas chambers by telling them that they were going to shower. My God, I thought. Do not let it happen. I looked around and saw panic in the eyes of the other prisoners. Motek Hoffstetter stood near me. "Showers? You believe it?" I whispered to him. Motek nodded his head slightly. "They did not have to drag us to Germany to kill us."

Using his truncheon, the Kapo counted the first twenty rows of our column. He commanded the hundred men to step forward and then shouted, "Undress completely! Leave all your things on the ground, your clothing, shoes, bowls, everything! Then run through that door! Fast! Run!" The first group of prisoners stripped off their filthy tattered clothes, threw them with their possessions into heaps on the ground, and ran toward the showers. Some prisoners tried to hide their personal things under their arms or in clenched fists. The Kapos checked the naked prisoners at the shower room door and took away all belongings. I watched what was happening and became frantic. I did not want to leave my photos. I had not memorized the address in New York. I took the packet from inside my shirt and rolled it as tightly as I could. I tried to put it into my mouth, but it was too big. I hid the packet in my hand. I was still a few minutes from going to the showers and tried to practice holding the packet against my palm with my thumb and my other fingers extended to cover it. I knew that I would have to keep the photos from getting wet in the showers, but for now I could not bear to give them up. My group was ordered to strip and run to the showers. I undressed quickly. I dumped my clothing, my cut-off boots, and my old enamel bowl into a pile on the ground. I gripped the packet in my right palm, holding it firmly with my thumb. I ran with the others to the showers. A Kapo stopped me at the door. He pointed his wooden club at my hand. "What do you have there? Gold?" he yelled at me. "Nothing," I said. But I knew that he had seen that I held something in my hand. I tried to plead with him. "It is not gold, just a few photos of my family. Please, please, Mister Kapo, do not take them away. They are of no value to anyone but me." "Leave it here! Drop it!" the Kapo yelled. Again I tried to plead with him, "Please. Please. These are the only photos I have." The Kapo smashed my right hand with his club. The pain was terrible; it felt like the bones in my fingers had broken. I screamed, my hand opened, and the folded packet fell to the floor.

The Kapo kicked the packet to the side. I bent down, picked it back up, and held it to my chest. I kept saying, "Please, please." The Kapo started hitting my arm with his club, but I held the packet to my chest and continued to beg. The Kapo stopped hitting me. "If this is so important, leave it with your things." He pointed to the packet with his club. "You will get your things back after the shower. Run back there, and run right back. I will be watching you!" I ran back to where I had left my clothing in a bundle on the ground and pushed the packet deep into the pocket of my shirt. I ran back to the shower room door. The Kapo was waiting for me. "You will get it later," he said to me. I thanked him. He pushed me through the shower door. The rush of the other prisoners carried me into the shower room. It was full of steam and water. It was not a gas chamber.

After the shower we were made to run out a door opposite from where we came in. I held my battered right arm and ran outside, frantic to find my packet. We were on the other side of the building, far from the piles of our belongings. I stood wet and naked among other prisoners, surrounded by Kapos and SS guards. I tried to sneak past the Kapos. One stopped me, and I pleaded that he should let me go for a minute to get my photos. He shouted at me, "Shut your mouth! Nothing from outside Flossenbürg is allowed in here. Everything will be burned!" He pushed me back with his heavy wooden club. An SS guard started coming toward us. The Kapo saw the SS approaching and started hitting me with his club. I ran into the crowd of naked prisoners. I approached another Kapo, desperate to get back my pictures. He screamed at me, "Back! Back! It is prohibited for you to talk to me!" Before long all the prisoners from the Wieliczka transport had gone through the showers. There was no going back.

We were made to run naked and wet to an area separated from the camp by a barbed wire fence. A German sign said in Gothic letters: "Quarantine Section." There were three barracks and a tall stone guard tower. We were rushed through the entrance, and the gate was closed behind us. The precious photos that I treasured and protected for two years were lost to me forever. I tried to remember and memorize the faces of my parents and my brother. In my desperate anguish I could not recall their faces. I knew that my uncle's name was Julius Tamar and that he was a physician. My father had written the letters *MD* after his name. I remembered that he lived in New York, New York, but I could not recall the house number or the street.

We were kept in a closed area under quarantine for several days. We had to stay outside the barracks from the morning roll call at dawn until after the evening roll call. We stayed outside every day, even in the pouring rain. The Kapos made us march back and forth, to stand at attention for long periods, and to do calisthenics for hours. We were not permitted to talk among ourselves. We were fed a slice of bread and a little ersatz coffee in the morning and a bowl of watery soup in the afternoon. We were naked for all the days of the quarantine, living like animals.

One day an SS physician accompanied by prisoners came into the quarantine area to conduct physical examinations. This was another selection. We had to stand at attention for a long time while the physician looked us over. He was selecting the prisoners with injuries or open sores and anyone who even looked ill. Those prisoners were sent off to stand by themselves on the side of the yard. I was afraid that the doctor would pick me because of the bruises and welts from the Kapo's beating. The SS doctor came to me and looked me over with interest. I filled my lungs with air, pushed out my bony chest, and held my breath. He moved on to examine the next prisoner.

He selected the oldest prisoner from our group, who had a terrible hernia. A large bulge protruded from his abdomen, and he tried to cover it with his hands. His name was Zimmerman, and he was the father of the painters who helped me clean the yellow paint from my eyes during my first days in the Reichshof camp. I felt terrible for the elder Zimmerman and for his sons, who had to remain silent while their father was taken away. The SS physician finished his examinations and left the quarantine area with the thirty or forty prisoners. The elder Zimmerman was among them.

One afternoon we were finally given striped white and blue prison uniforms. They gave us shoes with wooden soles, enameled red soup bowls, and tin spoons. Our names were written on a list, and we were given Flossenbürg prisoner numbers. We were given patches with numbers and red and yellow triangles to sew onto our uniforms. One had to be sewn on the left front of our jacket and the other on the right side of our prison pants, just above the knee. I was an inmate of the Flossenbürg concentration camp, prisoner 16019.

The next morning, after roll call, a Kapo came to our barracks. He counted off nearly a hundred prisoners and ordered us to follow him. He led us to the stone quarry at the edge of the camp. Prisoners were deep in the pit of the quarry, breaking and cutting off large pieces of stone from huge granite boulders. Others carried the stones to the edge of the quarry. The large stones were loaded onto trucks and the smaller stones onto iron wagons mounted on narrow metal rails. Small groups of prisoners pushed the heavy wagons up an incline and then unloaded the stones into large piles. The prisoners had to rush back to the quarry with the empty wagons. Armed SS guards and shouting Kapos ran in all directions, supervising and beating the prisoners to make them work faster.

The Kapo assigned us to jobs at the quarry. I was sent to work with a small group of men to push a heavy wagon up the incline. I followed the prisoners, put my shoulder against the side of the wagon, and pushed with all my might. It was backbreaking and exhausting. The wagon moved slowly up the incline toward the pile of stones. The German Kapo forbade any talking. He yelled and cursed, and whenever an SS man was nearby, the Kapo hit us with a long truncheon made from an electric cable.

In our group of prisoners were Frenchmen, Norwegians, Dutchmen, and Poles. They were in bad shape, emaciated and bruised. They were desperate for news from the outside. We could only whisper during brief, stolen moments when our Kapo was out of earshot. They asked me where I came from and if I had any news of the war. I said little about myself but told them that the eastern front was in the middle of Poland. They were surprised and encouraged. I asked them about Flossenbürg. They told me that it was a severe camp with many rules, and even the slightest violation was always punished by lashings and torture. The Kapos were mostly violent German criminals transferred to the camp from prisons. They wore green triangles next to their prisoner number. The skinny prisoner next to me whispered with

pride that the red triangles on our chest identified us as political prisoners. I looked up and saw that our Kapo wore a green triangle.

Flossenbürg was filled with violence and brutality. Unlike Płaszów,
the majority of prisoners were Gentiles from the European countries
occupied by the Germans. We were the first Jewish prisoners to come
into Flossenbürg. Working with Gentile prisoners kept me alive. The
Germans did not randomly shoot and kill the prisoners here as they
routinely did Jews in other camps.

I labored at the stone quarry from the first light of morning until
nightfall for many days. We stopped working at noon and lined up for
a bowl of watery soup. We quickly sat on the ground to rest our legs
and prepare for the long stretch of work still ahead. After a short break
the Kapo would shout at us to get up, and I would resume pushing and
pulling the wagon filled with stones. When I did not and could not
move fast enough, the Kapo hit me. My skinny shoulders were bruised
from pushing the iron wagon, my fingers were cut from sharp-edged
stones, and my back was marked by truncheons. I was always hungry
and felt weak. Every part of my body hurt. My gums were swollen and
began to bleed, and I realized that my teeth were becoming loose and
brittle. I remembered my reaction to the beating that the Germans
gave me when I was a boy in Tyczyn. I had changed. The beatings were
still painful, but I accepted that the whip and the truncheon were the
way of the SS.

In the barracks each night after roll call I quickly drank the watery
soup and climbed onto my wooden shelf to sleep. In the morning I had
to drag myself outside to line up. Some men could barely sit up, and
they were beaten in their bunks. I no longer sought out my friends. I
worried about how I would go on working at the quarry. One morning,
right after roll call, a different Kapo came to our area and asked for
workers experienced in paving gravel roads. A few prisoners stepped
forward, and without thinking I went to stand with them. I did not
know anything about paving gravel roads. I was desperate to get out of
the quarry and hoped that paving roads could not be any worse. The
Kapo looked over the volunteers and questioned them. He turned to me
and asked, "Are you strong enough for this kind of work?" "I am strong.

I work in the stone quarry," I responded. "Do you know about paving roads?" he asked. "That was my family's work at home," I lied. He nodded and motioned for me to stand with the others selected for the job.

We marched to an area in the camp where prisoners were hammering large stones into gravel. They spread the gravel on an old eroded road and then poured cement over it. Others were pushing a large cement roller. The first morning I was given a hammer and told to break large stones into gravel. Close to twenty other men were doing the same work. I sat on the ground and held a large stone and hit it with the hammer. The stones broke up, and pieces and chips left cuts all over my hands. Another prisoner handed me a torn dusty rag to wrap around my hand. The work was better than being in the quarry. I worked sitting down, at my own pace, and as long as I looked busy, the guards left me alone. At noon, kettles of soup were brought to our work area and set up on tables. We were ordered to line up in pairs. I had my red soup bowl ready. Next to me stood an older prisoner who I knew was from Belgium. The soup line moved quickly toward the Kapo holding the ladle. When we got to him, we both held out our soup bowls. The Kapo said, "We give only one bowl of soup for two." He poured a ladle of soup into the Belgian's bowl and barked, "Go! Move on!" I never heard of such a crazy thing. How could they give only one bowl of soup for two starving men? How will I force the Belgian to give me half the soup? The Belgian moved briskly to the side of the road. I followed him closely, trying to hold on to his sleeve. He turned to me and asked, "Have you never split a bowl of soup?" I shook my head no. He replied reassuringly, "Here we do it all the time."

He had me sit on the grass across from him, with the bowl between us. He dipped his spoon into the soup, lifted it to my lips and fed me. I swallowed hungrily, not sure what to do. He told me, "Get your spoon and feed me. If you give me half a spoon, I will give you half a spoon. If you feed me the watery part or dip to the bottom, I will do the same for you." I did as he told me. I looked around, and everywhere pairs of starved prisoners, most likely strangers, were feeding each other. Slowly, carefully, deliberately, the Belgian and I fed each other. First the watery part from the top, and then, when the few turnips on the bottom became visible, we divided them fairly between us. I worked at that job for a few days. At noon each day I shared a bowl of soup with a different prisoner. We always fed each other carefully so as to not spill a drop of the soup, and we did so fairly, as if the other man's hunger was our own.

The work at the gravel road was finished. I expected to be sent back to the stone quarry. On our last day the SS came to inspect our finished work. An SS soldier picked out three prisoners and me and said that we were assigned to a special detail. He led us from the road work site, and we followed him to the camp hospital. Inside he led us to a room where bodies lay piled on the floor. Our job would be to carry the bodies to the camp crematorium. He took us to the penal prison compound where more dead needed to be collected. Most of the dead were skeletal and must have died from starvation and sickness. Others bore severe wounds from brutal beatings. The dead at the prison almost always had bullet holes. We covered the bodies with dirty sheets of canvas and carried them on wooden pallets to the crematorium. It was between the inner and outer electrified fences of the camp, not far from the quarantine section where we still lived. By late afternoon we had taken all the dead to the crematorium. We waited on a bench outside the hospital for more bodies.

There was a small building surrounded by a wooden fence. I saw that women lived in it. They were young and looked well fed compared to the rest of us. They stood idly outside and were dressed in flimsy prison robes. We were passing by, and one woman heard us speaking Polish. She called out to us in Polish, and we spoke briefly. The women were Polish and Russian and had recently been transferred to Flossenbürg from another camp. The SS guards and the German Kapos had set this house up as a brothel.

A surprising thing happened. The old man Zimmerman, the one with the hernia, who had been taken away shortly after we arrived in Flossenbürg, was returned to the barracks well and seemingly had had surgery. His sons rejoiced to have him alive, and everyone else was shocked and happy to see him. None of us ever understood why the Germans decided to operate on and save an old sick Jew.

New rumors flew through the barracks. One prisoner had heard that without permanent jobs in the camp factories, we would be transferred to a smaller work camp in a few days. Soon after the SS examined us. We had to undress and stand naked while we were inspected and questioned. Several Kapos accompanied the SS and painted the numbers *1*, *2*, or *3* or the letter *X* on our foreheads with colored ink. Other Kapos copied the painted numbers into notebooks. An SS officer looked at my skinny body and asked me what my occupation was. I told him that I was an experienced lathe operator. The SS man spoke to a Kapo and went on to examine the next man. The Kapo painted something on my forehead. I could not tell what it was. Another Kapo looked at my forehead, asked me for my Flossenbürg number, and wrote something in a notebook. He moved on, and I asked the prisoner standing next to me—he had a large *2* on his forehead—what was written on mine. "A black *X*," he said. I looked around and saw that most men had numbers on them. Only a few of us, the younger prisoners in the group, had *X*'s on our foreheads. When the inspection was over, we were ordered to dress and wipe the numbers from our foreheads. No one knew and everyone worried what the numbers and the *X*'s meant.

The next day all the prisoners except those from the Reichshof group were sent away. We stood about, wondering what had become of them and what would become of us. Two days later we were told that we would be transported to another camp right away. We were rushed through the showers and given clean uniforms and wood-soled shoes. The SS guards lined us up and marched us to the railroad station at the bottom of the hill. We were counted and loaded into boxcars. A bucket with water and an empty bucket for our waste were placed in each boxcar. No sooner had we pulled each other in than the doors were shut and the train started moving.

❖ 17 ❖

We traveled in the boxcar for five or six days. Many prisoners were sick and lay dying. The train stopped often, and we would sit hoping for water or the chance to empty the latrine bucket. Hours turned into days, and I lost my sense of time. Finally, after one extremely lengthy stop the boxcar doors were slid open. SS guards stood outside, armed with guns and whips, threatening, shouting, and ordering us to jump out. We fell and stumbled onto the ground. We were at a small deserted freight station. On the station walls were white signs with black letters that said "Colmar." The name meant nothing to me—but a few men in our group knew where Colmar was and the whisper "France" spread through our ranks.

Our guards, using whips and kicks, arranged us into a formation of fives. On their command we marched out from the train station and onto the quiet streets of the town. The guards shouted and threatened us. We tried to get into step to avoid their kicks and punches.

We entered an older section of the town. Our wood-soled shoes raised a loud clatter on the cobblestone streets. Here and there a window opened, and people leaned out and looked down at us. We must have been quite a sight, four or five hundred skeletal men with shaved heads, dressed in ragged striped concentration camp uniforms, walking and stumbling and trying to keep in step under the guns and blows of the guards.

We marched on. Slowly, we passed from the cobblestone side streets and came to the center of the town where the streets widened.

There were stores, apartment houses, and official-looking buildings decorated with Nazi flags and swastikas. People were strolling and walking, riding on bicycles and trolleys. Our marching column sounded a great commotion in the square. The people on the streets and sidewalks stopped walking. They climbed off their bicycles. Soon groups of people stood shoulder to shoulder, lining the street and watching us. The trolleys stopped, and the riders stepped out. Windows and doorways opened, and hundreds of people looked on. I had seen such crowds before. They had watched us driven through their towns and villages. They were always mocking and hostile. In the beginning the hostility was hurtful, but I no longer cared.

Our column approached an official building draped with the Nazi flag. "Caps off!" shouted the guards. We snatched off our blue-and-white prison caps. We passed the building, and the guards commanded: "Caps on!" We thrust our caps on while we tried to keep step.

Strange sounds and whispers rose up from the people watching us. Our column approached another official building. Again came the command: "Caps off!" Again we obeyed. The sounds of the crowd became louder and angrier. We heard angry shouts in French and German. I understood the German and could clearly hear the people calling: "Shame! Shame!" I glanced at the crowds to comprehend their cry. We passed another official building, and through the shouts of the people, I could hear the guards again command: "Caps off!" Quickly, we removed our caps. The people on the sidewalks, on the street, in the trolleys, in the windows, the people everywhere started clapping. The clapping started slowly and quickly grew to a defiant, continuous roar. I realized that the most unbelievable thing was happening. The people of Colmar were on our side! Their shouts of "Shame!" were aimed at the Germans! With growing rage they shouted. It was a gift, a miracle. The people of Colmar felt our pain and gave us comfort, witnessed the injustice and protested, saw our despair and gave us hope.

Our guards reacted nervously. They lowered their guns and rushed us down the street. They no longer commanded us to remove our caps to salute the Nazi flags. The people kept clapping and shouting, and as we passed, some started tossing bread and fruit and cigarette packs into our marching ranks. We dared not pick up anything under the watchful eyes and guns of the SS. Their support and compassion were more precious than food. I turned to the onlookers and let them see my bruised and tearful face and smiled at them through my broken teeth. We marched out of town, but the cries of the people and the memory of their kindness stayed with us.

We reached the outskirts of Colmar. We came to a small empty camp with a few barracks on a grassy lot that was surrounded by barbed wire fences. We crossed through an iron gate, and the SS guards turned us over to a detachment of Luftwaffe soldiers and their sergeant. The sergeant stood by while we were counted and then assigned to barracks. He told us there was water for washing and drinking in the latrines and that we would be fed later that day or the next morning. The Luftwaffe soldiers locked us in the enclosed yard and stayed outside the wire fence.

No Germans or Kapos were inside the Colmar camp. We were left completely alone. I ran with the other prisoners to the latrine to find water. We stood and drank and poured the cool water over our hot filthy selves. I was starving and overcome with exhaustion. I went to my barracks and found an empty bunk. I fell asleep instantly and slept until a terrible hunger woke me. Many prisoners were sleeping. I went out into the dark night and joined the prisoners sitting and speaking to each other quietly. I saw some men from Tyczyn sitting near the barbed wire fence and joined them. "No, it does not look like we will get anything to eat today," said a voice filled with regret. "I do not know if I will live until tomorrow." "You will, you will," another prisoner answered. "The Germans promised that if they do not feed us today, they will feed us in the morning." "Since when can we believe the Germans?" another prisoner asked. "What choice do we have?"

The talk died down, and we sat silently in the darkness. I was hungry and worried about the next day, but for the first time in a long while I was able to just sit quietly and rest. Soon it was completely dark. A prisoner asked, "Why did they bring us here? Nothing is ready, and no one is here. Do they have work for us?" It was a question on my mind as well. A familiar voice responded, "I heard someone say that this is a temporary place, and they will keep us here until another German work camp is ready for us." We sat in silence, each man with his own thoughts and worries. The night was warm, and no one left to go into the barracks. Suddenly, we heard a muffled thud. "What was it? What is it?" we asked each other. We crawled on the ground and groped in the dark, and then one prisoner cried out, "My God, My God, it's a loaf of bread." He held it up. Another loaf landed in our midst. Someone was throwing food over the barbed wire fences! We had our Flossenbürg metal spoons, most with one side of the handle ground down to form a crude knife. We used our spoons to cut up the bread and divided the pieces among ourselves. I tore the bread into small chunks and ate it. It was not the moldy camp bread but a crusty fresh loaf of real bread.

The next morning the guards brought us slices of camp bread and some muddy substitute coffee. We were again left alone to roam the small enclosed yard. Late in the afternoon the guards returned with a large rusty kettle filled with a watery broth of onions and some greens. I was painfully hungry. Soon some prisoners started to pull up the roots of the grass and weeds and eat them. Without thinking, I walked over to them and started pulling up weeds to eat. The roots were thin and small, and they tasted bitter, but they were edible and all we had. The Germans stayed outside the fence and did not stop us from feeding on the grass. Within days the small grassy area was bare and brown. After that we had nothing to eat except for the meager rations that our Luftwaffe guards brought us.

We lined up twice each day for roll call. We cleaned the barracks, washroom, and latrine but had no other work. I was glad to have the chance to rest, but we worried that without jobs the Germans might decide that our lives were useless.

One night after an evening roll call the Luftwaffe sergeant told us that at first light the next morning we would be transferred to a work camp near Colmar called Urbès. We had only a few hours to get ready to leave. I had only the uniform on my back, my wooden shoes, and my soup bowl and spoon. I could leave on a moment's notice. Before going to sleep that last night in Colmar, my friends and I worried about the kind of work camp to which we were being sent. We hoped that Urbès would not be an extermination camp with mass executions and gas chambers. We convinced ourselves that this was unlikely because we were no longer under guard by the SS but by Luftwaffe soldiers.

We marched out of the Colmar camp at dawn. This time we marched to the Colmar railroad station through back streets and avoided the center of town. At this early hour no one was on the streets. The noise of our wooden shoes on the cobblestones brought people to the windows where they called out in French, which I did not understand. At the railroad station we were ordered to quickly climb into boxcars. The doors were closed, and the train started moving right away. Within a few hours the train came to a stop. The doors were opened, and Luftwaffe guards ordered us out. This time we were allowed to climb out and help each other down without being cursed at or beaten. We were at a very small railroad station in the country. We lined up into a formation of fives, and the sergeant counted us. No one was missing, and no one had died. He gave the order for us to march.

We left the small station escorted by the Luftwaffe soldiers and marched along a winding country road bordered by thick woods, cultivated fields, and orchards heavy with apples. All around us were hills covered with forests and meadows where sheep and goats grazed in the sun. It was a scene of incredible beauty. How I wished to run into the hills and be free. We marched on in step and formation.

After about an hour we came to a hamlet of old farmhouses. Some country peasants stood near the road and watched in silence as we were marched by. We passed through the small village and came to the concentration camp. It was a small camp surrounded by a barbed wire fence and a few high wooden guard towers. We saw only a few dilapidated barracks and no factories, construction sites, or work areas. We passed through the camp gate. Two German civilians and several men in SS and Luftwaffe uniforms were waiting for us. One civilian looked familiar to me. I remembered that I had seen him back at the Reichshof Flugmotorenwerk, where he was a Daimler-Benz official. He stepped in front of our group and told us that we would work in a Daimler-Benz factory near the camp. We would do work similar to what we had done at the Daimler-Benz factory in Poland. Working for Daimler-Benz was better than working in a mine or stone quarry. We were divided into two groups to work the twelve-hour day and night shifts. I was to start work the next morning. We went to our assigned barracks, and after being given a chunk of bread for our evening meal, we crawled onto the sleeping shelves and went to sleep.

Very early the next morning, after roll call and another meager morning meal, the day-shift group was assembled into formation and marched out the gate. The Luftwaffe soldiers stood guard at the camp gate as the SS escorted our formation. We walked about two miles along a narrow gravel road. The SS seemed to be leading us straight toward the steep face of a tall mountain. I was alarmed. I knew that Jews were often executed against a wall or mountain. We were within only a few feet of the mountain when I saw a narrow tunnel-like opening in the mountainside. Armed soldiers stood guard as the SS led us into the dark tunnel. A few weak electric lights hung in the darkness. The tunnel walls were rough and wet. The air inside was stale and moldy and worsened as we walked farther into the tunnel. About a half mile in, the lighting suddenly got brighter. A group of civilians was standing alongside a row of lathes and drill presses. The factory was inside this unfinished railroad tunnel. The German civilian foremen and supervisors asked us what work we had done in the Reichshof factory. I told the supervisor that I worked as a lathe and drill press operator. He ordered me and another Jewish prisoner to follow him. We walked deeper into the tunnel, past long rows of machines operated by civilian workers and men in some kind of navy uniform. The air was much worse than at the entrance to the tunnel.

After walking nearly a mile, the German stopped us at two large complex drill presses. He said, "Here we do the most important job. The main airplane engine blocks are drilled, bored, polished, and reamed on these machines. Your foreman will tell you what to do and how to operate these machines. We expect all the work to be done in less than nine hours. If you fail, we will find someone else and transfer you out. If you are careless and damage an engine block, you will be charged with sabotage!" He walked away. The other man was a Jewish watchmaker from Przemyśl whom I had met my first week in the Rzeszów camp.

A German foreman came over and hurriedly showed us how to use the small crane to lift an engine block onto the drill press table and how to operate the machines. He gave us a list of the procedures to perform on each engine block and briefly told us what to do. We could ask for help during the next few hours, but he expected us to work on our own and expected completed work on an engine block before the end of the day. He said as he walked away, "Starting tomorrow you are on your own. We will see if you filthy Jews are as smart as you think." I turned the machine on and started working. I worked with the other prisoner to decipher the instructions, and before long we were drilling holes and reaming out openings. We finished our engine blocks before the shift was over. I knew I could complete the work within the allotted nine hours.

The work in the underground factory was easier than pushing wagons of stones or carrying bodies at Flossenbürg. But the long hours in the wet and cold tunnel filled with moldy air was exhausting, and my health was suffering. At the end of each shift I rushed to the opening of the tunnel to breathe clean air and warm up. In the camp I ate quickly, spoke to my friends, and went to sleep.

One night in the camp the night-shift workers were at the gate, ready to march to the tunnel factory. The camp gate was unlocked and slightly open, ready for the night shift to leave. A young, blond Luftwaffe soldier stood guard. He had a reputation for treating the prisoners humanely. He motioned a young Jewish prisoner to approach the gate. The prisoner walked to the gate and stood before the soldier. I watched but could not hear what the soldier was saying. The soldier opened the gate wider and gestured for the prisoner to go through. The prisoner ran through the gate as fast as he could and headed for the nearby woods. Quickly, the Luftwaffe soldier aimed his machine gun and shot the prisoner in the back. Other soldiers ran to the gate. The young Luftwaffe soldier stood there smiling. I was angry that for the sake of a trick a prisoner had died. The dead Jew and his German killer seemed to have been the same age. We had no time to mourn. A whistle blew, and we were ordered into formation to march to the tunnel factory. I passed the body lying face down in the grass. Luftwaffe soldiers were no different than the SS.

One day I was rushing to get out of the tunnel after work when I saw a crumpled piece of a German newspaper in a pile of trash. I slowed to read the headline. In bold black letters it said, FESTUNG EUROPA (Fortress Europe). Quickly, I picked up the paper and stuffed it under my jacket. I pushed it up under my arm and held it against my chest as I marched back to camp. We were dismissed inside the camp, and I ran to my barracks. I climbed on my bunk and unfolded the paper. The full headline said: "*FESTUNG EUROPA ANGEGRIFFEN!*" (Fortress Europe Assaulted). I read and tried to understand the article. It was badly soiled and parts of the front page were torn off. My German consisted of commands and insults that I had endured, not the sophisticated writing of a journalist. The best I could decipher was that US and British forces had landed on the coast of France but would soon be pushed back into the sea. I could hardly believe it. I was in France, and the Allies had landed! I was shaking and crying. I had to find someone who could translate the German article to make sure that I was not mistaken. I found my friend Motek Hoffstetter from Tyczyn and showed him the torn page. He looked over the newspaper and embraced me. "Thank you, Lucek! Thank you!" he almost shouted. "You bring us great news. The Allies have landed. Germany will be beaten for sure." Motek studied the paper. There was no date on the portion that I had recovered. "Go tell your friends the good news, and I will tell mine," he said. "But be careful. If the Germans find out, they will kill us."

I told my trusted friends, and they told others. Hope was reborn. That night I dreamed of American cowboys and British cavalry soldiers. In my dreams I was not afraid. The few prisoners who were optimists predicted that the Allies would be coming any day, before the Germans could shoot us or carry us off to still another camp. I looked to the Germans' faces for signs of worry, but nothing seemed changed.

One evening at sunset I heard gunfire coming from the woods. Everyone stopped and listened. My first hope was that the Americans or

British had arrived. I turned to my friends and fellow prisoners and exclaimed, "Do you hear it? The English and the Americans must be here!" "Do not be foolish, and do not shout," they said. "It is probably the French Resistance fighting the Germans." I would be happy even if it was only locals fighting the Germans. That night I dreamed that the barbed wire fences were pulled down and that I joined the French to fight the Germans and seek revenge. We heard gunfire again the next night. I listened with excitement and hoped that freedom would soon be ours.

Two days later I heard that two Jewish prisoners had escaped. The Germans held endless roll calls, strengthened the guards around the camp, and increased the number of SS guards. We thought that the prisoners must have escaped from the tunnel at night. During the few hours when I was outside the tunnel, my eyes scoured the countryside. I imagined that they were there, safe and under the protection of the French Resistance. I decided to look for chances to escape. I was sure that it would be easier to get help here and avoid capture than in Poland. A few days later the German military police brought the two escapees back. They were wearing civilian clothing. Their hands were tied behind their backs. Some prisoners found an opportunity to talk to them. They had made it into the hills, and the French had given them food and clothing. At first they slept in the woods, but then a farmer let them hide in his barn. That night the Germans came to the barn and captured them. They had been betrayed. Late that night the SS took the two escapees out of the camp and shot them.

The German managers of the factory ordered that the work on an engine block now had to be completed in less than eight hours. The workers would operate the two large drill presses in three eight-hour shifts. Only six prisoners could work the presses. We were escorted to the tunnel and back to the camp separately from the other prisoners, who worked the normal twelve-hour shifts in the tunnel. The SS decided that we would work extra jobs for them each day. Before and after my shift in the tunnel, I had to clean and sweep the compound where the SS men lived, wash their cars and trucks, and polish their boots. Whatever I did, it never was good enough or fast enough for the SS, and they cursed and hit me.

I was working in the late afternoon inside the walled-in yard of an old farmhouse, where the SS were quartered. The SS housing was in a nearby village and surrounded by other farmhouses, barns, and stables. My job was to scrub some old wooden outdoor furniture. An armed SS man sat in a chair in the yard to watch me. I was given a bucket of water and a steel hand brush. The furniture was moldy and weathered black. I knew that I would not be able to clean it to satisfy the SS and expected a beating. I was wet and tired, and the capture and execution of the escapees lay heavily on my mind. I scrubbed the blackened table, my sleeves wet to the elbows. I heard a dull thud of something hitting the ground. The SS man had begun talking to someone and moved out of my sight. I turned back to the wet table and heard the dull thud again. I turned my head and saw a green apple rolling though the grass. I looked around the top of the wall encircling the yard but saw nothing but trees and the rooftops of neighboring houses. Then I heard two more dull sounds, and two more apples landed near the first one. I took a few steps and picked up the apples. I put them inside my shirt. I pulled off my tattered dirty striped cap and bared my shaved head. Holding my cap, I bowed, hoping that the decent and generous person could see and feel my silent but emotional gratitude. I could not resist eating one apple in a few bites, even with my broken teeth. The others I hid under my baggy jacket and shared that night with my shocked and delighted prisoner friends.

I worked at the drill press in the tunnel and as a servant of the SS. Then one day all work in the tunnel factory stopped. All the night-shift workers were brought from camp and joined us in the tunnel. The German supervisors and foremen ordered us to move the machines to the entrance of the tunnel, where we loaded them onto large trucks. There was not enough room in the tunnel to bring in lifts and trolleys. We worked hard by hand for days and nights without much rest or food. We did move the smaller machines to the tunnel entrance but could not move the larger, heavier pieces. We all understood that this was a repetition of what had happened at the Daimler-Benz factory in Rzeszów when the Russians were drawing near. The Allies must be in France and coming close to Urbès. Without planning or saying anything, the prisoners began to slow the movement of the machinery to a standstill. We hoped the delay might allow the Allies to get to Urbès and set us free.

The Germans gave up on the machinery still inside the tunnel. They ordered us to leave at once. Luftwaffe soldiers and SS marched us along the country roads, and after several hours we reached a small railroad station. We were packed into boxcars, the doors were shut, and the train started moving. After a few hours the train stopped at a railroad depot that I thought might be the Colmar station. There must have been an air raid, for many buildings were smoldering, and a train on the next track was still on fire. Someone climbed up to look out the small window of the boxcar and realized that the burning train was the one that had carried the Daimler-Benz equipment from the tunnel. At a short stop, the doors were opened for us to empty the latrine bucket, and we saw that the Luftwaffe soldiers were gone and only the SS guarded us. We had many long stops at different railroad sidings. We were given little food or water. At night the train was strafed and sprayed with machine-gun fire. We hoped that the Allies were here at last. Bullets hit our boxcar and killed three prisoners. The train moved on slowly, and many prisoners died of hunger and thirst.

One night we passed a very large city that we guessed was Berlin. An air raid was going on. Buildings were on fire, gunfire sounded without pause, and bombs exploded. I was too tired, hungry, and thirsty to care. I wanted a little space to lie down, some water, and a piece of bread. Not long after leaving the burning city, our train stopped at a blacked-out railroad station. I felt the boxcars being decoupled from the rest of the train.

· 18 ·

The boxcar doors were slid open. In the morning light we looked out into chaos. The SS swung their clubs and truncheons as we jumped and fell from the boxcars. They were shouting and cursing, and we cowered from their blows. We rushed to line up for the counting. Some prisoners had dropped their bowls and were beaten back in line as they tried to retrieve them. An SS guard climbed into the boxcar to count the dead and to finish off the nearly dead. On the grimy walls of the railroad station hung signs with the name Oranienburg.

We stood for the count, and the SS men began shouting for us to march. We marched out of the station and through the streets of the town. This time the pedestrians took little interest in us. From my place in the middle I looked up and saw many bombed-out buildings. The Russians must be coming from the east. I was exhausted and distracted and started to fall back from my row of prisoners. I felt a sudden blow of a truncheon on my back. A guard yelled, "Wake up! You filthy Jew!" I stumbled and forced myself to get in step and march. We were nearly running.

We slowed as we came to the camp. Ahead was a massive gate. It was as wide and as tall as a three-story building. Armed SS looked out from the windows on the upper floors. Above the entrance a sign in black letters said: "Arbeit Macht Frei." (Work liberates.) We passed through the gate. The SS men stopped us on a large paved lot next to the gate. In every direction as far as I could see were row upon row of prison barracks. On a small area of green grass in the middle of the square a formation of prisoners was marching back and forth. Some were stooped over, for they carried German army knapsacks on their backs. A Kapo stood nearby and shouted the cadence. The prisoners kept marching back and forth.

A Kapo came, used a wooden stick to line us into a formation of fives, and then counted us. He marched us across the camp, and we stopped in front of two large barracks. The Kapo paced along our column, waving his long wooden stick. "You are in Sachsenhausen," he said angrily. "You will live in these barracks. First you will be given a shower and be registered. Tonight, you will be fed. Tomorrow you will work."

We stripped and left our clothes in piles. We ran through a barracks with icy cold water running out of overhead faucets. It was not enough to wash the grime or filth from our bodies. I copied the other prisoners, who slowed their running and opened their mouths to drink the shower water. We came out through the barracks, and the Kapo and an assistant checked our names against a list and gave us two patches with black numbers and red and yellow triangles on them. We were given a needle and a length of thread and a few minutes to sew the patches to the front of our jackets and the side of our pants. I sat wet and naked on the ground and stitched my prison clothing. I was now prisoner 107,028 of the Sachsenhausen concentration camp.

We dressed and were led back to our barracks where we stood outside in rows for hours. Finally, our Kapo opened the barracks doors. The barracks were overcrowded with rickety three-tiered wooden bunks. We were to sleep two to a single bunk. My friend Julek Schipper and I agreed to share an upper bunk. It would be tight and uncomfortable on the narrow shelf, but we were both extremely thin. Many prisoners immediately lay down on the bunks to sleep. I was too hungry to sleep and lay awake for hours. I climbed off the bunk without waking Schipper and went outside and stood in the small enclosed yard. I watched as groups of prisoners marched back from work. In each camp I had learned to seek out experienced Jewish prisoners whom I could trust for advice about the camp. I always hoped to find someone from Rzeszów who might know something of Manek's whereabouts.

I walked by the edge of an open square where the prisoners assembled for morning and evening roll calls. I knew that it was of vital importance to quickly learn my way around the camp. I tried to walk in a purposeful manner and thought of excuses for being away from my barracks if a Kapo or the SS stopped me.

I came upon a narrow stretch between four small barracks. A small group of prisoners had gathered and appeared to be looking at something at the far end of the yard. I moved toward them, and my eyes turned to a terrible sight: several small barbed wire cages. Inside, haggard prisoners were chained to each other and a thick wooden pole anchored in the middle of each cage. The prisoners were chained with thick arm and leg irons and slowly shuffled around the pole. They struggled under the weight of the irons. Their bare feet and legs were grotesquely swollen above and below the tight and heavy leg irons. Their cheeks were painted with a large letter *T*. Some prisoners had fainted or were unable to walk. They were held up or carried by the other prisoners to whom they were chained. A Kapo stood in each cage and used a leather whip to keep them moving in the endless circles. I stood with a group of young prisoners. They were Poles, marked with a *P* on the red triangles on their prison uniforms. I whispered in Polish, "What is happening? Who are these people?" "They are resistance fighters from France," a Pole answered. "The Germans have already sentenced them to death. The *T* stands for *Tod*, death in German." "What will happen? How long do they have to walk in chains?" I asked. The Pole whispered back, "No one knows. Every morning the SS pick a few of them to hang. They do not know when their turn will come. That is part of the torture. They do it in the open to frighten us. To make sure we know what happens to resisters."

The Poles noticed that my prisoner number was high and that I must be new to Sachsenhausen. They wanted to know where I was from. They were from Warsaw and had been captured by the Germans during the Polish uprising. They had been in Sachsenhausen for months and worked the night shift in a nearby factory. I had not known of an uprising in Warsaw, and they told me about the valiant attempt and the ultimate failure.

I walked back slowly toward the edge of the camp assembly square. On the patch of green grass the same group was still marching back and forth. I stopped and asked a passing prisoner with a red triangle why they were marching. "They are from a punishment barracks," he told me. "For even minor infractions prisoners are sent there and have to march for hours each day before and after their regular work. They make them wear stiff new German army shoes to break in before they are given to the German soldiers and carry their heavy backpacks as an added punishment." The prisoner started to walk away. He turned and said, "You are new here. Do not go around asking questions or you will soon be with them." He gestured toward the punished marchers and walked on.

The next morning after a long roll call we were lined up to have our heads shaved. A group of prisoners had manual clippers and quickly took off any hair. They took a razor and shaved a bald stripe across the top of our heads, from the front to the back. "Why are you doing this?" I asked the prisoner who was shaving me. "It is to mark you if you try to escape," he answered. "The Germans call it the lice alley, a place for all the bugs on your body to roam."

When we had all been shaved, we were lined up and began our march to work. The SS shouted as we moved through the camp, out the entrance gate, and through the damaged streets to the railroad station. We climbed into empty boxcars and rode a short distance to a railroad siding where iron supplies were stored. There were railroad rails, field kitchens, tank and truck axles, rolls of wire, iron fences, and gates. We had to carry the large heavy iron pieces as we loaded and unloaded railroad cars. My hands were quickly bleeding from the sharp rusty edges of the iron. I was weak from hunger and tried to pair up with stronger-looking prisoners. When six prisoners strained to lift a huge iron piece, the SS ordered that only five prisoners carry it. We soon realized that the SS did this all the time. We learned to rally more prisoners than we needed to lift and carry and waited for the SS to reduce our crew. I kept my eyes to the ground to avoid eye contact with the Germans as I cursed them under my breath. This was my resistance, to declare in spirit what I could not do with might.

In the camp each night after the day of exhausting work, we were allowed a short break between evening rations and roll call. Prisoners used this short break to rinse their clothing in the latrine washroom or go to the camp infirmary to plead for a bandage or some medication. This was a desperate act, for many who ventured to the infirmary never returned. I went back each night to the compound of prisoners with the black *T* painted on their faces. I stood and watched the chained prisoners stagger in an endless circle in the wire cages. I watched them and took note of every detail of their suffering. I felt the need to memorize what was happening here. I looked to their bruised faces to remember them from one day to the next. When I recognized a certain prisoner from the day before, I was happy that he had escaped the hangman. On some days familiar faces were gone, and I knew they were dead. It was not curiosity or pity that compelled me to witness this terrible suffering. I stood to be among them, even though I was helpless to even call out a prayer for their sake. When I stood close to the wire cages, I sensed the physical pain and the anguish that they knew they were to die any day. I, a Jew, had also been condemned to death, with the day not yet selected by my executioners. I knew the struggle to walk under the heavy irons was useless in changing their fate and began to believe that all my struggles to survive were probably equally useless. During all my years under the Nazis I was sustained by the conviction and hope that I would survive. I was not certain any longer.

Whistles blew throughout the camp to announce the start of the evening roll call. I ran back to my barracks and got into line next to Julek Schipper. I leaned over and told Julek that I feared that our fate was decided and that our struggle was useless. Julek thought that I was joking and joked back that we should tell the Germans we did not feel like being counted tonight. I was silent, and he looked into my eyes and saw that I was serious. He spoke to me as firmly and sternly as my father would have.

"Listen, Lucek, and do not be stupid. The condemned Frenchmen are good men, and I am sorry for them, but our situation is different. They have tried to fight and lost. We have not lost yet. Do not talk about fate or giving up, or I will beat the devil out of you. We are more than friends. We are like brothers. We need each other, and I will not let you quit now." The Kapo blew his whistle and shouted for us to form straight lines.

One day a German freight train came to the depot. Many cars at the end of the train were on fire. We worked furiously until the burning cars were decoupled from the train. The train departed, leaving the burning cars at the depot. We continued to work, carrying and moving iron through the smoke-filled depot. I smelled something familiar but could not identify it. The others noticed the smell too. We looked around and sniffed the air. Then a prisoner cried out, "Baked potatoes?" Yes, I recognized the smell. The potatoes must be in a burning freight car. We chose a longer path as we carried the heavy iron so that we would be closer to the cars with potatoes. A German army sergeant saw what was happening. He ordered us to move several large iron stoves from the center of the depot to a spot next to the cars of potatoes. He supervised our work, but as groups of prisoners approached, he quietly said, "One of you—get some potatoes for the group. I do not want a stampede." We hurriedly did as ordered, and each of us got three large, warm potatoes. The sergeant organized us the same way the next day, and again we ate potatoes. For the first time since I could remember, I did not go to sleep hungry. We were grateful and surprised that the sergeant helped us and that the SS guards allowed it. They cursed us as we struggled with the heavy iron but allowed us our treasure of potatoes.

My friend Julek Reich injured himself at work. That evening our Kapo ordered him to go to the camp infirmary. He returned before the evening roll call and told us that he was given a job in the camp hospital. His work would not be hard, and he would be able to get more food. The next day he moved to a barracks with other hospital workers. We were sad to part from each other. We had been together since the Rzeszów ghetto. Schipper and I were happy that he had found easier work and wished him luck.

Our Kapo told us that our group would be divided and transferred to separate camps in Bremen and Braunschweig. Both camps were attached to factories in need of metalworkers. This was good news.

Sachsenhausen was a deadly camp with too many Kapos and SS. Doing skilled work in a factory would be easier and offer some protection from the coming winter and the murderous Kapos and SS.

I was worried about the decision to split up our group. We had been together a long time and grown close and dependent upon each other. I knew many of the prisoners from Tyczyn and the Rzeszów ghetto. I had developed relationships with many others during the years that we had suffered together. These were friends who would help me at every chance, whom I could trust to watch my shoes or bowl, and who would even lie to a Kapo or the SS to save my life.

We were ordered to line up outside the barracks. Two German civilians called out: "For Braunschweig we need thirty-five lathe operators and for Bremen, twenty-five lathe operators. For Braunschweig, twenty metal polishers and twenty foundrymen. For Bremen thirty smiths and ten locksmiths." I had no idea whether it was better to go to Braunschweig or Bremen. Prisoners gave their name, skill, and number and were then ordered back into the barracks. When the division was complete, most prisoners from the Reichshof camp, including Schipper, Ringel, Hafferflock, and I, were going to Braunschweig. Most prisoners from Budzyń were going to Bremen.

They sent us back to work at the iron depot. When we returned to our barracks, two lists of numbers were posted on the door. I looked to find my number, *107,028*, on the Braunschweig list. It was not there. It was on the list with prisoners going to Bremen. I was upset. I had felt sure that I would stay with my friends, and now things were messed up. I was not the only prisoner switched from the Braunschweig to the Bremen list. A large group of prisoners were upset, including my friend Julek Schipper. Another young prisoner from Przemyśl, Josef Singer, was unhappy to be placed on the Braunschweig list. A frail young German Jew named Kurt was from the Budzyń group and had been shifted away from his friends to the Braunschweig list.

Some prisoners were resigned to the change. Julek Schipper and I were frantic. Josef Singer was desperate about being separated from his cousin. The young German Jew, Kurt, went to plead with the Kapo to go to Bremen. The Kapo said no changes were allowed. That evening we were told that the Bremen group would leave the next day. Kurt went again to plead with the Kapo. The Kapo yelled and beat Kurt up. I saw Kurt outside the barracks, bruised and crying. His voice was filled with despair. "Nothing can be done. The Bremen transport leaves tomorrow." I sought out Julek Schipper. "Let us switch uniforms with those two prisoners. We will tell each other our names, ages, and parents' names, and Kurt and Singer will go to Bremen, and we will go to Braunschweig." We found the two prisoners and they agreed. That night, in the dark corner of the barracks, Julek changed uniforms with Kurt and I with Josef Singer. My name was now Josef Singer. I was born in Przemyśl, Poland. I was eighteen, two years older than Lucek Salzman, who was leaving for the Bremen camp the next day. I was now prisoner number 107,081 of Sachsenhausen concentration camp.

The next morning after roll call they told the prisoners on the Bremen list to stay in camp and prepare to leave. We said goodbye and wished each other good luck. Those of us not going to Bremen were taken to work at the iron depot. We marched back to camp that evening, and as we came back through the gate, our formation was ordered to halt by a group of SS. A senior SS officer walked up and down our ranks shouting, "Prisoner Schipper! Step out of the ranks! Immediately!" My heart sank. Our switch has been discovered. How else would they know that Schipper was still in Sachsenhausen? I waited for SS to demand that Salzman step forward. How can I conceal it? What will I say? What will they do to me?

The SS kept calling for Schipper. After a minute of hesitation Julek Schipper stepped out of rank. The SS yelled at him and led him away. We marched back to the barracks. I was worried about Julek and fearful that the SS would come for me. Something must have happened. Someone must have talked. If the SS did not know about me yet, they could get it out of Julek. All evening I expected the SS to come for me. Other prisoners asked why the SS took Schipper, but I pretended not to know. More time passed. We were given our evening ration and stood for another long roll call. I tossed in the bunk all night, wondering and worrying about my friend. The next day I searched the camp but could not find him. The Germans acted as if everything was normal. No word about or from Schipper. I worked at the iron depot all day. I carried the heavy load on my back and the heavy worry in my heart. After work we marched back into the camp. Again I was sure that today the SS would be waiting for me. Again nothing happened.

Three days after the group of prisoners had been moved to Bremen, we were told that we would leave for Braunschweig. I started to believe that the Germans did not know about my switch with Singer. We were inspected and counted. Our group had about 220 prisoners. Our numbers and names were called out. With apprehension I answered when they called Singer. They called out the next name on the list, and I nearly fainted when I realized that the feared moment had passed. We were given an extra portion of thick stale bread. The Kapo ordered us into formation and marched us across the camp toward the main gate. An SS officer came out of the gate building and halted our column. We stood and waited for nearly an hour. I was sure that this had something to do with me. Two SS came toward us with Julek Schipper limping between them. My heart raced. I was sure that they were coming for me.

The SS pushed Julek into our ranks. I looked ahead to where he stood. He looked haggard, and his shoulders were slumped forward. We were called to attention. The large gate was opened, and we marched. Armed SS escorted us to the Oranienburg station, where old boxcars painted red were waiting.

They gave the order to climb into the boxcars. I shoved and ran to climb into the boxcar with Julek. We embraced and sat together on the floor. "Julek, I am so happy to see you," I cried out. "I worried about you all the time. I thought that they would come for me too. What happened? How did you get back to our group?" He answered, "Lucek, if you are happy I'm here, I am a hundred times happier. I found out what happened, but I still cannot believe it. When the Bremen group lined up to leave Sachsenhausen, the Kapo spotted Kurt and remembered his constant pleading to go to Bremen. Kurt insisted that his name was Schipper and that he was on the list. The Kapo started hitting him, and Kurt told him about our switch. He must not have told about you and Josef Singer. I give him credit for that."

He stopped talking and closed his eyes. I moved to try to give him more space to stretch out. I wanted to hear the rest of the story but knew that he needed time to rest and recover from the terrible days that he had endured. After a few minutes he began to speak.

"The Kapo told the SS. They beat Kurt up but let him go to Bremen. I guess they did not want to change their lists." Julek smiled. "They waited for me that night and took me to the office. The SS gave me a whipping and kicked me until I could not get up from the floor. Then they asked me why I did it. I told them that I liked being in Sachsenhausen and wanted to stay. The SS had never had a prisoner who wanted to stay in Sachsenhausen. They laughed and said they should not be surprised that a dumb Jew did not know better. They assigned me to the punishment group at half rations and said that I would be shipped out with the next group. For two days I marched in German army boots, and then the SS took me to your group. The bastards did not know that this was what I was trying to do in the first place."

I tried to get him to take some bread that I had saved from our rations. I knew that he was starving, but he refused and wanted me to keep it for myself. I broke off a chunk of bread and wordlessly gave it to him. He hesitated and then he took it and ate it quickly. "The punishment group had a Kapo, a Pole who heard about my story but did not know that it was about me. Everyone was talking and laughing about the jerk who wanted to stay in Sachsenhausen and who would change places not to be shipped out." Julek closed his eyes, and I saw that he had fallen asleep. Our train started moving through the countryside and another miserable journey began.

• 19 •

We had been on the train for four or five days. We were starving, thirsty, and soiled from our own waste. At each stop some prisoners would bang on the boxcar doors and cry out for water. Every few days the doors would open, and we would throw out the dead. One night I felt the jolting and banging as our boxcar decoupled from the train. If this was Braunschweig, the doors would soon slide open and the SS would be ready to curse and strike us as they ordered us out. I stood and looked out the high, small window. It was still dark, and the SS would probably not come until daylight. These last hours were mine to rest. The other prisoners were sleeping, unaware that we had arrived. Julek was slumped over, and I looked at his thin bony body and then at my own. How would we ever live long enough to see freedom?

The SS came in the morning. They opened the doors with a bang and began shouting for us to get out. Many of us were weak and stiff after days in the crowded car. We tried to move quickly because the SS struck and shoved us into formation. We were counted twice and ordered to march. The SS were noticeably older than the guards in the ghetto and other camps. The countryside was flat and gray, and dense fumes rose from tall smokestacks in the distance.

We marched for a long time before we reached the camp. We came upon a large wooden gate densely covered with barbed wire and hinged to thick wooden posts. Next to the gate was a small building with a porch. Two armed SS guards watched as we approached. The gate was swung open, and we marched into the camp. We were halted, counted again, and told to stand in place. The Braunschweig camp was flat and lined with muddy, partially graveled streets with old barracks of different shapes and sizes.

An SS sergeant and two prisoners in clean, well-fitting striped uniforms came out from the building. A Kapo and a *Lager Ältester* (camp's senior) wearing a special identifying armband walked through our ranks and looked us over with obvious disgust. The Lager Ältester spoke. "This is a working camp attached to the Hermann Göring Werke. No one unable or unwilling to work hard and well will be tolerated." Pointing to the Kapo, he added, "This is your Kapo. He is your king, your lord and master." The sergeant and the Lager Ältester left. The Kapo led us to a small wooden building near the gate. A sign above the door said "Administration Office." He told us to go into the building four at a time to be registered. When my turn came, I went into the building. Two clerks sat behind a table. "Name?" one of them asked me. After the slightest hesitation I answered, "Josef Singer." He examined a list lying on the table before him and said, "Yes, a lathe operator. You will work the day shift this week." He reached into a small box and pulled out two small patches with a large red and smaller yellow triangles that formed a Star of David and had black numbers printed on them. He handed them to me: "Sew them on before you go to work tomorrow. You know where they go." I was prisoner 64,487.

Outside I stood next to Julek, who had gone through the registration before me. "What name did you use?" I asked him quietly. "I used my name, Schipper. They know who I am. And you? What name did you use?" "I used my own name too," I said. "Josef Singer." We both smiled. The 220 prisoners in our group were jammed into one barracks. The barracks was filled with rickety, narrow, three-level wooden bunks. It also had a row of narrow wooden tables and low wooden benches. At each end of the barracks stood a black iron stove. The Kapo and his assistants randomly assigned two prisoners to each bunk and ten prisoners to each table. We were to remember our table and be at it whenever the Kapo commanded. Our meals would be distributed, our work assignments issued, and our punishments meted out from these tables.

The Kapo told us that we would not get any food until the evening. In the meantime he did not want filthy Jews fouling up his barracks and ordered us to get outside fast and not wander away. We ran out, with the Kapo screaming for us to move faster and to keep our caps off until we were outside. He pushed and hit prisoners as they ran. He would not be an easy Kapo to live under. Next to his prisoner number was a green triangle.

We gathered outside and tried to make sense of this camp. Schipper stood with me, and we looked at each other in silence. We could have gone to the Bremen camp, and we took grave risks to be sent here. The camp was bleak and dreary and not very large. It might have held three or four thousand prisoners. Motek Hoffstetter walked over, and I asked him what he thought of this camp. He was always wise and encouraging but now shrugged his skinny shoulders and answered in a voice heavy with worry, "I do not know, Lucek. Something here is different. We will have to wait to see."

That evening, after a long roll call, we were ordered into the barracks. We sat at our assigned table with our bowls. Kettles of soup were delivered. The Kapo picked four prisoners to carry the kettles. He went from table to table and gave each of us a small ladle of the watery broth. The Kapo's assistant placed a small loaf of black bread on each table and picked a prisoner at the table to be the table leader. He handed the table leader a rusty knife and said, "Cut the bread into ten pieces and distribute them at your table. Then bring the knife to me. I do not want any fighting or arguing. If I hear any noise, I will take away all the bread and give the responsible swine-dog ten lashes."

We were starved, and I hoped that my slice would be the largest or, at least, not the smallest. Motek Hoffstetter was my table leader. He stood holding the rusty knife as the loaf of bread sat on the table. He looked at the small loaf and our hungry faces. He looked over at another table where the bread was being divided. A prisoner from the next table came over and quickly whispered something to Motek. Motek took the knife and cut the loaf into ten slices that were as equal as possible. The slices were laid on the table. He asked for suggestions about how to make the slices more even. Someone said that he needed

to cut a sliver from a larger slice and move it to the thinnest. He con-
sulted with the prisoner from the other table where they were already
eating. Then he chose a prisoner to be a questioner and another to be
the answerer. The answerer stood and faced the wall, and the questioner pointed to each slice and asked in Russian, "Komu?" (For
whom?) The answerer called out Yiddish numbers between one and
ten that corresponded to our positions at the table. The bread was
divided without fighting. We changed the process a few days later.
Some prisoners thought that the ends of the loaf were the most nour-
ishing, and we began taking turns getting the thick ends. The Kapo
demanded an explanation and, after cursing us, left us alone.

On the second day in camp we went to work. A Kapo came to our
barracks and ordered us to line up in a formation of fives. He marched
us to the camp gate. We were counted again and stood waiting as other
columns of prisoners left the camp. All the prisoners wore striped
prison uniforms and were gaunt and haggard. As they passed the SS
guards at the gate, they were commanded to remove their caps. Without hats or hair the bony faces and thin bodies foretold a difficult existence in this camp. As they passed, I saw that some had letters printed
next to their prisoner numbers. There were *P*'s for Poles, *R*'s for Russians, *F*'s for Frenchmen, *B*'s for Belgians, and so on. Every nation of
occupied Europe was represented. I saw no Jewish stars on anyone.

It was our turn to leave. The Kapo commanded us to march and to
remove our caps as we passed the gate. We crossed through and were
encircled by armed SS guards. We marched in step as we had in so
many other camps. The Kapo wanted us to sing and ordered us to
repeat the words after him.

Links by Hamburg liegt ein Lager, zwischen stacheldraht versteckt.
[To the left of Hamburg lies a camp hidden behind barbed wire.]

We followed his song and sang it on many marches.

The march to the factory took nearly thirty minutes. The Hermann
Göring Werke factory complex came into view, and I was surprised by
how large it was. It had tall buildings, giant halls, warehouses, and rail-

road sidings spread over a vast expanse. The Kapo led us to a giant hall. The SS guards remained outside. The hall must have been a half-mile long. It was filled with machines, overhead cranes, and foundries. Railroad cars sat on two rail lines that went inside the building. Some German civilians looked us over and then called for people with specific skills. They called for lathe operators, and I stepped forward with many other prisoners. A civilian came over to me and asked, "How many years' experience?" "Two," I answered. "Come with me," he commanded. He pointed to two other prisoners in the ranks. "You will be his helpers." He led us to the middle of the hall and stopped before a huge lathe. The machine had the features and controls of a lathe but was the size of a large truck. Next to it, in a neat row, were many dark cast-iron shells for large bombs. Each was about eight feet long and two to three feet in diameter. Between the lathe and the row of bombshells stood a crane to hoist the bombshells on and off the lathe. The civilian spoke to me. "Your job is to cut off the rough surface of iron, give each bombshell a smooth surface, and shape it according to the guiding jig in the machine. If you ruin any bombshells, you and your helpers will hang."

He spent some time showing me how to use the crane to place a bombshell into the lathe's grip and how to cut the rough surface off a shell. I had a quota to cut and shape two bombshells per hour. At Daimler-Benz I had made brass rings for an airplane engine or drilled engine blocks. I could pretend that I was not helping the Germans to fight the war. These were monstrous bombs that could kill scores of soldiers, sink ships, and level cities. I was forced to work for the Germans. Refusal would be suicidal, and other prisoners would take my place. Resistance was impossible and stupid.

I worked twelve hours each day, alternating between weeks of day and night shifts. Outside it was fall, and the days grew shorter and the weather colder. I marched back and forth from the camp to the factory in the windy cold darkness. My thin patched uniform gave no protection from the cold or frequent rains. I had no coat, gloves, or even socks. The factory hall was big and drafty, and I shivered at the lathe and stood near the motor to warm my cold stiff hands. I knew I was lucky and that others were laboring and freezing to death outside.

The misery and brutality of the camp got worse. The SS came to count us during roll calls, to inspect our barracks and the prisoners. They beat and tortured the prisoners for any trivial reason. The Kapos inflicted the worst beatings and abuse. They served as barracks leaders, assistant leaders, and labor team overseers, as well as overseeing the kitchen, sanitation, and other camp functions. Most were German criminals, prisoners who wore green triangles on their uniforms. They forced the other prisoners to do painful calisthenics, to sit squatting in the cold mud for hours, and deprived them of food and sleep for days. Some had special cruelties, like the Kapo who had been a boxer and impressed the other Kapos and SS men with his ability to knock out a prisoner with one punch. Of course, other Kapos claimed to be able to knock out a man with one punch as well and demonstrated on any prisoner who passed by.

The weather got colder, and the Kapo ordered us to build fires in the potbellied stoves in the barracks. A few prisoners secretly began toasting the bread from the evening rations. They gathered around the stove and waited for a space to lay their bread on the top. I always devoured my ration immediately. Once, before lights out, our Kapo saw the prisoners toasting their bread. He became angry and took the bread from the stove and the prisoners. He lectured that toasting the bread destroyed its nutrients and vitamins. He insisted that it was unhealthy and issued an order that no one should ever toast the bread again. A few evenings later he caught a prisoner toasting a miserable little slice of bread. The Kapo became furious and shouted that we would all get sick because we ignored his advice. He took his heavy wooden cane and beat the prisoner. When the poor prisoner fell to the ground, the Kapo placed his cane across the prisoner's throat and stood on both ends until he was dead.

One evening at the beginning of the shift, the German foreman of my section and a German civilian came over as I was hoisting a bomb-shell into the lathe. "Stop!" the foreman yelled. "We need you for another job." "What's your name?" the civilian asked.

"Singer," I said nervously. "Singer, your foreman told me you are quick, and I want you to operate one of the large overhead cranes. Follow me!" I followed him up a narrow iron ladder and along a high narrow walkway just under the hall ceiling. We walked to the side of the great hall and stopped at a small balcony suspended below the high walkway. It was much colder at this height. I followed the German down into the balcony where control levers and switches were mounted on the walls. Right below stood a railroad line with open roofless freight cars. "This is the control room for the overhead crane," the German said. "I'll show you how to work it and what you have to do. This is work that can only be done at night and is done six nights every week." The German showed me how to work the switches and pulleys that controlled the crane's massive metal claw. My job was to load scrap metal from a large bin into the freight cars. After a few minutes the German told me to start working and left. I was alone, high under the ceiling of the giant hall.

After a few nights I could load the scrap metal onto the railroad cars. A supervisor seldom came the long way to check on me, and I could see him in advance, coming across the walkway. At first I thought that working alone would be good, but the cold and isolation became depressing. I thought of my parents. I worried about Manek and despaired that we might never find each other. I spent the lonely hours thinking about my years as a prisoner and how hopeless my future seemed. I could not remember what freedom felt like, to walk where and when I wanted, to live for an hour without fear and hunger.

I was put on the night shift permanently. I was in camp during the day when the SS inspected the barracks and the Kapos were awake. It was dangerous and nerve-racking. The Germans decided to make room in the Jewish barracks for more prisoners by adding bunks and moving the stoves closer to the walls. This work would take several weeks during which several prisoners were temporarily transferred to other barracks in the camp.

I was transferred and told to report to a barracks on the other side of the camp. I went there with my soup bowl and spoon to report to the Kapo. He assigned me to a bunk and table for night workers. I quickly realized that no Jewish prisoners were in the barracks. It housed mostly Ukrainians and a few Poles and Russians. I knew that they hated Jews, and I needed to find a way to hide my identity. The two white patches stitched to my jacket and pants had my prisoner number, *64,487*, a red triangle with a black *P* and three yellow triangles to form the Star of David. The colors had faded. The blacks were gray, the red looked pink, and the yellow was faint. I went to the wash barracks and scrubbed the patches until the colors and star were shredded and unrecognizable. The other prisoners ignored me. The barracks was crowded, noisy, and smelly. The prisoners were withdrawn and unfriendly, and many were ill.

At the night rations the division of bread was governed by brute strength with no sense of fairness. The table leaders were the strongest and meanest prisoners. Each had a following of two or three large prisoners. When the loaf of bread was left at our table, the table leader cut it into ten pieces. He cut a big chunk for himself, a few large slices for his followers, and the remainder into tiny slices for the others at the table. I tried to protest in German and Polish. The table leader put his huge fist under my nose and bellowed in Russian: "Molchaj sobaka. Ely ja tebia ubiyu!" (Shut up, dog, or I will kill you!) I sat down and silently started to chew my thin piece of bread. Later I asked an older Polish prisoner if we could complain to the Kapo. He told me that the Kapo did not care and that the Ukrainian table leader and his thugs would kill me if they found out that I had complained. It seemed impossible, but I was even hungrier than before. I was lonely, for I had no friends in this barracks, and I still worked alone in the factory. Fortunately, the Kapo was unhappy at having me in his barracks. After a few days I was transferred to another barracks.

In the morning I reported to my new Kapo. He told his assistant, a Pole, to show me my bunk and to assign me to a table with the other night workers. At the morning rations I drank the weak substitute coffee and spoke to my table mates. They were all Frenchmen, as were most prisoners in this barracks. I was able to communicate with some German-speaking Alsatians. The French prisoners appeared frail and hungry. Even the young prisoners looked shrunken and aged. These prisoners were the opposite of the crude and brutish Ukrainians. The Frenchmen were polite, peaceful, and even cheerful on occasion.

I soon found out that they had a unique way of dividing the daily loaf of bread. Ten prisoners sat, and the Kapo and his assistant distributed the soup into our bowls. It was the same measly ladle of foul broth served throughout the camp. The loaf of bread was placed on the table. Our table leader cut the loaf into ten slices of different sizes. The first piece was at least a third of the loaf. The next slices were cut progressively smaller until the ninth and tenth slices were paper-thin slivers of bread. I thought that this was even worse than in the Ukrainian barracks. I looked around, but none of the prisoners at the table looked worried or unhappy. Everyone sat patiently and seemed to be content. A Frenchman saw my alarm and spoke to me in German. "Do not worry—the large piece goes to each of us in turn. Once every ten days each of us has the big piece for himself. Once every ten days we each have a day when we are not hungry. On the other days we get less, but waiting for the big piece helps us cope with the days of hunger." He smiled to reassure me. "Of course, the problem is that new prisoners start at the tenth position. But every day your slice will be bigger and in ten days you will eat like a king." This sounded crazy. But who could know? No one objected, and another Frenchman said, "You will like it. Anyway, that is how it is done in this barracks." I received the thinnest sliver of bread. That night, as I worked loading scrap metal into the railroad cars, I could think only of my fierce hunger. I kept seeing the large piece of bread, larger than I had had to myself in a long time, and remembered that it would be mine in little more than a week.

I was given increasingly larger slices of bread each night. I ate it all. There was not enough to save even a small corner for the morning. Every evening I envied the lucky prisoner who received the large portion. I could almost feel the weight of the bread in my hands and tried to imagine the feeling of a full stomach. After six days of constant hunger in the French barracks, I was transferred back to the Jewish barracks and the random system of getting bread. I could not believe that I had missed the day of reward in the French barracks, but I kept dreaming of that huge piece that I almost had.

Allied planes began to fly sporadically over the factory at night. They dropped a few bombs, which caused the air-raid sirens to wail.

When the air-raid alarm sounded, the machinery was shut off, and the civilian workers rushed to the underground shelters. Normally, the concentration camp prisoners would not be protected, but the SS guards wanted to take shelter and had to take us along. At the alarm the camp prisoners ran to the shelter entrance, where we lined up and the SS quickly counted us. The SS were eager to get into a shelter quickly and raged at any prisoner who was late for the counting. This put me in a dreadful predicament. I worked high up under the hall ceiling and had to run along the narrow high walkway, climb down the high ladder, and run across the giant hall to the shelter. I arrived panting and breathless but always was the last one there. The other prisoners had been counted, and the SS angrily paced as they waited for me. I was slapped and kicked every time I arrived. I pleaded that I worked high up at the crane and could not get to the shelter any faster. The SS men were angry but luckily did not want to waste much time giving me a beating. Still, the SS were experienced, and it did not take much time to hurt me. The air raids were over within twenty or thirty minutes. The "all clear" would sound, and we would return to work.

The air raids began to happen three or four times each week, usually around midnight. I tried to anticipate the start of the air raids and climbed down from the crane to the floor of the hall sometime before midnight. I would pretend to need to use the toilet but would try to linger by the entrance. This scheme worked sometimes, but at least twice a week I had to race like a crazed monkey to jump and swing down from the high platform, only to arrive late and accept the SS slaps and kicks.

One time the alarm sounded, and I slid down the ladder and ran as fast as I could. I was last at the shelter, and I tried to run in quickly and duck the blows of the SS. As I was running into the formation, the "all clear" sounded. The SS decided to make everyone wait to return to work while they taught me a lesson. I had to stand at attention, facing the other prisoners, while the SS slapped and punched my face. Between the blows of the SS I saw a tall thin Dutchman in the formation of watching prisoners. His jaw was clenched, and his large bony hands were in tight angry fists. Our eyes locked, and I saw his hate for the SS and what they were doing to me. Aroused by the anger in his eyes, I felt a growing rage against the Germans. I stood as the Germans bloodied my nose and bruised and blackened my cheeks and eyes. After a few minutes the blood flowed down my face and jacket, and the Germans did not want to bloody their gloves. We were dismissed back to work.

I climbed back up to the crane control cubicle. My jaw throbbed, and I could feel that my face was grossly swollen. I tried to stem the flow of blood with the sleeve of my jacket. I stood there trembling, cold, and alone, my face full of bruises and tears running down my cheeks. Out of the darkness two women quietly came into the control cubicle. They wore heavy winter clothes and babushkas, Russian kerchiefs around their heads and tied under their chins. In the dim light I looked into friendly and sympathetic eyes. One handed me a cloth to wipe the blood from my face. She motioned that I should sit and rest in an empty corner of the cubicle. I collapsed on the floor, and one woman covered me with her coat. The other stood at the control panel and began to operate the switches that ran the crane. I felt the floor vibrate as the crane swung down. I must have slept on the floor for hours. They shook me gently. My face was aching, and my eyes were swollen into slits. The two women were leaving. I tried to say something, but I could not speak. They smiled at me and disappeared into the darkness. On the floor lay a piece of cloth stained with my blood. I looked down below the crane and saw that the railroad cars had been filled with scrap metal.

It was mid-December 1944. The Germans began to talk and plan for Christmas. Inside the electrified barbed wire fence of the camp, the hunger, suffering, brutality, and pain did not diminish. A prisoner from the Rzeszów group worked as a carpenter in the camp wood shop. He remembered that I could draw and paint. One day he told me that he had spoken to the shop Kapo and arranged for me to work in the carpenter shop for a few hours every afternoon. My job would be to draw pictures on wooden boards that the carpenters would cut out and make into toys for the children of the SS. It was warm in the carpenter shop, and I would get an extra portion of soup. I thanked the

Rzeszów prisoner for remembering me and promised to go to the carpenter shop the next day at noon.

The carpenter shop was a small building standing alone in a corner
of the camp. The Kapo was a master carpenter. Eight other prisoners
were working there when I arrived. The shop was filled with work-
benches, tools, and piles of lumber. A wood-burning stove stood in
one corner. Everyone was busy working, and the shop was warm and
peaceful. The Kapo took me to a workbench piled with wooden boards
and a large carpenter's pencil. He told me to draw pictures of animals
in different sizes. I drew pictures of rabbits, dogs, and roosters. Later
these pictures were cut out, painted, and mounted on wheels. I drew
large ponies that would be made into simple rocking toys. My drawings would be transformed by saw and brush into colorful Christmas
presents for the children of the SS that guarded and beat us. I tried to
visualize the children, blond and pink-cheeked, playing at their father's
knees. I had not been close to a child in years. I thought of Belzec and
Auschwitz, the gas chambers and pits of fire, and that no Jewish children were alive anymore. I hated the German murderers and was angry
at myself for taking an extra portion of soup to make toys for the SS
children. Tears came to my eyes as I sketched the childish pictures and
mourned the innocent Jewish children. The German children would
never know that these toys were stained with Jewish tears.

The Kapo inspected my work and told me to return the next day.
He filled my bowl with soup that I took back to my barracks and shared
with Julek Schipper. He had been working the night shift and was very
ill. He coughed constantly and complained of pains in his chest. We
could do nothing for him, and we knew that if he went to the infirmary, he would never return. He thanked me for the soup, and I
reminded him that we had promised to always treat each other as
brothers. It was painful to watch him suffer in the damp cold barracks,
and I worried about him when we were apart at our jobs.

I continued to work at the carpenter shop, making Christmas toys
for the German children. Two days before Christmas an SS sergeant
came to the shop and asked to see me. He told me to make a colorful
star for the top of the Christmas tree in the SS dining hall. He showed

me with his hands how large it should be. "I need it by tomorrow. Do not make it a four-pointed star—that is just a cross—or a five-pointed star, which is Bolshevik, or a six-pointed Jewish star." I drew an eight-pointed star. A carpenter cut it out and attached a metal clasp to mount it on the Christmas tree. I painted the star in bright colors, and I felt a bitter irony that on that Christmas night, on the other side of the wire fence, the SS guards would sit under my star and sing of peace and holiness, while on this side of the fence they would continue to murder us. The SS sergeant came to the carpenter shop to pick up the star. He gleefully slapped the Kapo on the shoulder and gave each prisoner a cigarette.

"Wonderful news!" he shouted. "Our German armies have won a great battle in Belgium! We are pushing the Americans and the English-men out of Europe!" The SS sergeant liked the star that I made and gave me another cigarette. I found a piece of waxed paper and carefully wrapped up the cigarettes and put them in my pocket. Later I might trade these to a Kapo for some extra bread or soup.

My work in the carpenter shop was finished. I sought out the Jew-ish carpenter and thanked him for getting me the job in his shop. "I was glad to help," he said. "It was a good job, wasn't it?" "Yes," I answered. "I was warm and got extra soup just to draw and paint. I just felt funny making toys for Christmas." "Do not be foolish," he said in Yiddish. "Christmas is the birthday of Jesus. If Jesus lived today, the Germans would gas him like any other Jew."

The winter of 1944–45 was bitter cold. We were stung by the freez-ing winds as we marched to the factory. As cold as I was up high in the big hall, I knew that I was lucky to be indoors. The only clothes that I had were the thin uniform issued at Flossenbürg the previous summer. No coat, underwear, socks, or gloves. I knew that the prisoners laboring in the freezing rain were in worse shape. Even after just a march in the rain to the factory, my soaking clothes froze, and I would secretly remove my shoes in the cubicle for a few minutes and rub the circula-tion back into my feet. I could only hope and pray to survive the winter.

The Hermann Göring Werke factory operated around the clock every day and night, except for Sunday afternoons. That was the only time that we did not work in the factory and could see our friends. It was bad because we had to endure various inspections and selections and do extra jobs that the Kapos and SS found for us. One Sunday in January all the prisoners were inside the camp. The Germans and foreign civilian workers were allowed to leave the factory to go to their homes. The prisoners from the Jewish barracks stood outside waiting for our Kapo to give our Sunday assignments. It was sunny but very cold. I huddled with a group of friends from Tyczyn. We were freezing in our thin summer uniforms. We leaned into each other to turn from the stinging wind and find warmth from each other's bodies. Suddenly, I saw a faint pattern moving across the distant sky. It looked like schools of tiny black fish. They moved in unison, leaving thin white traces and trails. Before I could grasp what I saw, the air-raid sirens wailed through the camp. "Air raid! Air raid!" the prisoners started shouting. They pointed to the distant sky and cried out, "Look, airplanes! Ours! So many coming this way!" I could see the formations of silver planes in the sky. The blasts of anti-aircraft guns sounded from the factory. My eyes beheld a wondrous sight as the planes dropped rows and rows of black bombs. In seconds flashes of explosions burst from the factory. We heard loud booms, and the blue sky was filled with black smoke. The anti-aircraft guns were silent, but the bombs continued to drop and explode. We stood and watched the sky fill with fury and fire. After a while the airplanes flew out of sight, and the factory complex was left with raging fires. We looked about at the chaos as the alarms continued to sound. We dared not show our joy, but I felt tears in my eyes and looked about my group of starving, freezing friends and saw that the pain, misery, and hunger that had deadened our spirits had been replaced with a glimmer of hope.

The Kapo ordered us into the barracks without counting us or conducting an inspection. We were given rations and allowed to go to our bunks. A few prisoners spoke about our future. They worried that we would not be useful to the Germans if the factory was destroyed. I felt my aches and pains again on the hard wooden bunk and wrestled with myself about whether I should save a piece of my bread for an uncertain tomorrow.

· 20 ·

The first snow fell during that night and covered the grounds, barracks, and roads. An icy wind blew the snow into deep drifts. Winter stalked the weak, the hungry, and the ill. We stood in frozen rows during the morning roll call. The snow reached over my old shoes and sank in around my bare ankles. I pulled my cap down over my ears and hoped that the Kapo would not persist in the usual repeated demands for us to remove our caps. An SS guard counted us and moved toward the next barracks. Our Kapo told us that all prisoners would work the daylight hours to clear away rubble in the factory. We would work outdoors in the cold, wind, and snow.

Our Kapo and his assistants led the prisoners from our barracks in a march toward the factory. Other large columns of prisoners were marching toward the gate. The SS were present in larger numbers than I had seen before. At the factory everything in sight was destroyed or severely damaged. Sections of walls and parts of buildings stood, but most roofs had collapsed. The buildings were filled with twisted steel, blasted masonry, and smoldering rubble. The roads between the buildings and the railroad tracks were blocked with rubble, overturned trucks, and derailed railroad cars. Everything was covered with a thick layer of snow. I was overwhelmed that we would have to clear the wreckage with our bare hands in this wintry cold.

Groups of German civilians in high boots, thick long overcoats, and fur hats directed the work. We were divided into smaller groups and assigned to specific jobs. I was with a group of about sixty prisoners ordered to clear a road. We picked up big heavy segments of brick walls and carried them to a vacant lot. We labored for hours in the cold and the snow. I tried to work fast to keep from freezing. I never got warm, only tired quickly. At noon we were given a short break and a small portion of soup. We stood about, stamping our feet, and rubbing our hands to keep from freezing. Soon we were ordered to resume clearing the rubble. I carried cold bricks and stones with my stiff, aching, frozen hands. My shoes were soaked, and I felt pieces of ice form between the wooden soles and my naked feet.

It was dark when we stopped working. The Kapo and SS counted us, and we were marched back to camp. We did not really march; we limped and staggered. Several prisoners could not walk all the way back to the camp, and we carried them among us. At the gate each group of prisoners had to stand and wait until we were counted again. Nothing in the rubble was worth stealing, but the guards, dressed in military winter coats, boots, and fur gloves, stripped down some prisoners and searched them.

In the barracks a fire was burning in the potbellied stove. The soup and bread were distributed at the tables. No one debated the sizes of the bread slices. I was worn out and eager to lie down. I swallowed my bowl of soup, stuck my slice of bread into my jacket, and almost ran to the bunk that I shared with Schipper. He was already lying down. He looked horrible, and his coughing was much worse. I pulled my tattered blanket over my head and quickly fell asleep.

The Kapo awoke us early the next morning with the blast of his whistle. It was dreadful to wake up knowing that I had to face another day in the cold and snow. I was horrified to realize that I had lost a button from my threadbare uniform. My shoes were still wet and cold from the previous day's exposure. We were ordered outside for roll call. In the darkness of the breaking day we marched through the snow to the factory grounds. I was again assigned to dig in the icy rubble with my bare hands and carry bricks. All around me prisoners stumbled and slipped on the icy roads. The SS cursed and yelled for us to work. Sometimes they pushed a prisoner to make him slip and fall while he carried the heavy loads. I thought for sure that this would be the final day for many of us to survive. I was lucky that afternoon. I found a few pieces of torn cloth from the factory blackout curtains. I wrapped some of the rags around my hands and hid a few pieces inside my shirt. In the morning I would use them to wrap my feet inside my shoes.

In the night the dying began. A few prisoners simply did not wake up. At work some picked up a heavy load and just fell down dead in the snow. They were left in the snow until the command to halt work was given. We marched back to camp in the evening, supporting the weak and carrying the dead. Those of us still alive in the barracks urged each other not to give up.

I worked for many days in the freezing cold. I started to feel that I would not be able to keep up for much longer. I had to try anything that I could to get another job that would allow me to preserve my little strength and would get me out of the cold. Many other prisoners working in the rubble had the same idea and tried to volunteer for every alternative job that came up. I would need to be aggressive and even take the risk of being discovered and punished.

Late one afternoon I was trying to move a large piece of rubble. I noticed a broken door on the side of the damaged factory building. From the doorway I looked down a flight of stairs that must have led to a basement or air-raid shelter. I was cold and tired, and I needed to rest. I looked around to make sure that no one was watching. I quickly ducked into the doorway and ran down the cluttered stairs. I came to a large room filled with bricks and broken concrete. I looked around for any rags that I could wear under my clothing. I found nothing of use, but the room gave me shelter from the wind and cold snow. I slumped down against a wall and pulled my arms inside my jacket to try to get warm. I had to stay awake. I had to sneak back out before the march back to camp. If I missed the formation, the Germans would think that I was trying to escape and hang me for sure. I stayed hidden in the basement for several hours. I kept my eye on the light that fell across the staircase and climbed out as the shadows of evening fell. A Kapo saw me step out from the doorway and demanded an explanation. I told him that I went inside to relieve myself. He began to hit me across my back with his club and yelled, "This is a factory, not a latrine, you stupid swine dog!" The pain from his beating was a small price for the hours of rest out of the harsh wind. From then on I looked for any chance to get away from clearing the rubble. I needed to build up a little reserve of strength to go on for another day. Sometimes a Kapo or the SS discovered me, and I was beaten and chased. At other times my ruse worked, and I was able to march back to the camp without the support of other prisoners.

One day I saw a group of prisoners building a brick wall to seal off the corner of a factory building. The workers were sheltered from the wind and snow by the partially built wall. About twenty prisoners were working there. A few men were on the ground, and others stood on ladders, handing bricks up to bricklayers on a scaffold. I walked over and joined the wall-building crew as if I belonged there. I spent the rest of that day handing bricks to another prisoner standing a few rungs above me on a ladder. It was easy and slow work, and I was out of the cold wind. I marched back to camp that evening feeling less tired and physically beaten than I had for many days. The next day I went back to building the wall. I knew what to do and went directly to my position on the ladder. No one questioned me, and I worked all morning. We were given a short break at noon, and sometime that afternoon I looked around and saw close to fifty prisoners building the wall. An SS guard called a Kapo over; the Kapo checked his list and drove away those of us not assigned there. In the commotion I ran off and went back to clearing the rubble.

Another day I saw some Polish and Russian prisoners sitting on the ground behind a pile of fallen bricks. They were using sharp stones to chip away the mortar cemented to the bricks. It looked like easy and quiet work. Without saying anything I sat down and started beating on a brick with a stone. Another prisoner sitting next to me hissed at me through his teeth, "Get away. You do not belong here!" I continued to hammer at the brick. Another threatened, "Get away, you son of a whore, or we will break your neck!" I was not going to leave. "A Kapo sent me," I told him. "Should I tell him you are chasing me away?" One whispered back, "We will get you later, you son of a bitch."

I was there for two or three hours before an SS guard saw us. He ran over, his club swinging and yelled, "I told you not to do this! I chased you away before!" He started hitting us with his club. I could not jump up fast enough to avoid the furious German and took several hits before I could run away. The side of my face was badly battered, and my nose was bleeding. I went back to clearing rubble again.

During the days that followed, the weather worsened. The temperatures were below freezing, and howling winds pushed the falling snow into high drifts. I cleared the rubble and could not find any other work or a chance to turn my face from the stinging winds. I was exhausted and trembling from the cold. I was worried, for many prisoners were falling ill. Prisoners who had been strong and hardy turned into gaunt skeletons. Dozens of prisoners died every day at work and in the camp. I kept telling myself that I would not give up, that I was young and strong, that I would survive, that spring would come and things would be easier. I tried to carry smaller pieces of mortar when the Kapo's back was turned, to walk slowly when I could, to brace myself against the cold. A few times I sneaked through the same shattered door and down into the basement storage room. It was cold there too, and the snow had blown in through the doorway and covered the floor and stairs. I would clear the snow from a corner of the floor and sit and shiver and try to convince myself that it was still better than being on the street above. Then one day a Kapo caught me coming out. He hit me a few times and took down my number. He shouted, "I will report you to the SS as a slacker and saboteur, you lazy swine dog!" He hit me as he chased me to a large truck where prisoners were unloading big sacks of cement. Two prisoners stood on the truck and put a cement sack on the back of a prisoner, who then carried the sack about three hundred feet to a wooden hut. "This is what I want you to do!" the Kapo shouted. "I will keep an eye on you!"

I got in line with the other men waiting for their load. When my turn came, the men placed the sack high on my shoulders, and my knees buckled. I staggered under the heavy weight of the cement sack. The Kapo watched me, and I had to carry the sacks from the truck to the hut many times. It was getting dark when the prisoners placed a sack on my shoulders, and my knees gave way. I fell on my face with the sack on top of me. Other prisoners lifted the sack off me, and the

Kapo had them drag me to the side of the road where they dropped me in the snow. I lay in the soft snow and thought that this was the end, that I would close my eyes and die. For a moment I did not care. I no longer felt the cold or wind or the melting snow inside my leaking shoes. It was so simple and so peaceful to give up, to accept the giving up and no longer struggle. In that moment I remembered my parents' sacrifice and that my brother was waiting for me. I felt the urging of the people who had helped me along the way and the luck that had kept me from the gun and the gas chamber. I had no right to give up when everywhere the fight was to live. I raised myself from the snow and stood. The Kapo looked over at me but then turned away to deal with the other prisoners. It was getting dark, and the prisoners would soon march back to the camp. I stood alone and afraid to move without the Kapo's orders. The prisoners began to line up, and I made my way over and joined the formation. The Kapo ignored me. He probably thought my life was nearly finished anyway. In the barracks I drank the foul soup and chewed on a piece of bread. I climbed onto my bunk and was soon asleep. I dreamed of my mother and that she asked me to live and grow up to be a mensch.

I started to have horrible pains in my mouth and around my teeth. My gums were swollen and spongy. They bled all the time. My teeth felt wobbly and loose. Some of my teeth started to fall out, which made it harder to chew the tough stale bread. I did not know why this was happening, and I could do nothing to ease the pain and bleeding. Then my left hip started feeling stiff and sore every morning after I climbed out of my bunk. In the beginning I would rub and massage my hips and legs until the stiffness went away and the ache lessened. But soon the pain persisted, and my hips hurt throughout the day. I tossed and turned and moaned in my bunk at night, as did most of the prisoners.

Another day started badly. In the morning I found out that another prisoner I knew from the Reichshof camp had died during the night. At work the day before, one of the five prisoners carrying a heavy wooden beam with me suddenly fell down and lay on the dirty ice and snow even while the Kapo kicked and stepped on him. I was cold and tired, and it was only morning. My mouth hurt, and I was spitting out blood. My left hip hurt with every step. I was assigned to carry large pieces of wood with another prisoner. I saw a small group of prisoners sitting on the ground with a pile of broken boards before a roaring fire. Some were pulling nails out of the boards. Others were then straightening the nails by hammering them against flat stones. I had to join them if only for a short time and even if I would be beaten afterward. Instead of carrying the wood to the junk pile across the road, I took it to the woodpile by the fire and sat down. I picked up a board with nails, took a stone, and started knocking the nails out of the board. The heat of the fire warmed every inch and bone of my body. I put my feet in my soaking shoes close to the flames. I kept battering at the nails. The other prisoners glanced at me but remained silent as they worked. Maybe a half hour passed. An assistant Kapo from my barracks came near the fire and took off his gloves to warm his hands. He reached into his pockets and took out a stump of a cigarette. He leaned over and lit it from the fire. He looked around, and as he saw me a puzzled and stern look came over his face. I knew that he could order me back to the rubble. He took another puff on his cigarette. I stood up and carefully took out the two cigarettes I had earned in the carpenter shop before Christmas and still carried, waiting for a moment like this. "I see that you smoke, Mister Kapo," I said. I unrolled the waxed paper and offered the cigarettes to him. "I do not need these. Do you want them?" He looked surprised. "Why?" he said. "In the camp you can sell them for soup." "Yes," I answered. "But I was hoping that maybe you would remember me when you need another *Kessel* [kettle] washer. My name is Singer, Josef Singer. I am in your barracks."

"Maybe, maybe," he said as he took the two cigarettes. "But only for a week or so." "Thank you, Mister Kapo," I answered as I sat back down near the fire. He put the cigarettes in his pocket and walked away. I stayed by the fire for several hours. I hammered on the nails with the stone and stayed warm.

Just before the noon break for soup, our Kapo came over to the fire. He put his club down, turned his back to the flames, and rocked on his heels. I dropped my head down low and kept banging with the stone. "You there, lazy dog!" he shouted at me. "You do not belong

here! Get back to the rubble! Immediately! Before I show you something!" I stood up and went back to the rubble. My shoes were warm
but still wet. The cold wind again blew through my tattered uniform.

The next week the assistant Kapo called out my name in the barracks. "Singer. Starting tomorrow, you will work as one of the kettle
washers. For maybe ten days. I expect that our Kapo will bring someone
else for the job in a week or two, but in the meantime you will have it.
You know what to do?" "Yes, and thank you very much, Mister Kapo," I
answered. He looked me over and said, "You do not look well. Are you
strong enough to carry a full kettle of soup?" "Yes, Mister Kapo, I can do
it," I assured him. "Good. You start tomorrow," he said and walked away.

I was overjoyed. I ran to tell Julek Schipper. He was sitting on our
bunk waiting for the evening soup and bread. He was coughing and
looked horrible. But then no one in the barracks looked well anymore.
I told him that I had gotten the kettle washer job for a while and that I
should get extra soup for us. He was cheered but said that I looked too
thin and should eat the extra soup myself and give him only what was
left over. I was heartened by his words and became even more resolved
to share every drop with him.

To work as one of the four kettle washers was every hungry prisoner's dream. The evening soup was brought to the barracks in six or eight
covered kettles. Each was about two feet high and carried by the big side
handles. During the meal two kettle washers held a kettle for the Kapo
to ladle soup from. The other kettle washers stood ready with the next
kettle and brought it to the Kapo when the first was empty. The four
kettle washers were given soup after everyone else was fed. Our job was
to wash the kettles in the washroom. And the kettles were not really
empty. The Kapo's ladle was shaped like a large flat bowl and did not
scrape out all the soup from the bottom. Enough remained in each to
fill a bowl, and it was the thickened soup that coated the bottom of the
kettle. The extra soup was enough to help a prisoner recover his strength,
build a little reserve, and to help a friend.

I worked as the kettle washer for a week. Every evening I had an
extra bowl of thick soup to share with Julek. For the first time in years
I did not go to sleep starving. I could save my slice of bread for the

morning and was stronger to tolerate the hard work and the cold. For a bit of the soup I bought a vest from another prisoner that was made from an empty paper sack. It was stiff and tight but helped keep out the cold wind. This was a good week for me. I knew that the job would not last long, but in the meantime I relished my good fortune.

On a Sunday afternoon, the only hours of daylight during the week when we did not work, we were waiting outside the barracks for the Kapo to let us in. I was walking by the side of our barracks when I heard a croaking angry voice call out to me. "Lucek, you ungrateful son of a bitch, I hope you die!" Surprised, I turned to see who was saying such hateful words to me. Sitting in the snow against a fence, his cheeks sunken, his eyes red and swollen, his face burning with both illness and hate, was a vaguely familiar prisoner, seemingly young and at the same time terribly aged. The prisoner looked at me with a terrible, crazy anger and muttered, "Yes, you, Lucek, you ungrateful murderer. You have all the food that you want. You eat and stuff yourself with soup but do not repay your debts to those who saved your life. You should die. I curse you. You should die." I did not know who this prisoner was and why he hated me so. To survive I had done some selfish things in the camps but not anything that deserved such anger and hate. I looked more closely at the muttering, cursing, sick man and suddenly I knew who he was. He was the strong and kind young man from Nowy Sacz, my friend who helped me and carried me when I was so sick and so disabled by the injury to my knee, way back in the Reichshof camp. He was my friend from Nowy Sacz. I bent down to him and tried to interrupt his mumbling. "No, no. Do not say that. Please do not say that," I pleaded. "I do not have all the food that I want, and I did not know that you were so sick." He kept repeating, "You ungrateful boy, you ungrateful dog. I curse you. I curse you." And I kept pleading, "Please do not say that. Please." The doors to the barracks opened. The Kapo was letting us in. I had to go in right away to be there when the kitchen wagon brought the kettles of soup. I said to my friend from Nowy Sacz, "I am sorry that I did not know that you were so sick. Please. This evening I will bring you soup. I promise." As I ran to the barracks door, I heard him calling, "I curse you, I curse you."

That evening after the kettles were washed, I went looking for my friend from Nowy Sacz. I carried half a bowl of soup, my share of the take after I divided it with Julek. I could not find him anywhere, and no one knew where he was. Finally, I went outside to look where I had seen him last. Yes, he was there, half-sitting and half-lying in the snow. "I have soup for you," I said. When I got closer, I saw that his eyes were open and he was dead. I went back into the barracks, sat down at one of the tables, and started eating the half bowl of soup. But it tasted bitter, and I could not swallow it. I gave it to a prisoner I knew from Tyczyn. He was surprised and most grateful. I was too upset that I had been too late to help my friend and rescuer from Nowy Sacz.

One evening I held the kettle, and as the Kapo ladled out the soup, he told me that he did not need me anymore as a kettle washer. I pleaded with him to let me continue. I told him that I carried the kettles well and washed them very clean. I pleaded with him that I was recovering from a sickness and needed the extra food from the empty kettles. "No!" he told me roughly. "This is your last day! Now shut your mouth and leave me alone." That was it. My job as kettle washer had lasted for twelve days.

At the destroyed factory I worked outdoors again, clearing the mounds of rubble. Working hard in the cold and again hungry all the time, I was quickly back to my state of exhaustion and weakness. My legs and arms did not function well, and I could not lift or carry much or walk very far. I felt like an old, weak, and sick man. My feet had swollen badly, and my old leaky shoes were now too tight to hold both my swollen feet and the rag wrappings that I used to keep my feet from freezing. At first I tried to stretch my shoelaces but only succeeded in breaking them. In camp this was a desperate problem, for there were no laces or string to be found. I had to keep my shoes from falling off, especially during the marches, when the SS would not let you stop and pick up a lost shoe. Another prisoner suggested that I use wire to keep the shoes laced. On the way to work I shuffled to keep my loose shoes from falling off. I found wire in the rubble and managed to break off small pieces to hold my shoes closed. I still could not fit my swollen feet and the wrappings into the shoes. I dreaded pulling the tight, wet, and cold shoes on my bare, swollen, and sore feet.

I looked to get away from the hard work of lugging shattered mortar and lumber through the cold and snow. One day I succeeded in joining a group of prisoners who were pulling thick electric cables through tight underground ducts. The ducts were narrow, dark, and filthy, and the cable was thick and heavy. I spent most of that day inside the ducts, protected from the cold, wind, and snow.

The conditions in the camp were deteriorating. The food was getting worse. The soup was like water; the bread seemed to be made of sawdust as well as dark flour. A plague of lice was everywhere. They were in my shorn hair, on my body, in my clothing, in my blanket, in my bed. I tried to shake them out, sweep them out, to kill them. They tortured me with thousands of bites and an unending itching that nothing could stop or cure. Worst of all, their attacks kept me awake during the nights, robbing me of sleep, my only escape from the cruel reality of my life.

Many prisoners were now afflicted with the loss of hope. They simply gave up trying to resist and survive. They were the muselmen. They wandered about in a state of delirium, uninterested in food or warmth, not caring about the shouts and blows of the Kapos and the SS. They lived only for a day or two and just fell dead. I kept promising myself that I would not become a muselman. But in my heart I was unsure. At roll calls in the mornings and in the evenings the SS and Kapos counted the living and the dead. We, the living, stood shivering in the cold, forming tight formations in the hope of sharing a little body heat. The dead lay in frozen rows, their mouths and eyes open toward the sky. They were free of the SS and the Kapos, the cold, hunger, and misery. We were still alive, still cold and hungry, fearful, and suffering. I had become insensitive to death. The dead foretold what awaited me in another day or another week. My thoughts did not turn to the prisoners' families, waiting and praying for them somewhere in Norway, Poland, or France. I was more interested in their stained uniforms and old shoes and made silent, secret plans to switch my torn rags and leaking shoes with those no longer needed by the dead.

Most factory roads were free of rubble and wreckage, and we started to clear the debris from inside the bombed-out buildings. We loaded debris on trucks parked near the buildings. Inside a building Julek Schipper found a packet of official German food ration cards. He was clever and brave enough to approach a Polish civilian driving a truck and arrange to trade some ration cards for bread. He shared the bread, which gave us both the strength to go on for a few more days. I had helped my friend Julek when I could, and now at a critical time he was helping me. The extra bread helped Julek to improve his physical condition somewhat, but he was still very sick. The camp hospital was crowded with sick and dying prisoners and had no space for him. We knew that few prisoners accepted into the hospital lived for more than a few days. The SS now used the hospital as a means to dispose of prisoners no longer able to work.

Because so many prisoners had died, the Kapos transferred other prisoners into our barracks. They now sat at the tables with us and slept in the vacant bunks. So many prisoners were dying that for a while some prisoners had a bunk to themselves. Sleeping with Julek had become impossible. He coughed continuously and tossed and turned. He lay awake and complained of pains in his chest. I thought that it would be better for us both if I found another bunk to sleep in. I saw that Hafferflock, my old friend from the Reichshof camp, was sleeping alone. I asked him if I could share the bunk with him, and he was glad, for he expected the Kapo to assign some sick muselman stranger to his bunk. Hafferflock was about nineteen, from Dębica or Przemyśl, and had been a nice friendly young man. Now he was as hungry, tired, cold, lice-ridden, and as close to death as any of us.

Hafferflock worked in my group, carrying rubble out of buildings and loading it on trucks. A few days after I started bunking with him, he collapsed at work and had to be helped back to the camp. That evening in the barracks I told him that he needed rest and that I would sleep with Julek again that night. "No, Lucek. Please, stay tonight," he asked. "I feel bad and I do not want to be alone. Please stay with me." "Good. If you want me to, I will sleep here," I said. "But do not worry about what happened today. You will feel stronger tomorrow. This happened to me not long ago." I took off my shoes and wrapped them in my jacket to use as a pillow and to keep them from being stolen. I climbed into the bunk, covered myself with my part of the shabby blanket, and tried to sleep. But Hafferflock continued to talk. "You know, Lucek. I have strange dreams lately," he whispered. "About mezuzahs."

"Mezuzahs?" I answered. "That is crazy. If I dream, it is about huge bowls of thick hot potato soup."

"No, no," he said. "I dream about living in a house with a mezuzah on the doorpost."

"Why? Don't you feel Jewish enough here? You need a mezuzah?" I said. "Go to sleep—you need rest and not to worry about mezuzahs."

"You do not understand," Hafferflock insisted. "Placing a mezuzah on your door is more than a religious obligation. It means that one is not afraid to be Jewish, that it is safe for everyone to know that you are a Jew. This is what I wish for, what I dream about."

I understood. He was right. But now we both needed to sleep. "Do not worry," I said. "One day you and I will live in houses with mezuzahs on the doorposts. Now go to sleep."

"You think so? You really believe that?" he asked in a weak, child-like voice.

"Yes, I believe it will happen. I promise," I said. "Now go to sleep."

"You promise?" he asked, sounding very young and very desperate.

"Yes, I promise. I promise," I answered. He sighed and turned his back to me. I was asleep in minutes. I awoke in the night and felt that something was not right. I quickly realized that Hafferflock was still, not scratching or moaning. I reached out to touch him. He was cold and not breathing. Hafferflock was dead.

I lay next to him until daylight came, and the Kapo blew the morning whistle. The lights were turned on. I looked over at Hafferflock in the narrow bunk that we shared. His thin bony body, shaved head, and scarred hands told of his suffering. I knew that the Kapo would order us to drag his body outside to the roll call yard. The dead were still counted with the living to ensure that no prisoners were missing. Then later, while we were at work clearing the bombed factory, his body would be taken to the crematorium and burned. His ashes would be dumped into the river or thrown to the wind.

At work the pulling, carrying, and lifting of rubble continued. Each day was marked by increased abuse by impatient and angry SS and the vicious Kapos. More prisoners collapsed and died in the snow. During the weeks after the bombing, many Reichshof Jews died. We did not realize how weak and vulnerable we were, how limited the margin of our endurance. Each morning we had more dead bodies to carry out to the roll call yard. Each night we had to carry bodies back from the factory to the camp. So many died, and so many were dying. I saw it all around me, and I was frightened. I forced myself to wash, to find buttons for my clothes, to guard that my shoes were not stolen. I clung to the hope that warm weather would arrive, that I would find easier work, that by some miracle I would find a way to get more food. I kept telling myself that Manek was waiting for me. I did not want to die. I was afraid to become a muselman. I did not want my body thrown in a pile in the snow and then burned like garbage. "I will not become a muselman," I kept saying to myself. "Not I. Not I."

My condition was getting worse. The millions of lice kept me up for hours every night. I was always tired and sleepy. I was less alert and found myself falling asleep on my feet. One evening I marched back to the camp, and I began to hallucinate. Next to the road was a muddy and snow-covered field. But I saw a huge pile of straw-filled mattresses, all plump and fluffy. There was a small, dark opening in the side of the mountain of mattresses. I felt myself run to the mattresses and crawl through the opening. I stretched out on a mattress, and other mattresses covered me. I was hidden and safe here in the warm darkness. No one could see me. I was happy and carefree. I could rest and sleep. I wanted to stay here forever. I closed my eyes and slept. Something began to wake me, to annoy me. Something was shoving me on my right side. I tried to ignore it, but I could not. Something was hitting me again and again.

I opened my eyes, and a burly SS guard was kicking me in my ribs. He screamed, "Get up, you filthy dog! Right now! Or I will shoot you!" I was lying in the snow. He kicked me again, but I could not move. Two prisoners pulled me up. I was disoriented and could not walk. They supported me and dragged me back to the camp. Some Jewish prisoners from Tyczyn and Rzeszów helped me get from the camp gate to the barracks. They sat me at the table and made me drink my soup.

Motek Hoffstetter came and sat by me. He looked like a skeleton in his uniform. "Motek," I whispered. "Motek, I do not know what is happening to me. I am afraid. I do not have the strength to make it." He leaned over and shook his fist at me. "Do not give up, Lucek! You must try! You are young, and the war cannot last much longer. We must survive to tell the world what they did to us!"

"Does the world care?" I asked. "I will try. I will try." I stood, and Julek helped me walk to my bunk.

"Get some sleep," he said. "You will be better tomorrow."

I slept through the night. I did not feel the pain in my side from the SS kicks or the constant bites of the lice. In the morning I drank the substitute coffee and ate a slice of bread that Julek had saved for me from the evening. I was weak and unsteady but strong enough to walk outside without help. At roll call the weather seemed milder. It must have been March 1945. At work I was tired and worried. I kept telling myself to stay alert. I tried to convince myself that I could make it. I remembered the words of my friends in the barracks the previous night, but deep in my heart I had already begun to lose hope. I was becoming a muselman.

A few days later, standing in roll call, we heard faint explosions. Was it artillery fire or the bombing of Braunschweig? We whispered among our ranks, but no one could really know. The Kapo ordered us to return to the barracks. We stood by the doorway and looked to the skies for planes, but none came. That day the SS did not march us to the factory. No one told us why. The next day the SS ordered us out of the barracks. Many prisoners were dead in the bunks or too weak and sick to move. The prisoners who could still stand were given an extra ration of bread and marched to the nearby railroad siding. The sick, the muselmen, and the dying were left behind. Boxcars were waiting for us. The SS crowded us into the boxcars and slid the doors shut. Another miserable journey would begin. I could no longer stand. I moved to the back and slumped down to the floor.

✦ 21 ✦

The train traveled for three or four long and miserable days. Many prisoners died during the trip and lay among us in the boxcar. The crowding, stench, and our thirst were unbearable. At one stop we heard the familiar shouts and whips of the Germans as the doors were unlatched and the prisoners were driven out. It was night. We jumped to the ground and left the dead in the boxcar. The railroad siding was surrounded with barbed wire fences. Dim electric lights were mounted on the tall wooden posts of the wire fence. The SS arranged us in a formation. They did not count us but gave the command to march, and we started off through the dark corridors of barbed wires. After several minutes we came to a gate. The weak lamps cast a faint light on a big mound next to the gate. As I got closer, I realized that it was an immense pile of human bones and skulls.

The gate swung open, and our formation passed the pile of bones. I was entering the gates of hell. I remembered and understood Dante's words in my mother's book: "Abandon all hope, ye who enter here." A prisoner mumbled that we were in the concentration camp called Ravensbrück.

We were marched to a small primitive camp with one row of barracks on a wet sandy lot. We saw no administrative buildings, kitchen, or medical facilities, workers, trees, or even grass. The Kapos randomly assigned us to barracks and then assigned two prisoners to each wooden bunk. The barracks were shabby, small, and crowded. In the rush and confusion I was separated from Motek and Julek. They were sent to another barracks. Emil Ringel, another old friend from the Reichshof camp, was with me, and we agreed to share a bunk. I had learned to always cling to friends I could trust and not to rely on strangers. I could count on Emil Ringel, and he could rely on me. In all except the most desperate circumstances, we would not steal each other's shoes.

It was still night, and we were permitted to lie down for a while. At dawn the Kapos and assistants drove us out of the barracks with shouts and sticks. There was no roll call, and we were allowed to walk around or just lie down on the sandy ground. The weather was mild. Many prisoners were in terrible shape and staggered around until they fell to the ground. The Kapos were meeting in a barracks and left us alone. I was starving and wanted to know when we would be given some food. I asked some prisoners from another barracks. The Kapo had told them that we would be fed soup at noon and a slice of bread in the evening. Noon was still six hours away. I walked about the small camp. I discovered that our train had also carried Jewish prisoners from another camp. We were actually in a small subcamp of Ravensbrück, the largest German concentration camp for women. I saw women in striped prison dresses working beyond the barbed wire fences. Some looked over at us. A few waved. We must have been a sad and pitiful sight, a group of skeletal men, stumbling and falling down, looking sick and ready to die. I looked at the women watching us and hoped that they felt pity.

At noon women prisoners brought kettles of soup. SS guards forbade us to speak to the women. They unloaded the kettles and left. The Kapos ordered us into the barracks. Many prisoners lying on the ground did not get up to go into the barracks. They were dead or too weak to stand, and the Kapos just left them lying there. Inside the barracks we were lined up at the door, given a bowl of rancid soup, and then sent back outside. Those prisoners who remained outside were not fed.

In the afternoon the women prisoners returned with a wagon filled with baskets of bread. The women unloaded the baskets, collected the empty kettles, and left. The Kapos and assistants carried the baskets into the barracks. The prisoners had to wait outside. After a while the Kapos ordered us into lines outside the door. The bread had been sliced and set on a table by the door. Each prisoner was given a slice as he went inside. The process was slow but orderly. After nearly half the prisoners had received bread, some made a sudden rush toward the table. The basket was overturned, and the slices spilled into the sand. The Kapo raised his hands in disgust and went into the barracks with the empty basket. Outside there was a desperate fight as the prisoners fell upon the bread lying in the sand. I snatched a piece from another skeletal prisoner who tried to run off with several slices. A few prisoners grabbed two or more slices, some got only one, but many prisoners got no bread at all.

I found out that the same thing happened at some of the other barracks. Prisoners made a sudden rush for the basket, bread was thrown to the ground, and a scuffle erupted among the crazed prisoners. I was sure that the Kapos had a hand in the disaster. The next day Emil Ringel and I made sure that we were at the front of the bread line. We got our slices and were inside the barracks when the prisoners again rushed at the basket and spilled the bread. I was near the door and saw it happen. I thought that I recognized the prisoners rushing the basket as the table leaders back in the Ukrainian barracks in Braunschweig.

I had been in camps a long time and understood the tricks and crimes that selfish and desperate prisoners used to gain an advantage. The Kapos and assistants probably stole many loaves before they sliced the rest. Staging the rush on the basket and the spilling hid the fact that there was not enough bread for everyone. I told Ringel what I saw and thought, and he agreed. We also figured out that the stolen bread must be hidden in our barracks.

After the lights were turned out that night, Emil Ringel and I watched as a prisoner from the bunk above us left and quickly returned with something that he stuffed under the straw on his bunk. He climbed down again and then returned to push something more under the straw. He left again and did not come back. "He is an assistant Kapo," Emil whispered. "What do you think he is hiding?" "I do not know," I answered. "Can you touch it?" Emil reached up and pushed his fingers through the slats of the bunk and into the straw. "What is it?" I asked. "It feels like bread," Emil whispered. We knew that we would steal the bread. It was dangerous, but bread meant life, and our lives were already filled with danger and death. "Get it," I said to Emil. "Then I will hide it outside so that he cannot blame us." Emil got the bread and gave it to me. It was wrapped in paper and felt like half a loaf. I climbed out and quietly went out of the barracks. Outside I saw bodies on the ground. I walked between our barracks and the next and quickly dug a hole in the sandy ground. I buried the bread between two bodies. I struggled to pull the bodies over the hole and memorized the spot where the bread lay hidden. I went back into the barracks and climbed next to Emil. The assistant Kapo must have returned after I had fallen asleep. I was awakened when the barracks' lights were turned on, and the Kapo and assistants began shouting threats and searching bunks. No bread was found.

The next day Emil and I dug up the bread that I had buried under the bodies. I could tell from the prison uniforms that one of the dead was Jewish and the other Norwegian. We sat next to the bodies and secretly ate the bread. That evening we stood at the front of the bread line and again got our slice before the rush and spilled baskets. That night we waited for the same assistant Kapo to hide bread under his bunk. He went to sleep without hiding anything. There would be no more extra bread for us. The half loaf that we got was a few days' worth of nourishment. It helped keep us alive as prisoners were starving and dying all around us.

One afternoon I was wandering around outside the barracks, waiting for the bread line to form. I passed a barracks window and saw the reflection of a face in the dirty glass, a familiar prisoner who looked like a muselman with sunken eyes, hollow cheeks, broken teeth, a skinny neck, and shaved head. I turned to see who was standing beside me, but no one was there. I was looking at myself.

I despaired. I had sworn to myself and tried so hard not to become a muselman, and now I could see that it was too late. I opened my jacket and lifted my shirt. My body was thin and wasted. My ribs stuck out under my skin. My legs were scrawny, and my knees were bigger than my thighs. I was scared, and I ran to find friends who would tell me that I did not look as bad as I thought. But when I looked at Julek Schipper, Motek Hoffstetter, Emil Ringel, and the other prisoners from Tyczyn and Rzeszów, I saw that they also looked like muselmen.

We had been in Ravensbrück for a few days. We were given little food, and sometimes we did not get our slices before the breadbasket was overturned. I knew that I was starving. I watched as other prisoners began to die in larger numbers. They did not seem ill or in pain. They just lay on their bunks in the evening or on the ground during the day and quietly died. The rotting corpses were not collected or moved, just left all over the grounds for us to walk around or stumble over. I went on living among the dead and dying, aware that any day could be my last. I still tried to be at the front of the bread line, still washed myself as I could, and got as much rest in the sun as possible. I made sure not to look at my reflection in the barracks windows.

The SS ordered that certain prisoners be transferred to specific barracks according to their nationality. All the Jewish prisoners were put into two small barracks. We felt more comfortable and safer sharing the barracks with other Jews. The next day all the prisoners were ordered to stay inside the barracks. The SS surrounded the Jewish barracks and ordered us outside and into formation. They counted us, and a sergeant inspected our ranks. He sent the sickest and weakest prisoners back into the barracks and told the rest of us that we were being sent to another camp. I was greatly distressed. I knew that being singled out as Jews and separated from other prisoners was dangerous.

The SS marched us out of the camp and toward a hangar-size warehouse. We were ordered to go quickly through the building in two lines. I was amazed to see the warehouse filled up to the ceiling with thousands of cardboard boxes marked with the symbol of the Red Cross. Some were torn open and full of metal cans and cellophane packages. The sergeant stood among the boxes and said, "These are American Red Cross boxes with food and provisions. You can take as many as you can carry. Quickly! You have a few seconds!"

It was unbelievable. I reached for a large box and discovered that I was not strong enough to lift it. I reached for a smaller box. I could lift it but not carry it. I put the box down and broke it open. I took out some cans, but the box was still too heavy to carry. I took out the rest of the cans. I cradled the box in my arms and went out of the warehouse. Prisoners were already outside. Some were carrying the smaller boxes, while others had filled their pockets and hands with cans and packages of food. A few of the weaker prisoners carried one small package or nothing at all. Some prisoners started tearing into the packages and stuffing food into their mouth. It looked like crackers and chunks of cheese. I was impatient to dig into the box but did not dare put it down.

We walked in formation to boxcars at a siding nearby. The Germans loaded us into the boxcars slowly and put only about forty men in each car, less than half the usual number. The Germans did not shout or hit us, and we took the Red Cross packages with us. Inside the boxcar I leaned against the wall and dug into my package. It was full of wonderful things. I found crackers and cookies, small bars of yellow and brown cheese, chocolate, and dried fruit. I also found a pack of cigarettes and a small box of matches. I devoured the crackers and some cheese, chewed some dried fruit, and ate a chunk of chocolate. The delicious foods with long-forgotten flavors were like a dream. I wanted to eat everything, and yet I wanted to save it all. Someone cried out in amazement that his Red Cross box had the word *kosher* written on it. He held it up for us all to see. We shook our heads in disbelief. It was beyond my imagination that anyone cared enough about Jews to include kosher food.

The boxcar doors were closed, and the train started moving. It moved slowly, and we made many stops. This trip was different from the others. We had our Red Cross food packages and space in the boxcar to lie down. At many of the longer stops the SS opened the doors, letting in fresh air and sometimes even allowing us outside for a few minutes. The SS guards were restrained. They did not curse or beat us. I was happy but also concerned. I had learned that unexplained changes were more likely to lead to bad ends than good. In the semidarkness of the boxcar someone spoke in Yiddish. "This is nice, but what is happening? What does it mean? Have the SS changed so suddenly?" "The

SS would not change that easily," another responded. "They must have a plan and reasons for this. And when the SS have a plan, Jews should worry." This conversation went on for much of the journey.

Our train stopped at the siding of a busy railroad station. Through the open boxcar doors I saw trains full of German soldiers passing by. At one point an army train carrying wounded German soldiers came to a stop on the rail line next to ours. We were only about fifteen feet from their train, and I could see them clearly. The soldiers' heads and arms were covered with bloody bandages. They were young but looked tired and beaten. I hated the Germans and all they stood for: arrogance, cruelty, and murder. I looked at these wounded soldiers and saw that they were broken and defeated. I was glad to see their suffering, which was not punishment enough. Maybe payback was coming.

On the second day our train stopped at a siding in the middle of nowhere. The boxcar doors were opened, and with SS guards posted on both sides of the train, we were allowed to get out, move around, or even talk to prisoners in other boxcars. My left hip hurt again. I got out and slowly walked over to the next car to speak to friends from the Reichshof camp. They were uneasy with the different way that we were being treated. We had no answers. I went back to sit and rest in my boxcar. A gaunt sickly prisoner from our boxcar repeated a rumor. "The people in the boxcar behind us say the Germans will hand us over to the Swedish Red Cross in exchange for German officers and diplomats." "The Swedish Red Cross?" an older prisoner asked doubtfully. "Who told them that?"

"No one is sure," said the prisoner who had repeated the rumor. "But someone said that it came from an SS guard."

"I do not believe it," another prisoner said. "And if it came from the SS, I do not believe it at all. The Germans would rather shoot us than hand us to the Swedes."

Other prisoners brought back the same rumor. A discussion ensued between the committed pessimists and the less pessimistic. There were no optimists. I tried to find and hold onto a tiny spark of hope that maybe the behavior of the SS did foretell something good. I needed that little hope to go on.

In the afternoon a bucket of water and a latrine bucket were put in our boxcar. The doors were closed, and the train started moving again. I sat in the darkness and thought about the rumors. No, I did not believe it. I remembered the story of the abandoned Ukrainian farm that they had told us about in the Rzeszów ghetto. I remembered the promise and the lie and thought about my parents in Belzec.

I woke up before morning. Our train was not moving. It was dark outside and pitch black inside the boxcar. I rubbed my sore hip. I felt around to make sure that my nearly empty Red Cross box was next to me. I felt for the cigarettes and matches and put them in my jacket pocket.

◆ 22 ◆

I awoke to the noise of the boxcar doors as they opened. I heard the angry, shrill German voices outside the boxcar. "Out! Out! Fast! Fast!" the voices commanded. "Out! You stinking damned Jewish swine!" I tumbled out of the boxcar into the harsh daylight. We were at a railroad siding between two rows of tall barbed wire fences. Armed SS guards and Kapos were yelling and striking out with rubber truncheons. This was what I should have expected. Gone were the dreams of Sweden and rescue. The terror had not ended.

The Kapos lined us up in front of the boxcars, and the SS counted us. They ordered us to drop everything to the ground except our soup bowls. I dropped my Red Cross box. The cigarettes and matches were still in my pocket. A gate in the fence swung open, someone shouted orders, and we marched into the camp. The camp looked small and was surrounded by double barbed wire fences and guard towers. Weeds grew waist high on the swampy ground, and the air was filled with dense gray smoke. Gaunt and sickly prisoners dressed in tattered uniforms sat or lay on the ground or leaned against the dingy barracks. Rotting corpses lay in heaps, and the stench of death was heavy in the air.

A Kapo marched us to two unfinished buildings in the center of the camp and told us that these were our barracks. The buildings had rough brick walls and a tin roof. They had no windows and no door, just an opening that served as a doorway. Inside, the building was barren. It had no flooring, just the dirty ground. It had no bunks, tables, straw, or blankets. There was no need to claim a place in the barracks.

The building was empty, dirty, and wet. I saw Julek Schipper sitting on the ground across the room. He did not look well. I went over and sat down next to him. "Julek, I am glad that we are together," I said. "I am sorry that we were in different boxcars. How do you feel?"

"I do not feel well, Lucek." His voice was filled with pain. "My stomach and chest hurt. I tried to eat some of the Red Cross food, but I vomited everything out. I do not think that I can last more than a few days."

I looked at him and knew that he was right. But I could not let him believe that. There was always hope. "No, Julek, do not think that way," I said. "I have known you for a long time, and I know how tough you are. You do not look that bad. No worse than the rest of us. Do not give up. You will feel better after you rest." I said these things to my friend Julek, as I said them to myself. "Can I do something for you?" I asked.

"I do not know if you can get it, but I would like some hot water to drink," he said.

"Let me try," I answered and went out of the barracks.

The conditions in this camp were primitive and worse than any camp that I had been in. Piles of dead bodies and prisoners on the verge of death were everywhere. I was weary of trying to fight death. My strength and my health were waning, and I felt that this camp would destroy me. The haunting reflection of me in the window returned with a brutal force, and I knew that I was a muselman. It was not hope that I was losing, for I had not enough hope left to hang on to, but the faith that struggle and hope made any difference. I knew how dangerous my despair could be and told myself that. For the moment I did not give up, but the doubts remained, like monsters waiting at the edge of a bad dream.

Life in this camp had no order or purpose. No prisoners worked, no one gave commands, and no one cared about the ill and dying. Skeletal prisoners from many nations stood idly near the unfinished barracks. Others sat or lay on the muddy ground or wandered around aimlessly. A few prisoners built small fires from twigs and branches. Some prisoners were cooking something in their metal soup bowls and rusty cans. I asked some prisoners who were lying on the ground about this camp. They told me the camp was called Wöbbelin and that it did not have any sanitary or medical facilities, that the camp construction was not finished. Worse, they said that the prisoners were not fed every day. I asked them if I could get a little hot water for a sick friend. One said that I might be able to heat water in my soup bowl at one of the small fires if I had something to trade. I kept the pack of cigarettes inside my pocket as I opened it and took one out. I approached some prisoners at a small fire, showed them the cigarette, and asked for some hot water. They wanted three cigarettes, but I told them that I had only one, and they agreed to let me use the fire. I got a bowl full of water from the washroom, returned, and put my bowl on some bricks on the fire. The men lit the cigarette and took turns puffing on it. I brought the hot water to Julek. He drank in small gulps. Soon he curled up on the ground and went to sleep.

We were not given anything to eat that day. In the evening we lined up outside our barracks for roll call. It was not like those that I had suffered through in other camps. The SS men and Kapos had counted every prisoner to make sure that no one was missing or had escaped. When the count was off, the roll calls lasted into the night while the Germans searched the camp. In Wöbbelin, with so many dead and dying, counting those of us still able to stagger to roll call had no purpose. The Germans just stood and screamed insults and beat us, the last standing prisoners. The SS strutted in their fancy uniforms, shouting orders and striking out with their truncheons and canes. The roll calls were long, exhausting, and depressing. The camp was deteriorating, and we could barely stand, but the Germans acted with arrogant cruelty.

At night I slept on the bare cold earth inside the crowded barracks. Many prisoners were sick and in pain from some of the Red Cross food, which was too rich for our malnourished bodies. The prisoners moaned, and the air was heavy with foul odors. No one was allowed outside at night, but some prisoners, because of illness or despair, stayed outside with the dead. The SS shot at them from the guard towers. I tried to sleep, but the cold sandy floor, my hunger and lice, and the cries and smells kept me awake. I knew with certainty that I would not live for many more days.

It was still dark when the pain in my hip woke me. At daylight I went outside. I found a dry place on the marshy ground and lay down. The warm sun felt good on my aching body. I was tired and hungry. I looked out toward the woods beyond the fence. Spring had arrived. The trees were full, and wildflowers colored the landscape. The sounds of singing birds filled the air. I was abandoned and starving, and all around me men were dying. The dead lay scattered throughout the camp like a cemetery unearthed. I lay and dreamed that I was free as I prepared for my death, which I sensed was coming.

At some point those strong and aware enough to get in line were given a bowl of watery soup. I drank the dirty watery soup from my bowl. I hoped to find some solids at the bottom, but there were none. I was still very hungry. In desperation I wandered through the camp looking for weeds and grass with roots that I could eat. The ground was bare. Behind one of the older half-finished barracks I came upon a group of Russian prisoners sitting around a fire and contentedly eating something that looked like a stew. The smell was enough to drive a starving man mad.

I took two cigarettes from the pack in my pocket and held them out. I walked over to the Russians and spoke to them in a mixture of Polish and broken Russian. "Will you sell me some soup for cigarettes?" I asked.

"Four cigarettes for half a bowl," one answered.

"What is in it?" I asked.

"Potatoes with meat," he answered. "Very good. We have access to the kitchen hut. Four cigarettes for half a bowl." "I have only two cigarettes. American," I bargained.

"American?" the man said. "Let me see." I held my hand close enough for him to see but not snatch the cigarettes. "American?" he repeated. "Hold up your bowl." I did. The Russian poured half a bowl of the thick soup from his bowl into mine. I gave him the two cigarettes.

I walked a short distance from the fire, sat on the ground, and ravenously ate the stew. An older prisoner came over and stood over my shoulder. I waited for him to ask me for some stew. I had no intention of sharing. "They are cannibals," he said in Polish. "Do you know what you are eating?" "Potatoes with meat," I said, hoping that he would go away. "No. Not meat. Human flesh cut from the dead. They are cannibals."

"I do not believe it," I said. I did not want to listen to him. "Go away!" "Come with me and I will show you the mutilated bodies. Come," he insisted.

"I do not believe you! Go away!" I shouted. He shook his head and walked away. I did not know if it was true. I did not want to know. I finished eating the delicious stew, and I did not care whether it was true or not.

We were not given any food the next day. I went looking for the Russian prisoners from whom I had bought the stew. I looked everywhere but could not find them. I spent the day wandering and dozing on the ground. The next morning, starved and desperate, I bought a quarter of a rotting yellow turnip for three cigarettes. I offered a piece to Julek, but he was too sick to eat.

Without work or purpose the SS and Kapos were angry and frustrated and brutalized us. Gunshots rang out at all hours. I ducked the whips and kicks, searched for food, and tried to keep dry and warm. I was in Wöbbelin for four days, or maybe seven, or maybe twenty. I never had access to a watch or calendar in any camp, but at least work and rations gave our life rhythm. Now I had no sense of time, and the days and hours melded into an endless haze of misery.

One morning the shrill blast of a whistle and angry shouts of the Kapo shook me from my troubled sleep. My cheek was against the dirt floor of the barracks, and I could smell the stench of filthy prisoners packed into the hot airless building. I sat up quickly, still driven by the instinct to survive. Other prisoners were pulling themselves up from the dirt floor, adjusting their frayed uniforms, wrapping bits of rags around their feet, and pulling on their tattered wood-soled shoes. Some prisoners did not get up. They were dead or dying. I tried to shake the dust and sand from my clothing and tied an old piece of rope around my waist from which I hung my rusty soup bowl. I put on my torn shoes and tried to rub and massage the searing pain out of my hip.

I felt a terrible gnawing hunger. I had not eaten in two days. I knew that I was getting weaker and was almost to the point where I would have to give up and spend my last days like the prisoners at my feet, lying on the muddy floor.

Julek stood close to me, fumbling with a button on his jacket and scratching at the lice that infested our clothes and bodies. I looked at him and saw myself. We were both close to being muselmen. For so long we had shared the suffering, work, and the beatings. At one time we had shared hopes for our future. Now we were hungry skeletons living like beasts. I feared that our friendship, my only true human relationship, might deteriorate to something based on need and survival.

The Kapo stood in the doorway and shouted, "Out! Everyone out! Immediately! Dirty dogs! Out and line up for roll call!" I ran through the door behind other prisoners to dodge the blows of the Kapo's truncheon. I had learned to never be first or last and to never, ever let myself be singled out. We lined up for roll call, five men deep. The Kapos made sure that our lines were straight and that we stood at attention. The SS arrived with a senior sergeant. He stood up on a chair and told us that the Wöbbelin camp was being closed. All prisoners able to walk would march to another camp later that day. All those unable to march would be transported by truck. He ordered any prisoner unable to march to step out of the ranks. My hip hurt, and I was in no condition to march or even walk very far. I knew that I would put myself in grave danger if I admitted that I was too weak to march. I stayed in the ranks. I would have to find a way to make it on my own.

A few prisoners stepped out of the ranks. The SS counted our remaining group. We were instructed to wait near the barracks for the order to leave. We sat on the ground and quietly wondered where they would take us and even why they would bother to drag our half-dead bodies anywhere. The SS reappeared and ordered us back into formation. They marched us to the railroad siding where boxcars painted red stood waiting. There was no locomotive to drive the trains.

The Kapos packed almost one hundred prisoners into the boxcar. I was with Julek and some other prisoners from Tyczyn. The Kapo let us leave the boxcar doors open while we waited for the locomotive to arrive. He told us that the SS would shoot any prisoner who left the boxcar and that they would ask no questions before they did so. There was barely enough space to sit down. I dreaded the miseries that lay ahead. I sat without even a wall to lean on. At least I was not on foot, marching to the next camp with my bad hip.

Hours passed and night came. The boxcar doors stayed open. The locomotive had not come, and we sat in the dark and listened to the sound of distant gunfire. It was too crowded to lie down or sleep. I heard shots from outside the train. A prisoner sitting close to the open door said that he could see a boxcar filled with turnips and that some prisoners were sneaking out and stealing them. The SS were shooting at them. Sometime that night three prisoners jumped down from our boxcar and ran. Again we heard gunshots. Two prisoners came running back and quickly climbed into the train with turnips in their hands. They said the third prisoner was hit. I was starved and could not stand to watch them eating.

During the night more prisoners slipped out to get a turnip. Most came back. The sound of chewing and the smell of turnips filled the boxcar. I could not resist, and I lowered myself from our boxcar and ran behind another prisoner to the freight car two cars behind ours. I ran hunched over and stumbled on bodies on the ground. Several prisoners were pulling turnips from the freight car. Gunfire came from a guard tower near the rail siding. I grabbed a turnip and ran. I climbed into my boxcar and pushed my way to an open space to sit down. With the sharp edges of my broken teeth I pulled back the thick skin of the turnip. It was sweet and juicy and tasted of life.

I could not sleep. I thought about the next camp. Many prisoners spent the night whispering and worrying about what lay ahead. For better or worse, no one knew.

During the long black night we never heard a locomotive arrive.

· 23 ·

Dawn came and the sun rose. The train had not moved during the night. The boxcar doors were still open.

The SS and Kapos stood in a line outside the boxcars and shouted for all the prisoners to come out immediately and line up. They herded us into a tight mass between the boxcars and the barbed wire fence. The SS surrounded us. They held machine guns. I had never been put on a train and taken off without going somewhere. A great panic spread. The prisoners huddled together, fearing that the SS were going to start shooting. Some prisoners whispered, "The bastards changed their minds. They will march us out of here." "The locomotive never arrived." I stood there, worried and hoping that the SS would load us back into the boxcars. I would either have to try to walk or admit to the SS that I could not make it. The SS stood with their guns ready, waiting for their commander to issue an order. Some prisoners sat or fell to the ground. The SS ignored them and did not even order them to stand up. Finally, an SS sergeant approached and began shouting, "All prisoners stand at attention! Anyone on the ground will be shot." The prisoners struggled to stand. I straightened up a little to try to appear to be standing at attention. The SS sergeant bellowed, "All camp Kapos of German nationality, leave the formation, and stand next to that boxcar." Twenty or thirty Kapos left the formation and gathered next to a boxcar beyond the SS guards. The SS sergeant commanded, "All Jewish prisoners, step out and line up to the left. Fast!" A few Jewish prisoners stepped out of the ranks. Most of us stayed where we were. The sergeant grew furious and screamed his order for the Jews to step out. Some SS began dragging the Jewish prisoners they recognized out of the formation. A few Christian prisoners started pointing out the Jews or shoving them out of the ranks. The Jews resisted the Christian prisoners. Other Christian prisoners tried to help the Jews by pulling them from the grasp of the SS collaborators. The Germans were cursing and beating the prisoners with their clubs. The prisoners were yelling, shoving, and fighting.

Suddenly, we heard the blast of artillery fire. BOOM!!! Everyone froze. The guards and the prisoners turned and in the distance saw a huge tank near the railroad line. Clouds of smoke poured from the tank's cannon. All eyes were on that tank. The cannon moved to the left and the right. With a lurch the tank rolled out of our sight and into the forest.

The Germans came back to life. The SS sergeant commanded that the camp gate be opened. All the prisoners, except for the Kapos, were ordered into the camp. The SS closed the gate behind us and then began to fire their machine guns at us. Prisoners cried out and fell to the ground. We started running away from the fence and toward the barracks. The SS started shooting from the guard towers.

I ran as fast as I could, forgetting the pain in my hip. I ran to the closest barracks, threw myself to the ground, and crawled around behind the corner of the building. I hoped the SS would not follow us with their guns. Most prisoners sought shelter inside the barracks. A few other prisoners were outside with me. Some were cursing the Germans, and others were praying. An old prisoner on the ground next to me hissed, "The sons of bitches want to kill us all. We are not safe! We need to hide!" The gunfire from the guard towers went on. Bullets hit the barracks wall above us. "They can see us! They can see us!" a prisoner cried out. The others near me scrambled away. I was so weak and the pain in my hip was so piercing that I could not move quickly enough to stay with them. I crawled into a small ditch a little ways up and dug at the ground with my hands to get down lower. I pulled some dried and broken twigs and weeds over me, trying to hide. I knew that if the Germans came upon me, they would see me. I heard steady gunfire and then yelling and screaming as prisoners were shot. I thought that this was the end of my life. I could do nothing more. All the years of suffering and struggle were for nothing. All they had bought me was more wretched time alive. I closed my eyes and wanted it to be over. I tried to remember, for one last time, the feel of my mother's touch, the love in my father's eyes. I yearned for them with all my heart and soul, and if longing was enough, it would have brought them back to me. I whispered to the earth, "Mommy, Daddy, *Mamusiu, Tatusiu*. I should have gone with you. I should have been there with you. I do not want to die alone." My heart ached. The words of Julek Reich's song came back: "Stone, dear gravestone, at one time you were my dear mother." My tears ran, and I cried the pain of all the despair and sadness that had been my life for so long.

After a while the shooting stopped. The camp was completely still and silent. I knew the Germans would soon come into the camp to kill the rest of us. I prayed: "Dear merciful God of my people Israel. Blessed be your name. Forgive me my sins. I know I have had doubts and questions, but I still have faith in you. You are my staff and my salvation. Have mercy on me, God. Take my soul to my parents. Protect my brother, Manek. And punish the killers. Amen."

I listened for the coming of Death. I heard a strange noise. It was like the steady beating of a muffled drum. I listened, and then I knew what it was. It was the sound of men running in wooden shoes. I raised my head and saw prisoners running in the distance. I saw them in their dirty striped uniforms. First, I saw two, then groups of prisoners, all running toward the corner of the camp where the latrine and the great piles of bodies were. I could not imagine why they were running. I heard no gunshots, no Germans. Maybe they had found food. I pulled myself up and slowly ran toward them. Other prisoners were coming out of their hiding places and running and hobbling in that direction.

I ran through the pain, and when I felt that I could not go on, I pushed myself not to give up. I ran past the last barracks before the corner of the camp, and there I came upon a miraculous sight. A small group of soldiers in olive uniforms stood quietly among the piles of bodies. Around them hundreds of skeletal and half-dead prisoners were dancing, embracing, laughing, and shouting with joy.

"Americans!! Americans!! Americans!! The Americans are here!!"

I stood there, unable to move or believe my eyes. My heart was pounding, and I was weeping. This was the impossible dream come true. I had lived with the Angel of Death, and now I stood among angels of life. I had given up on rescue, and liberation had come as a complete and shocking surprise. The guard towers were empty. I was overcome with joy. I joined the celebrating prisoners, dancing and jumping, embracing strangers and old friends, and shouted until my voice was hoarse: "The Americans are here! My God, we are free!"

I wanted to touch the Americans, their shoes and uniforms, their hands, as if to make sure that this was real. The soldiers were young and looked tired, but they were not repulsed by our ugliness, craziness, and stench. They were shocked at the sight of us and by all the dead lying about. They spoke in reassuring and soothing voices, in English, which I did not understand. One took photographs.

The ill and feeble prisoners, the muselmen, made their way to where we stood with the American soldiers. Some of the stronger prisoners helped or carried the weak and sick so that they too would see that this day had come. Julek Schipper was laughing and shouting. We embraced and cried together. We told each other that we had survived and that we should never have given up hope. This was our day of glory.

The American infantrymen were in a small detachment that had come upon the camp while on patrol. They had cut open the barbed wire and found us. After a short while they shouldered their rifles, waved to us, and left through the same opening in the fence.

Some Russian and Polish prisoners opened the front gate of the camp and walked back to the boxcars that held the turnips. There was no sign of the SS. The French prisoners gathered and sang the "Marseillaise." I stood together with Julek Schipper, Motek Hoffstetter, Moishe Ziment, Mola Tuchman, and Moses Verständig. The Germans were gone. I was not sure what to do next. Someone said, "In Poland, during the first war, towns and villages changed hands every few hours and days. Why did the Americans leave?" His voice held worry. Someone else blurted out, "The Germans may come back! Who would stop

them? Let's run! Before the Germans come back! The wires are cut!"
The six of us ran out of the fence and into the woods.

After so many years I was outside the fence. No SS or Kapo to tell
me what to do. I was in the forest, and I was free. I could run to the left
or walk to the right or lie down behind some bush. But I was still afraid.

I followed the others on a dirt path through the grass and underbrush. I felt anger and hate toward the Germans who had run away.
They were so brave, so arrogant, and so cruel when they were in charge.
They were ruthless with the helpless prisoners in the camps and the
families and children in the ghettos. Now they had run like cowardly
dogs. I remembered the song that I had foolishly sung in Reichshof in
front of the SA guard Lafferenz: "The day of payback will still come."
That day was here.

We came to a road marked with tire tracks and littered with abandoned German military equipment. We found helmets and belts, some
with bayonets, and empty army rucksacks. A small German army van
had crashed into a tree. The engine was still on fire. We looked into the
back but saw only a mess of papers, empty wooden footlockers, and a
case of green bottles. One man took a bottle, pulled out the cork, and
sniffed. "Wine," he said as he put it in his pocket. I took a bottle, pulled
out the cork, and took a few swallows. It was sharp and sour, but I was
thirsty and drank. Immediately, I felt lightheaded. Julek took a bottle
too and drank too. "Stop or you will get drunk," warned Verständig,
the oldest of the group. "Let's get out of here before the engine blows
up."

I was drunk. I tossed the bottle back into the van and followed the
others back into the woods. We came upon a German submachine
gun, a Schmeisser, and an ammunition belt lying in the underbrush. I
picked up the heavy gun and slung the strap over my shoulder. I was
too weak, and the gun was too heavy. I was falling behind and stagger-
ing under the weight. I dropped the gun and moved to catch up with
the others. I told myself that I would wait to find a lighter weapon.

We came to the edge of the woods and a narrow, paved road. We
saw several large farm wagons, piled high with crates and furniture,
standing across the road. Huge horses were hitched to each wagon. A

group of elderly men, a few women, and young children stood near the wagons. The men were feeding and grooming the horses, while the women talked. The children were running around and playing. Two pretty little blonde girls were picking flowers on the grassy shoulder. I was amazed at the sight of children. I had not been close to a child in years. I had forgotten how they looked, how small and beautiful they were. The Jewish children had all been gassed. Probably by the fathers or uncles of these children here.

I walked slowly toward the children. They saw me and were not afraid. I remembered my fantasy from the Reichshof camp, the day the Nowy Sacz boys were murdered. I had thought of making Oester suffer by tormenting and killing his children in front of him. Now I realized that I could never harm these or any children. I would never sink to the level of the Germans. I was better than they. I was human.

The Germans around the wagons saw me near the children and maybe the others behind me. They shouted for the children to come back. An old man pulled a rifle from a wagon. I went back to my friends, and we turned and walked back into the woods.

We came to the outskirts of a town. We were hungry, and our first job was to find some food. We had drunk water from a stream in the forest but had not come across any gardens, wild berries, or trees bearing fruit. The town looked deserted. We hid behind a tall overgrown hedge above the road that led into town. We decided to stay hidden until after dark. Then we would go into the town to find or steal something to eat.

Two men came walking up the road. They were pushing bicycles loaded down with sacks and boxes. I saw that they were civilians. They had diamond-shaped patches with a *P* stitched onto their coats. They were Polish civilians who had worked as forced labor for the Germans. "Stay here," I whispered to my friends. "I will talk to them." I slid down the embankment and surprised the two Poles.

"*Polacy?* Poles?" I asked them. They looked me over. "A Pole? Are you from a *Katzet*? Concentration camp?" they asked. I nodded yes. "What do you want?" they asked. "Something to eat," I said. "Aha, today that is easy," one said and pointed down the road. "That way and then to the right a hundred meters is a broken-down abandoned train. It is full of clothing, furniture, and food. Everybody is looting. Since the Germans ran, the taking has been good." He patted the bags mounted on his bicycle. "The chance will not last long."

My friends had come out from the embankment and stood behind me. "You say the Germans have run away?" one asked. "Yes, yes," the Poles answered. "The German army and police ran away this morning. The German civilians are hiding in their houses. Today, the town of Ludwigslust is wide open." They waved and went on, pushing their loaded bicycles.

We walked in the direction of the train. The road was empty. The houses were shuttered. We reached the corner and turned to the right. Walking toward us were two uniformed and armed German soldiers. They had a young woman between them as they came up the opposite side of the street. It was too late for us to run or hide. The Germans looked at us with surprise but walked on without saying or doing anything. We stood and watched them walk away and disappear around a corner. "Oh, my God, the Germans are still here," someone said. We were shocked and upset. One of my friends said, "We better hide until it is dark and then sneak out of this town." We crawled through a sparse hedge and came out on a grassy yard with a small stone shed. We ran around to the back and lay down in the grass.

The hours passed slowly. As day turned to dusk, we heard trucks and people on the street on the other side of the hedge. I crawled over with another fellow and peeked through the hedge. We saw a convoy of green trucks painted with white stars coming down the road. Two columns of soldiers were walking down both sides of the street. They wore the same olive uniforms and helmets as the soldiers that had been at Wöbbelin. The Americans had come to Ludwigslust!

We stood and walked back behind the shack. Our friends who were still lying there, pressed to the ground, looked up in surprise. "Do not worry, do not worry," we said. "The American soldiers have come to town."

That night we slept inside the small stone shed. The door was unlocked, and we took advantage of the opportunity. Inside, we found a large table splattered with paint and shelves filled with paint cans and brushes. Julek Schipper was very sick again. We convinced him to sleep on the wooden table. The rest of us lay down on the cement floor. Within minutes I was asleep.

During the night we were awakened by loud noises that sounded like trucks driving by. In the darkness we wondered what was happening. A voice asked, "Do you think the Americans are withdrawing?" Uncertainty and fear crept back into my heart. We left Julek lying on the table and crept outside and looked through the hedge. Lots of large American trucks, their headlights dimmed, were driving in both directions. We went back to the shed and went to sleep. It was my first night in three years as a free man.

I awoke in the morning and looked around at the other sleeping men. No one woke us or shouted at us to line up for roll call. No SS or Kapos were beating us with their truncheons. No guns were pointing at us, no gas chambers waited for us. But I was still dirty and hungry, and thousands of lice still lived in my clothes and on my body. I was hungry and weak, and my hip still hurt, and my teeth had almost all fallen out.

I went outside and stood in the morning sunshine. I walked over and looked across the hedge and out into the street. The American soldiers were staying in a large house next door. They had set up a field kitchen on an adjacent empty lot, and a soldier in a tall white hat was serving food to soldiers standing in a line. I crossed the street, took off my cap, and held out my soup bowl. I walked toward the front of the line and made begging motions and noises to the soldier in the white hat. He shouted something and waved me away. I felt pangs of fear, the old fear of soldiers and uniforms, and ran dejected back across the street. I stood and watched the soldiers fill their plates with food. Two soldiers came across to me and gently put some food from their plates into my bowl. I did not know what to say, and I knew no English. I took the bowl, bowed quickly, and sat down on the grass and ate.

I went and got my friends and told them of the Americans' food, generosity, and kindness. We went and stood on the same spot on the side of the street. All the soldiers must have eaten, for the line was ended. The soldier in the white hat beckoned for us to approach his kitchen. Julek Schipper went first to get the food. The soldier must have looked at our skinny bodies and realized that we were starving. After that, we went and waited patiently every day for the soldiers to finish. After the first two days Julek was too sick and weak to climb off the table and come with us. I got him food and tried to feed him, but he could not eat. Motek was somehow able to communicate to the Americans that one of us was very ill. Two Americans came into the shed and examined Julek. They must have been medical specialists, for they checked his temperature and pulse and listened to his chest through a stethoscope. A little while after they left, an American ambulance came, and two American soldiers prepared to take Julek away. He was awake and terrified by what was happening. I walked with him to the ambulance. He looked at me with the greatest sadness that I had ever seen. I took his hands and told him to go with the Americans. He would get well, and we would come for him. The ambulance took him, and five of us were left in the shed.

I was getting stronger. I spent hours sitting in the warm sunshine. One afternoon as I sat half-dozing, an armed American soldier approached me. I jumped up, pulled off my cap, and stood at attention. The soldier was just a teenager himself and seemed embarrassed by my reaction. He fumbled in his pants pocket and pulled out a small dark brown paper package with *Hershey* written on it in large letters. He handed it to me, motioned for me to sit and eat, and he walked away. I sat on the stone steps and ate the delicious chocolate bar. I felt foolish about how I had acted. I still did not know how to be free.

We had been living in the shed for nearly a week. One morning two German police officers came looking for us. They wore the same German uniforms that I had seen in Tyczyn and in the ghetto. An American soldier who wore a helmet with *MP* painted on it accompanied them. He waited as the police came and spoke to us. They said that we could not stay in the shack and must go with them to town where foreigners were being assembled. We tried to persuade them that we wanted to stay in the shed and that we were not doing any damage. They would not listen and told us that they were following the orders of the Americans. We did not seem to have any choice but to leave with them.

The German police escorted us through the town as if we were their prisoners. In Ludwigslust they led us to a cluster of buildings that resembled a German military garrison. We went in and saw many American soldiers, Poles who had been forced laborers, and Jews in concentration camp uniforms. They took our names and then gave each of us a large piece of bread. We were told not to leave the compound. My instincts to be cautious and suspicious resurfaced.

An hour after we arrived, everyone in the compound was told to climb onto several military flatbed trucks. The American soldiers drove us out of town, and after a few miles we were stopped at a roadblock manned by Russian soldiers. The Americans got out and argued with the Russians. After a while the Americans got back into the trucks and drove us back to the compound. We got off the trucks and were given no explanations or instructions about what to do next. I was liberated but not free.

We sat on the ground and waited for an hour. Then several flatbed trucks with canvas covers pulled up. Someone mentioned that the soldiers driving these trucks were British. A burly redhead with a handlebar mustache was in charge. He told us through a translator to get on the trucks. Once again we headed out of town. The convoy drove slowly for hours and stopped often to let other military vehicles pass. At each stop the redheaded sergeant walked around to inspect the trucks and check on the drivers.

About twenty others were on the truck with me. Most were other Jews liberated from Wöbbelin. I sat back and listened to them converse in Yiddish. At several stops the driver of the truck behind us seemed to be listening to our conversation. During the next stop the redheaded sergeant again walked around and then stopped to speak to the driver of the truck behind us. I saw them pointing and looking at us.

The driver and the sergeant walked over to our truck. They both wore uniforms and carried guns in their holsters. They walked over slowly and looked at us with great seriousness. We saw them coming, and the conversation in the truck abruptly stopped. The soldiers came over and stopped next to the truck. The redheaded sergeant looked up and spoke Yiddish in a voice filled with wonder, "*Yidd'n*, Jews, my God, are you Jews? I did not believe that any Jews survived. My God, my God."

"Yes, we are Jews," someone answered. "We should thank God we survived."

I could not believe it. Jews in uniforms with guns! Jews who commanded troops, ordered trucks to stop or go, and served in the armies that beat the Germans. The other Jews on the truck were astonished and could not even speak. "Are you really Jews?" the sergeant asked.

"Yes, yes, yes," we answered in a chorus. "We are Jews."

The sergeant spoke again in Yiddish. "From what we heard about the camps, I did not think there were any Jewish survivors."

"The bastards did not kill us all. A few of us are still here. *Am Yisrael Chai*, the people Israel live," said a skinny man in the truck with me.

"Am Yisrael Chai," the sergeant answered back. "We need to go now. We will talk later." He went back to the front of the convoy. The driver ran back to his truck. In a moment we were moving again.

"We have survived," said the skinny man in the truck. I looked around at all of us still dressed in our shabby striped uniforms. Yes, we have survived, I said to myself. I have survived. In that moment the fear began to fall away from my heart. I no longer had to be afraid. It was finally safe to be Jewish. I felt something stir deep within my soul. It was my true self, the one who had stayed deep within and had not forgotten how to love and how to cry, the one who had chosen life and was still standing when the last roll call ended.

I was Lucek Salzman, and I was free.

◆ EPILOGUE ◆

The English trucks brought us to the city of Lübeck and a displaced persons (DP) camp established at an apartment complex that had housed Nazi officials. I was assigned to an apartment with several other survivors. Our soldiers were now British instead of German, and their eyes bore no hatred, only sympathy at our desperate and shocking physical condition. Survivors from all across Europe arrived every day. They were ragged and thin, filthy, and covered with sores. They came still dressed in their striped camp uniforms, and many were without shoes. After three years I took my first real shower with a bar of soap and a towel. I scoured the lice from my body and hair and put on clean clothing. I was given a mattress to sleep on and a pillow and blanket for comfort and warmth. No shouts and barking dogs woke us at dawn. No long and torturous roll calls to endure. No whips or truncheons to break our bones and our spirits. The respect, decency, and kindness that I received from the British felt like the miracle of a new dawn. I felt the first traces of my dignity restored with my newfound freedom.

I ate my first real meal served on a plate and held a fork in my hand. I sat at a table and ate at my leisure while I conversed with other survivors. I sat outside and rested while I slowly regained my weight and strength. I felt the sun on my face, looked up at the blue skies, and realized that for the first time in years, no clouds of human ashes were drifting overhead.

It was also a time of great anguish and sorrow, a time to try to accept and mourn the death of my parents and relatives. I tried to recall all the names and faces that I would never see again. I tried to remember the wonderful days of my childhood, my father's voice, and my mother's embrace. I had dreams of finding my parents and my brother and returning to a home filled with love and laughter. I fantasized of our tearful reunions, which would truly mark the end of this nightmare and the return of my former life. I did not want to accept that my parents had been gassed at Belzec, and I still hoped that they would come for me.

I held firm to the belief that Manek was alive somewhere and searching for me. I turned all my hope and efforts to finding him. I remembered the instructions from my father on our last day together. We promised to locate each other after the war by contacting our aunt Pauline and uncle Julius in New York. I got some writing paper and envelopes from the DP camp office and wrote dozens of letters to my relatives in the United States. I was seventeen and had received only a few years of elementary school education. With a shaky hand I held a pencil and wrote my first words:

Dear Aunt Pauline and Uncle Julius,
I want to tell you that I am alive and now reside at UNRRA
DP Camp in Germany. I do not know for sure what happened to my parents or where my brother Manek is. Please
let me know if you have heard from them.
Your nephew,
    Lucek Salzman

I did not know their address in New York. The slip of paper with their contact information had been taken from me in Flossenbürg. I addressed the letters to Julius Tamar, MD, New York, New York USA. I pleaded with every British and American soldier to mail the letters for me. They took my letters and promised to send them. I checked with the camp administrative office every second day for any mail that might have arrived. Weeks passed with no response. I wrote to former Polish friends and neighbors in Tyczyn, asking for any news about my parents and Manek. I also wrote to Mr. Gliwa, hoping to retrieve at least some of the family papers and photographs that we left with him for safekeeping. I never got any replies.

One day in the fall of 1945 I was summoned to the camp administrative office. A telegram had come from the United States. I ran and prayed the whole way for good news. The secretary in the administrative office translated the brief English telegram:

FROM NEW YORK—TO LUCJAN SALZMAN—POLISH CAMP LÜBECK HAPPY WITH NEWS. YOU WERE REGISTERED 1939 FOR AMERICA. WILL TAKE YOU TO US. KISSES JULIUS PAULA TAMAR 360 WADSWORTH AVE NEW YORK CITY NEW YORK USA

For the first time in years I knew that I was not alone, that I had not been forgotten. The telegram said nothing about Manek or my parents. I tried to come up with every reason that the telegram had not mentioned Manek. I felt absolutely sure that he was still alive and that we would find each other. Having the New York address was a great relief after so many months of worry. I began writing letters to the Tamars and waited anxiously for their replies and any news of my brother. I visited and moved to other DP camps but kept in contact with them.

My aunt and uncle wanted to bring me to America. Living in the DP camps in Germany was becoming increasingly difficult. The French, Norwegians, Poles, and Czechs who had been held in concentration camps had returned to their towns and families. Then the Jews from Hungary, Romania, Belgium, and Italy left to go home. Only the Jews from Poland remained in the DP camps. We had heard stories of Jewish survivors who had gone back to their villages, only to be murdered by the Poles who had taken over their businesses and moved into their homes. Eventually, the DP camps were mainly filled with Polish Jews and some Nazi collaborators from the Ukraine, Lithuania, Latvia, and Estonia who also feared going back to their towns.

I heard that the Red Cross had compiled lists of survivors and posted them in some DP camps. I hitchhiked, walked, and rode trains to the Neustadt and Belsen DP camps and searched through the long lists posted in the camp office. I asked every survivor and soldier about

Manek. No one knew of him, but they wished me luck with my search. At Belsen I met two of the Zimmerman brothers who survived the war and their father, whom I knew from the Reichshof camp.

One day in Lübeck I heard that a ship was taking sickly concentration camp survivors to recuperate in a hospital in Sweden. I ran to the docks in the Lübeck harbor. The Red Cross ship was docked there, and an official at the gangplank agreed to help me. I gave him my brother's name, and he checked his list. Manek was not on the ship roster. I asked if anyone from Rzeszów, Poland, was on the ship. He studied the list and told me that a very sick young man named Julius Schipper was aboard. I told him that I was Schipper's friend and begged to see him. Another Red Cross worker took me aboard the ship. We went into a makeshift hospital room, and I found Julek lying in a bed. He was washed and clean but still looked like a skeletal muselman. He was so weak that he could hardly lift his head or speak. When he saw me, his eyes shined with recognition. He whispered that he was glad that I looked so well and that I had gained some weight and again looked like a young man. He told me about his horrible sickness, about his heartache and fear that he would not survive. I held his hand and cried with him. I told him that the doctors in Sweden would make him well. I could see that he did not believe me. I stayed with Julek until evening, when the visitors were asked to leave the ship. When I returned to the harbor in the morning, the hospital ship was gone.

Months later I heard from someone who had a friend in the same Swedish hospital that Julek had died. Sensing my sadness, the person tried to comfort me and said, "At least your friend died a free man." Yes, that was true, but during the years of terror our dream was not to die as free men but to live as free men.

I continued to search for my brother. I met up with other prisoners who had been with me in some of the camps, including Emil Ringel and the two Zimmerman brothers. I met a few other survivors from Rzeszów. We were all desperate to find out about our lost families and friends. No one had any news about my parents or Manek. The Tamars wrote from New York that they still had not received any word from him. Finally, in September 1947 they were able to arrange my transport to America. I would have to leave Europe and hope that Manek would find me across the great ocean.

I traveled alone to the United States in October 1947. I boarded a ship at Bremerhaven, Germany. It was a long journey on a ship filled with other survivors who were also leaving behind a land that had betrayed us, a land that had become a graveyard of our past. At night I looked up into the black sky and wondered what my future would bring. I was nineteen. I spoke little English, had barely any education, no money, and only a few belongings other than the clothes on my back.

When our ship entered New York Harbor on October 2, 1947, I cried as I caught sight of the Statue of Liberty. I raised my hand to salute the torch that seemed to be held out for the hundreds of survivors aboard our ship. Suddenly, the ship was filled with laughter, singing, and joyful cries as we claimed our freedom in this new land. My uncle Julius was waiting for me at the 57th Street pier. He helped me fill out the English forms that would register my arrival in the United States. An immigration official asked me whether I wanted to change and Americanize my name. I remembered the danger, under the Germans, of having a Jewish name. In an instant I, Lucjan Salzman, became George Lucius Salton.

New York City was indeed a new world. The tall buildings, thousands of cars, throngs of people, and shops and restaurants were an astonishing sight after war-torn Europe. When I got to my uncle's apartment, my aunt and two cousins met me at the door. I was shocked to see how much my aunt resembled my mother. I tried to hide my heartbreak behind my nervous smile. They welcomed me into their home and said that they wanted me to live with them while I adjusted to my new life in the United States. They bought me new clothing and shoes and took me to a dentist to fix my broken teeth. My days were filled with new wonders and excitement as I explored the world-famous city. I checked the mail every day for news from Manek. There was no news, and my hope of being reunited with him began to fade. I had terrible nightmares in which I saw my parents drifting over pyres as I desperately tried to save them and never could.

In a movie theater one evening I was surprised and elated to run into my old friend Emil Ringel and his new wife, Clara. They lived in an apartment just a few blocks from me. Together we reminisced about our happy days as children and then struggled to overcome our terrible memories of the camps. I registered as Lucjan Salzman with an organization of former concentration camp prisoners. A few weeks later I received a letter saying that the German government had challenged my registration. Their records showed that Lucjan Salzman had died in a concentration camp in Bremen. It must have been Josef Singer, who had taken my name and then lost his life. I knew that I was not responsible for Josef's fate, but I bore a great guilt and sadness over his death. With the help of Emil Ringel I was able to convince the survivor organization that I was the real Lucjan Salzman.

My uncle was busy with his practice, my cousin Henry was at college, and my cousin Erika was in high school. My days were empty, and my uncle offered to help me find a job. Without an education or experience and little knowledge of English, my choices would be limited. I found a job as a delivery boy in the garment district. I enrolled in morning classes to learn to repair radios and televisions, made deliveries all afternoon, and went to night school to learn English. I finished the trade school after nine months and began work as a television repairman. I rented a furnished room near my uncle's apartment and slowly began to adjust to life on my own. I still saw Emil and Clara, who often invited me for dinner or out to a movie.

In 1950 I received a draft notice. I was summoned to take a physical, passed it, and was inducted into the US Army. I was to be an American soldier and serve and wear the uniform of the country that had given me my freedom. I would no longer be a stranger in America. I was stationed in Augusta, Georgia, for basic training and radio school for six months. After that I was sent to Fort Monmouth, New Jersey, where I served the remaining eighteen months of my army service. The soldiers in the barracks were like family to me. I took classes in communications and earned promotions for my diligence and achievements. I was given an honorable discharge and went to work for a company in Philadelphia as a radio technician.

Emil and Clara introduced me to a lovely Jewish girl named Ruth, who had also come from Poland after the war. She knew of the misery and loss that I had survived and encouraged me to work hard and build a new life in the United States. We had met while I was still in the service, and she waited for me to finish my training before she would agree to marry me. We were married in a small ceremony in New York City with our friends and family there to celebrate with us. This was a joyful day. I had found new love in my life. I wished that my parents and brother could have been there, but I knew that they would be happy for me.

In March 1953 I became a US citizen. I was overcome with emotion as I took the oath. My company sent me to work as an electronics technician at Griffiss Air Force Base in Rome, New York. Ruth and I left New York City and moved upstate, where I took and passed the New York high school equivalency test. With Ruth's encouragement and the GI Bill, I enrolled as a night student at the Utica College of Syracuse University.

In 1955 our son Henry was born. I looked with wonder and love at the beautiful tiny baby. Henry, named after my father, was for me the first blossom on the tree of life. As I held him lovingly in my arms, I imagined the immense pain felt by Jewish parents who could not protect and save their children from the Nazis. In 1957 our second son, Alan, named after Ruth's father, was born. And in 1959, our daughter, Anna, named after my mother, arrived. I was happy and fulfilled as a man, a husband, and a father.

In 1960 I earned a bachelor's degree magna cum laude in physics and in 1963 a master's degree in electrical engineering from Syracuse University. In 1964 I accepted a position on the staff of the secretary of defense at the Pentagon and moved my family to the suburbs of Washington, DC. I worked at the Pentagon for eighteen years and became the director of the Communications Systems Office. My work was overseeing the development of satellite systems. I eventually left the government to work in the aerospace industry and accepted a position as an executive manager for TRW Systems. We stayed in the Washington, DC, area for nearly thirty years; during that time our children grew into adults, got married, and made us proud grandparents.

During a trip to Israel in 1970 I was reunited with Motek Hoffstetter and my old friend Julek Reich, whom I had not seen since our days in the Sachsenhausen concentration camp. They told me that I had a cousin, Julek Birman, living in Israel. Through him I found out that I had another cousin, Joe Taler, a physician who lived in Annapolis, Maryland, a mere thirty minutes from my new home. I called Joe when I returned home, and we had a wonderful and emotional meeting. Ruth and I developed a lasting, sincere, and loving friendship with Joe and his wife, Bronka.

I had decided that in raising my children, I would live as if the Holocaust had never happened. I would put the past behind me and give them a happy childhood free from the horrors of my camp experience. Ruth created a warm and loving home where we taught our children to live with courage and conviction and to care for family, friends, and even strangers in need of kindness and compassion. We raised and educated our children to embrace our Jewish traditions and faith. The chain would not be broken.

I rarely spoke of the Holocaust or my life before the war. But children are curious, and they began to ask questions and demand answers. They claimed my past as part of their own and wanted to know about the grandparents and uncle whom they had never met. In 1998 they left their children and spouses behind and traveled with Ruth and me back to Poland. I had been there once before on business but had not ventured to many places from my past. Together we visited the camps and ghettos, the remnants of synagogues, and cemeteries all across Poland. We returned to my town and even to my old house. I met the widow of my childhood friend Jurek Roskiewicz. She told me that Jurek had died in 1990 and that his brother, Toniek, was living in Warsaw. We went to the Belzec camp, where my parents perished, and wept together as we said the Kaddish, the Jewish prayer in memory of the dead. My children took my memories and made them their own. They vowed not to forget and to teach their own children about the heritage that they had nearly lost. They told me that the pain of my past could not be borne solely on my shoulders, and with their love and support I began to tell my story.

My life is good. I appear to be a happy and secure man, living the American dream. That is true but only some of the time. My past, filled with the pain and trauma of the ghetto and camps, is with me always. Beneath the thin veneer that I have built during the last fifty years, ugly scars remain, ghosts hide, and painful wounds fester. I want to believe that Manek, whom I never heard from, survived and that we might still find each other. I sometimes see a vaguely familiar old man on the street or in a restaurant and look at his face. Could it be Manek? It never is. I see children playing in a park and wonder how men could shoot little children because they were Jewish. I see an old man when I travel in Germany, and with an accusing glare I wonder whether he was the Nazi that pushed my mother into the gas chamber. And in the restless nights I am haunted by dreams of Germans with their shouts and truncheons, of the desolate camps and piles of dead Jews in striped uniforms.

I struggle to convince myself that I am untouched. I have learned how to love, how to laugh, and how to be happy. And when the painful memories intrude and spawn doubts and strange regrets, I seek solace in my memories of my past and in the knowledge that I have kept the promises that I made: To fast on every Yom Kippur after the war; this I promised Manek, when he persuaded me to eat an egg on the first Yom Kippur in the camps. To live in a house with a mezuzah on the door-post, as I promised Hafferflock on the long and lonely night that he died in the Braunschweig camp. To live as a good and decent person, to be a mensch, as I promised my dear mother and father on the day that we parted, the last time in my life that I saw them.

◆ AFTERWORD ◆

T he following passages have been excerpted from speeches and interviews given by George Salton between 1995 and 2011.

ON FREEDOM

[At the Wöbbelin concentration camp] I noticed many prisoners yelling and screaming and jumping and dancing and there standing amongst them were seven giants, young people, they must have been eighteen or nineteen, American soldiers . . . standing inside the camp. . . . I also joined the crowd and yelled and screamed and somehow knew that the day of liberation has come. It was a strange feeling for me, however, because, as I remember it, on the one hand, I was overwhelmed by this unexpected and unhoped for encounter of freedom, but at the same time, what was happening was outside of me. I didn't really know what to make of it.[1]

And five of us Jewish young men who knew each other from home, left through the hole in the fence and through the forest. . . . So while

---

1 United States Holocaust Memorial Museum Oral History, February 23, 1995, https://collections.ushmm.org/search/catalog/irn511063 (video); https://collections.ushmm.org/oh_findingaids/RG-50.470.0018_trs_en.pdf (transcript), pp. 8–9.

we were free and while the Germans were gone, we were not really free because freedom didn't come like a sunrise where one day we were in the dark and the next day there was light and warmth and nurturing and rejoicing and celebration. . . . So we went into the forest not knowing what to do. . . . And we came to a little town . . . Ludwigslust. Only to discover . . . that the town was still in German hands. I remember us walking . . . around the corner and on the opposite side of the street there were two German officers . . . and they were still in uniform and armed. They looked at us and we looked at them and they moved on and we jumped over a hedge and hid in a little shack, and we were just hiding over there waiting for darkness to leave the town and hide in the forest again. . . . And toward the evening . . . American GIs came walking into town.[2]

And we were liberated, we were liberated. We then knew that the times of oppression and pain and beatings were behind. . . . I really didn't know what the future held. I recognized that most likely I was alone . . . that most likely my parents . . . did not survive. . . . I was obviously unprepared for freedom and self-sufficiency, and I was driven only to contact my relatives in the United States in the hopes that my brother might have survived. . . . [When] the family was separated back in early '42 my father instructed us all . . . to contact our relatives in Europe because this is how we will find each other. So that is how it happened. [It was a] day I remember with great joy and great pleasure, but it wasn't a day that held the kind of excitement that one would expect to see in the movies. It was a day when freedom came, liberation came unannounced and unexpected. . . .

The British came and put [us] on their trucks and took us to a town called Lübeck . . . into that part of Germany which was to be the British zone. . . . Something happened on this trip that I remember with great emotion. . . . Because even though it happened a week or eight days after liberation it was that punctuation mark that really made me realize that I'm whole again or that I can at least hope to be whole

---

2 Transcript of United States Holocaust Memorial Museum Oral History, pp. 9–11.

again. We were sitting on the back of the truck . . . and behind us was obviously another truck with two British soldiers . . . and the trucks would stop every once in a while . . . and a few of us that were sitting in that truck spoke Yiddish to each other. . . . And at one point, the drivers of the trucks behind us started blowing the horn. The trucks stopped and they came out running. Speaking Yiddish to us. Telling us that they were Jews, and being surprised and happy that they had found some Jewish survivors because somehow they didn't expect to find any and I remember the feeling of seeing people in uniform with authority, with guns, with hands on the wheel that could make a truck turn left or right that were Jewish, and it was the moment when I realized that I was equal. That was the moment when I realized that the days of humiliation and days when I was treated as somehow subhuman were behind me. . . . That is how long it took for me to really comprehend that liberation was more just being able to . . . go out of the camp and cross barbed wire. [It] was also a feeling of sufficiency and equality.[3]

All the people that loved me were dead. It was for me both a good time and a bad time. It was a good time because I was free. And I believe that freedom is like good health; only those who lose it can appreciate it. Freedom, you have to lose freedom to appreciate how sweet it is to be free. I, who for years could not say no (if I was sitting in a barrack and people said to me "Out!" I ran out; if people said to me "Do this!" I did it). Now, I could enjoy the sweetness of being allowed to say "No" and being able to have a choice. If people said to me, "Do you want to go out?" I could say "No!" So it was wonderful, and it was sweet.[4]

---

3   Transcript of United States Holocaust Memorial Museum Oral History, pp. 13–15.

4   Undated speech, Oakland City University, available at www.youtube.com/ watch?v=qOuxL8Wa_yM&t=1.

ON LIFE IN AMERICA

In October of 1947, I came alone to the United States. Here in America was a time for me to be reborn, a place to start a new life. And here, looking at a place with all the tall buildings and all the thousands of people and thousands of cars and prosperity, I, who felt like an old man, made a decision. I made a commitment to myself and also to my murdered parents that I would make my life what it could have been if the war had not happened to me. I would try to become what my parents would have wanted me to become. It was not an easy commitment. I was still a teenager. I was alone. I had no education, no means, and I did not speak English. But it was for me a crucial commitment— an act of defiance. I would not yield another victory to the forces of evil that destroyed my family and derailed my life.

And I did succeed. I did succeed because I had a special partner in my life, and the partner was and still is America. I was in America, and I had great hopes. And I did create a new life for myself. I learned a trade and worked hard. I was drafted during the Korean War and served two years in the US Army. Then, armed with a high school equivalency diploma and the GI Bill, I went to college to earn undergraduate and graduate degrees in physics and engineering. I married my lovely wife; we raised children and were blessed with grandchildren. I truly live the American dream.

But the memories of the Holocaust were never far away from me. I remember being awarded my first college degree. It was for me a day of achievement, a day of happiness. It was a wonderful time for me and a threshold of achieving my dream. I was married to the love of my life, my two sons were five and three years old, my little daughter was one. But somewhere at the fringes of my soul, there was a great, great sadness. For my parents who were murdered when I was fourteen could not be there to be proud of me.[5]

---

5   Unpublished speech at [unspecified] Jewish Community Center, January 22, 2005, pp. 4–6.

ON *THE 23RD PSALM:*
A HOLOCAUST MEMOIR

When the questions about the Holocaust came to me from my children, from friends, and from strangers, I felt an obligation to tell and record my story, to make it available to everyone, and especially to my children who wanted to know about my past and about their grandparents and uncles and cousins, all of whom were murdered during the Holocaust.

And thus, with the support of my family and with a sense of duty, I have written this book, *The 23rd Psalm: A Holocaust Memoir,* to describe my experiences during the Holocaust and to recall the lives of our people, of my family, my friends, and the fellow camp prisoners I barely knew, who tried to live and survive in the most horrible of circumstances. I have written this book to leave it as a legacy for my children and a legacy and warning for others. For the Holocaust is a cautionary tale! And unless we know about it and remember it, it may happen again. It is sad, but history forgotten may repeat itself.

While the story in the book is told against the overwhelming background of the Holocaust, it is not a story of the Holocaust. It is rather a story of a young boy and his descent from the happiness and innocence of childhood, through suffering and deprivation, into the shadows of the pit of horror where nothing but survival mattered.

I have written the book to tell what I have seen and experienced during the Holocaust and to speak of the days when we knew no mercy and sometimes believed that both man and God had abandoned us.

In the book I remember and recall my mother and my father, my older brother Manek who, until we were separated in 1942, was my guide and my protector. I remember my friend Chaim who was shot in the Rzeszów camp, my kind friend Yossel who was beaten to death in the Płaszów camp, my friend Josef Singer who changed places with me in the Sachsenhausen camp and did not survive, my dear friend Julek Schipper who never allowed me to consider giving up during the long years in the camps but who himself did not live long enough to enjoy liberty.

It was difficult and painful for me to write this book. I wanted to write it from the perspective of the day: and so had to be eleven again when I wrote about the arrest of my father by the Gestapo, fourteen when my parents were murdered, sixteen when my friends died in the camps.

And I did not only write about and describe the terrible things that I saw and witnessed—the suffering, cruelty, and killings. I also wrote about the things that were in my heart. About feelings, and fear and hate and hope and love. About the days when I needed to and did pray to my God and about the days when I felt that if the terror and cruelty that was happening about me were not sufficient to evoke God's mercy or fury, then maybe, maybe prayers were not necessary.

What was the hardest for me to write about were not the things I can remember but about all those terrible things that I am unable to forget.

For my memoir I chose the title "The 23rd Psalm," because I lived the words of David's psalm: "Though I walk through the valley of the shadow of death, I will fear no evil, for Thou art with me. . . . Surely goodness and mercy shall follow me all the days of my life." These words were and still are my prayer today.[6]

The 23rd Psalm is something that meant something to me after I survived in the camps. I did believe in God. I did hope God would have mercy to help us, and I did wonder if God had forgotten us. But after the war, especially with the passage about "the shadow of death," I felt that David, who wrote the psalm, must also have gone through some terrible experience. I wanted to acknowledge the psalm had special emotional meaning for me.[7]

---

6   Unpublished speech at [unspecified] Jewish Community Center, January 22, 2005, pp. 8–12.

7   Interview, *Milwaukee Journal Sentinel*, April 6, 2004.

ON CARING ABOUT OTHERS
AND THE HOLOCAUST

During the Holocaust, during the years of misery and suffering, of struggle and despair, there was neither compassion nor mercy for us. No one seemed to care. And after the war, when I came to America, people, good people, did not really want to talk about the Holocaust.

Seeing our pain, people urged us, survivors, to make peace with the past. But how could we make peace with the memories of millions who were murdered? Of desperate parents and crying children in the ghettos, in boxcars and concentration camps? Of cruel Nazis, barking dogs, endless roll calls, the killing factories and selections? How could we make peace with a past that held not only the terrible memories of the camps, but also the memories of our beloved parents, sisters, and brothers?

Our American friends meant well when they urged us to look ahead, but we could not make peace with our past. In our hearts and souls, painful wounds festered beneath the thin veneer built up during the post-war years.

But now, so many years later, things have changed. Now people do want to know about the Holocaust, do want to hear the stories of the ghettos and the camps. Now, after all these years, after so many deaths, what happened to us has to be told and remembered.[8]

I want to remember a promise made by me and my friends during the darkest days of the Holocaust. When people died every day and every tomorrow seemed a lifetime away, when we felt alone, isolated, and forgotten. We who were without hope promised each other that an unbelievable miracle would yet happen. That on some distant days, in some distant places whose names we could not even imagine, good men and good women, without fear in their hearts and without any reservations, would gather to hear what happened to our people in the

---

8 Unpublished speech at [unspecified] Jewish Community Center, pp. 6–8.

ghettos and in the camps. To hear and to remember and to care. Yes, care.[9]

We should not commit the sin, the unforgivable sin, of being silent bystanders when other people are abused and persecuted. . . . The sin of saying, "I don't care." So if we hear of something happening in Rwanda or something in Darfur, we have to care. Maybe we don't know exactly what we can do about it. But we shouldn't be silent bystanders. It should affect how we think, what we say to our friends and our colleagues, what letters we write, what contributions we make. Don't say, "I don't care."[10]

ON HOPE

As a Holocaust survivor, I was asked to come tonight and speak about hope. And I must say that in some ways I am an expert, for I have lived many very difficult days with hope and sometimes without hope.

And I can . . . assure you that life with hope is much better.

Although hope by itself never changed my circumstances during the Holocaust, its very presence . . . allowed me to survive the horror, the brutality, and the uncertainty that was my life for three years in ten different concentration camps.[11]

But, somehow, my hope refused to die. Hope remained in my belief in the goodness of man, as I suffered at the hands of evil men. In the belief in love and mercy and life, when I was surrounded by hatred and death.

I hoped, even in those horrible conditions, to survive another day.

---

9   Unpublished speech at [unspecified] Jewish Community Center, pp. 13–14.

10 Undated speech at Oakland City University, available at www.youtube. com/watch?v=qOuxL8Wa_yM&t=1.

11 Unpublished and undated Yom Kippur talk.

One day at a time. I chose life and chose to hope that one day the gates would open and I would be free.[12]

I was some years ago the guest of the United States Holocaust Memorial Museum in Washington. . . . There were 7,000 people there; 2,000 were survivors looking to find friends and relatives and without any success. The other 5,000 were their children, and therefore to me it was a mountain of strength, that these people like me, that we who have gone through this hell had the resilience, had the faith, had the hope to have families, to have children, to look to the future, something that can be glorious and wonderful. . . . I think that people who go through terrible times and a terrible experience if they are able to put it behind them and build a new positive constructive life, that's an important lesson for all of us. . . . And if somebody, any person, has had some difficult and troublesome and frightening experience and looks for some lessons of hope, look to us. Look to us.[13]

---

12 Unpublished and undated Yom Kippur talk.

13 Interview, University of South Florida, October 31, 2011, available at https://digital.lib.usf.edu/content/SF/S0/02/20/17/00001/F60-00053.pdf.

◆ ABOUT THE ◆
AUTHORS

George Salton survived ten Nazi concentration camps and, after living in a displaced persons camp in Germany for two years, emigrated in 1947 to the United States. There he changed his name to George Salton and forged a new life. He proudly served in the US Army and became an American citizen. He met the love of his life, Ruth, also a Holocaust survivor. They married and raised three children, Henry, Alan, and Anna. Using the GI Bill, Salton attended college classes at night, earning a bachelor's degree in physics and a master's degree in electrical engineering at Syracuse University. George Salton had a distinguished career with the Department of Defense, eventually becoming director of Defense Communications at the Pentagon. After thirty-five years of government service, George became an executive in the aerospace industry. In 1998 he traveled with his family to Poland to share his Holocaust story and to grieve his beloved parents at the Belzec camp where they were murdered. In 2002 George and his daughter, Anna, co-wrote his bestselling memoir, *The 23rd Psalm*. He spent many years speaking about and teaching the lessons of the Holocaust. He died after a sudden illness at the age of eighty-eight on March 13, 2016.

Anna Salton Eisen grew up in a home where her parents' Holocaust experiences were not discussed. When as an adult she moved to Texas, she became active in the Jewish community as a founding member of Congregation Beth Israel in Colleyville, Texas. She served as a docent for the Dallas Holocaust Museum and an interviewer for Steven Spielberg's Survivors of the Shoah Visual History Foundation. In 2002 she co-authored with her father *The 23rd Psalm: A Holocaust Memoir.* Anna also authored the memoir *Pillar of Salt: A Daughter's Life in the Shadow of the Holocaust*, which, along with *The 23rd Psalm*, is the subject of a forthcoming documentary film titled *In My Father's Words.* Salton Eisen and her family reside in Westlake, Texas.